CRAFT CLASSICS SINCE THE 1940s

Ivan Bohnin April 1991

AN ANTHOLOGY OF BELIEF AND COMMENT

# CRAFT CLASSICS
# SINCE THE 1940s

SELECTED AND EDITED BY JOHN HOUSTON

CRAFTS COUNCIL
1988

ISBN 903798 96 4

First published in Great Britain
by the Crafts Council
12 Waterloo Place, London SW1Y 4AU

Copyright © Crafts Council and
authors and publishers as stated
1988

Designed by Richard Hollis
Typeset and printed in England
by Redesign Print Limited,
London

# CONTENTS

# PREFACE

This anthology is published to accompany the Crafts Council's exhibition *Craft Classics since the 1940s* at the Council's London gallery from 19 October 1988 to 8 January 1989. Book and exhibition each review the changing states of the crafts in Britain. The exhibition shows the conclusion of some pioneering careers alongside the young and maturing work of crafts people who began their careers before the crafts boom of the 1960s.

Several crafts people contribute both to the exhibition and the book: Dora Billington, Peter Collingwood, Hans Coper, David Kindersley, Bernard Leach, Ethel Mairet, Breon O'Casey and David Pye. John Houston has been another link between these events: as researcher for the exhibition and as the editor of the book. The Crafts Council is especially grateful to him for his valuable work and the way in which he has given so generously of his time. Neither book nor exhibition is claimed to be comprehensive. Half a century of crafts activity has created a rich, deep hoard of material. We hope that these samples will lead to further investigation.

Ralph Turner
Head of Exhibitions
Crafts Council

# Introduction

This book samples expert opinion about the crafts in Britain since the Second World War. The experts are craftspeople, teachers, museum officials and critics: people professionally committed to discussing the aims and means of a past or present crafts world. The circumstances of war helped to invest the crafts with special qualities associated with national survival. The traditional crafts, especially the rural and least complicated ones, served best:

> One could not come away from the basket-maker without feeling, in a serious and unusual way, that what is meant by grit and English character has not nearly so much to do with Cabinet Ministers and their slogans as with such men as this: who really never have admitted defeat, who still persist in the thankless, inglorious task of making something of common use rather better, and all the time with less profit to themselves out of it, than those who rule and those who patronize them.[1]

The traditional crafts were not alone in gaining potency and meaning. The special feelings provoked by war-time danger and uncertainty could find refuge and release in all the arts and entertainment. War-time scarcity and intensity promoted the post-war appetite for the arts and crafts as healing forces in the new world of peace. The 'creative' crafts – the inventive, expressive works of the artist-craftsmen and women – benefited from the romantic glow of the fading traditional crafts. The pioneering artist-craftsmen and women of the 1920s and 1930s had taken on (in the public's eyes, at least) the essential qualities of the traditional craftsmen whose materials and techniques had inspired them to become this new kind of hyphenated craftsperson.

This book begins with excerpts from books that were read and responded to in those hopeful post-war years. Ethel Mairet's *Hand-Weaving Today* (1939) and Bernard Leach's *A Potter's Book* (1940) were each the result of working and teaching, as the head of their own workshop. Although both of them had attended art schools, their knowledge of their crafts was substantially self-taught. Acutely conscious of the failing powers of the traditional crafts – especially in England, as the initiator of the industrial revolution – Mairet and Leach had been part of a widespread artistic curiosity about folk arts and crafts. They searched abroad as well as at home: Mairet discovered her career as a weaver in the early 1900s through studying textiles in India and Ceylon; Leach's conversion from etching to pottery took place in 1911 at a raku decorating ceremony in Tokyo. All over Europe artists as well as ethnographers were interested in vernacular arts and crafts: dance, song, stories, customs, as well as artefacts. There was much recording, notation, and attempts to revive or protect these arts that had become so fragile as their social contexts were changed, usually by industrialisation. But Mairet and Leach, along with some other artist-craftspeople, were most concerned to try and absorb the essence of these folk arts. In studying and adapting materials and techniques and collecting traditional objects they were inventing a tradition: a consciously developed hybrid of pre-industrial substance and post-industrial sensibility.

The question of tradition *was* central to the artist-craftsman's role. In this anthology Bernard Leach continually refers to the need for a tradition, or

1. Thomas Hennell: 'The Basketmaker', Architectural Review, January 1941; the first in a a lengthy series that included 'The Windmiller', 'The Hedger', and Michael Cardew at Winchcombe as 'The Potter'. They were all reprinted as The Countryman at Work in 1947, all with illustrations by the author.

a standard, or universal principles which would, at the very least, be a common language for makers and users. His famous chapter from *A Potter's Book* is entitled 'Towards a Standard': its influence has been colossal, both as a fully rounded account of how to be a potter, and as a statement of belief based upon the crafts as a whole-hearted expression of everyday culture. That belief joins him to the first hopes of the Arts and Crafts movement: that 'social impulse with aesthetic consequences' that still resounds through this anthology. Readers who want to fine-tune their awareness of *that* movement while studying these excerpts, which are central to the Crafts movement, should read Alan Crawford's splendid essay in *By Hammer and Hand*[2].

To put it crudely: the Crafts movement *is* the Arts and Crafts movement *after* the architects had defected. Not only were architects prime movers in the earliest days of the older movement, but it was their overall view of all the arts and crafts developing harmoniously within a building, within a city, within a world unified by the art that lovingly bound all the others, that lent the movement social, as well as aesthetic conviction. Their defection made each craft autonomous: free to evolve; free to stagnate. As industrial design became the new crafts, developing harmoniously within the new Modern Movement architecture, the hybrid artist-craftspeople scattered in their separate searches for the new authority of their own traditions, their own aesthetics.

Taken as a whole, this book can be read as an account of some of that searching in the post-war period. The excerpts are arranged in chronological order and each one is prefaced by a note about the writer.

As to the choice of excerpts: I wanted variety and balance, judged by the best standards of the whole period; I quickly found that complete pieces of writing – a whole essay, an entire chapter – were the only guarantee of true variety. I have cut into Bernard Leach's journal, but that is already a patchwork of impressions. I have done worse to Soetsu Yanagi's essay about the tea-bowl, but I would claim only to have cut the writer's equivalent of establishing shots. The vital, emotional close-ups remain. I determined to avoid retrospection, but David Kindersley's memoir of his apprenticeship to Eric Gill was as solid, and unsentimental, as anything either of them might have made. However, the retrospection rule and the whole piece of writing rule combined to push out Bernard Leach's *Hamada: Potter* (1975). It certainly should be read whole; it has splended pictures of people as well as pots, it is as vigorous and vivid as a good novel and would make an intriguing 'buddy' movie. Another regret that I hope readers will repair by going to the original is the omission of David Pye's chapter 'Critique of "The Nature of Gothic"' from his *The Nature and Art of Workmanship* (1968).

These lengthy excerpts are accompanied by a spatter of contemporary comment: some of it fictional; but many of the liveliest comments coming from the admirable *Crafts Review*. I hope that one day, with more space and a different set of criteria, someone will do justice to the various voices of all the crafts magazines that I had to ignore.

2. Alan Crawford, editor, *By Hammer and Hand*, Birmingham Museums and Art Gallery, 1984.

John Houston

# Ethel Mairet

1872-1952

Mairet's life as a self-taught weaver stretched from the centre of the English revival of Arts and Crafts to the truth-from-materials fringe of the Modern Movement. Her first marriage (in 1902) to Ananda Coomaraswamy took her to India and Ceylon and aroused her interest in various textile arts. In England they lived in the Norman Chapel at Broad Campden, close to C.R.Ashbee and his Guild of Handicraft, who had renovated and extended the exquisite Chapel. Ethel's jeweller brother Fred worked for the Guild, as had her second husband (from 1913) the draughtsman, designer, actor, writer, Philip Mairet, with whom she ran the New Handworker Gallery in London from 1927 until the end of their relationship in 1930. From 1920 she lived at Ditchling in Sussex, as did the calligrapher Edward Johnston and the sculptor Eric Gill.

Mairet was a challenging personality and a welcoming, though sometimes fierce, teacher. No paper designer, she found her fabrics on the loom as her intuitive response to the expressive qualities of different materials. It was this delight in the different expressive properties of her raw materials – just the yarns and dyes, natural and synthetic – that made her so sympathetic to the colour and textural innovations of the Futurists, the Bauhaus, and modern architecture in general.

There is a good biography by Margot Coatts: *A Weaver's Life: Ethel Mairet 1872–1952*, 1983.

FROM

## HAND-WEAVING TODAY

# 1939

## [INTRODUCTION]

Extracts from *Hand-Weaving Today: Traditions and Changes*, Faber & Faber, London 1939. The whole introduction; part of Chapter 1: 'Hand-weaving and industrial development'; part of Chapter 2: 'Post-war weaving and the new architecture'; and the whole of Chapter 4: 'Spinning'.

Hand-weaving to-day is a rediscovered craft in England, for during the last century it had succumbed to the machine; at the beginning of this century not more than half a dozen hand-loom workers were in existence. In the remoter parts of Scotland, Ireland, and Wales the trade persisted, partly to meet local needs, partly to supply a luxury demand. The public had become gradually accustomed to the deadly machine finish which makes things look so much better than they are.

In the growth of any civilization there comes a time when the human element finds itself subordinate to the mechanical. If the process continues the civilization (as in Egypt, Crete, and Greece) disappears; but if the danger is realised and combated (as in India and Europe at the present moment) it may be averted. The reform does not develop a machine boycott but a machine mastery; men begin to use the machine which had begun to use them. It has to cease being a money-maker and to become a means for the better ordering of life, easing hard and laborious work, making for the appreciation of beauty in city, village, and home. Machinery is for the enrichment of life, not for the exploitation of the many by the few. It cannot yet be said that we have turned on our tracks and brought the machine into this service, but the consciousness that it must be done is everywhere manifest. The machine age of freedom is

9

upon us because the demand for speed, beauty, efficiency, and leisure are insistent. We do not ask for leisure now without beauty, speed, efficiency, nor for speed without leisure, nor for beauty without speed, efficiency, and leisure.

Hand-weaving has been in danger of developing on the wrong lines. It has set itself up on a pedestal as an art, instead of recognizing its immense and interesting responsibilities to present needs and to the machine. But it has more responsibility to the machine than any other craft. It is harder to become a well-trained weaver than a well-trained metal or leather worker or a printer. There are more things to be learnt and more varied technique to be acquired. The essence of hand-weaving is in its continual creativeness and flexibility (this is also its danger) based strictly on traditional knowledge. It is dependent on architecture and clothing; it must work in close collaboration with both. It cannot ever be an art by itself (as a beautifully printed book can be, or a fine piece of metal work) for always it must be part of a building (curtains, rugs, hangings, et.) or associated with the necessities of life (clothes, table-cloths, towels). It is far from just throwing a shuttle. Hand-weaving is a craft that looks easy and fascinating on the surface, but it is very exacting, involving many considerations. Here are a few:

1. A wide knowledge of raw materials and a strictly critical and aesthetic attitude to them.

2. A knowledge of the chemistry of colour and a strong colour perception.

3. An aesthetic appreciation of rhythm, balance of design, spacing – not only in the weaving of wall hangings, rugs, and curtains, but also in the structure of a piece of material and in the relation of yarns.

4. The correspondence between the various kinds of raw materials and a knowledge of their origins and structure must be understood.

5. A kind of mathematical precision is needed in being able to see the relation of a draft design on paper to the finished product, to be able to compose a draft from a visualized design.

6. Much technical knowledge and vision is required for dealing with Jacquard, dobby, and draw-looms (all of these looms require the most careful handling of design and represents the means to the highest expression of textile art). When the biotechnics of the necessary raw materials are understood, and the same amount of training is given to a designer for weaving as is required for a painter of pictures, there will be big development in these more advanced hand-looms.

7. The keeping in touch with fashion in clothes being alive to the future of dress.

8. An understanding of modern architecture and how to keep textile production in touch with it.

9. Constant creation of new yarns, new colours, new materials for the various purposes of architecture and dress.

10. A cultural background is essential; the balance of art has been upset by separating the crafts (and not only the crafts but knowledge generally) into little compartments, each with a wall around it, the unity of the whole has been forgotten. (The start of this unification was emphasized in the experiment of teaching at the Bauhaus in Germany after the War.) Professor Gropius collected together in one great school all sides of knowledge needed for the production of a fundamental artist-worker-thinker-human being. The world was not ready for such an obviously right step, but so great a creative idea cannot be lost. It points the direction for the future, and although it failed as an entity at the moment, the idea has been started and the influence of the school is to be found in all parts of the world.)

11. Hand-weaving influences the textile trade. This is notably seen in countries where hand-weaving and the trade are not so separated as in England. The production of hand-woven goods in other countries is very large and holds its own in spite of the factories. By this means the standard of machine goods is kept high with the constantly new ideas (cf. Rodier in France; Elsa Gulberg in Sweden; the large output of German hand-weaving), the cheaper manufactured goods being as a rule more interesting and alive.

The craft of weaving can only be acquired by long practice. It is not to be found in books. It is no longer a traditional craft in England. Everywhere, though, it has its roots and from these roots it can spring again into vitality, to run parallel with the birth of modern architecture. Weaving has its new materials and new ideas just as architecture has. It is for the hand-weavers in every country to realize this and to work toward a new expression in textiles.

## HAND-WEAVING
## AND INDUSTRIAL DEVELOPMENT

*The machine itself makes no demands, and holds out no promises; it is the human spirit that makes the demands and keeps promises. In order to reconquer the machine and subdue it to human purposes, one must first understand it and assimilate it. So far, we have embraced the machine without fully understanding it, or, like the weaker romantics, we have rejected the machine, without first seeing how much of it we could intelligently assimilate. The machine itself, however, is a product of human ingenuity and effort; hence to understand the machine, is not merely a first step towards re-orienting our civilization.*

Lewis Mumford: *Technics and Civilization.*

The craft of weaving (the textile trade) is, and always has been, with the craft of agriculture, at the beginning of any civilization. Among nomad tribes of Asia and Africa weaving was practised even before agriculture; early finds indicate a high development and knowledge of the raw materials of which cloth of various kinds was made. In Egypt, before 2000 BC, exceedingly fine linen cloths were woven; while in the Far East, earlier still, have been discovered examples of the finest craftsmanship. In the Stone Age, in Europe, not only remains of woven materials have been found but quantities of spindle whorls, showing that spinning was an accomplished and necessary craft before man even thought of architecture. The principle of spinning, the stuff turning upon itself, is the same to-day as it was then. It may have left the spindle for the spinning wheel, and passed from the spinning jenny of the nineteenth century to the elaborate machines of the present day, but the essential process is the same.

The earliest thread that is known to have been used is linen. Then, in the colder countries, came wool. Silk and cotton were first introduced into Europe in the Middle Ages; but they were known in Asia many centuries before Christ. In South America (Peru) cotton was woven centuries before the European invasion in the sixteenth century. (Some of these early cloths, preserved in the tombs, are incredibly beautiful; the essential quality of cotton was understood, both in the spinning and weaving of it.)

Sheep breeding, for which the English climate is particularly suitable, was an important industry during the Middle Ages. England was the chief supplier of raw wool to the then known world. In the fourteenth, fifteenth, and sixteenth centuries the wool industry produced great wealth. The Cotswolds particularly provide many evidences of this wealth, both in the magnificent churches and the beautiful stone houses built by the wool-staplers. Gloucestershire was indeed one of the most prosperous parts of England. Farmers specialized in the breeding of sheep for the production of various kinds of wool with the same care as they may now devote to pedigree stock or to the rearing of race-horses. The tradition of weaving in England has this important wool industry as its basis. This is different from what has happened in other parts of Europe where the weaver depended mostly on a mixture of linen and a very hard spun (usually coarse) wool. As there has been very little break in the continuity of Continental weaving, handwork developed chiefly in furnishing materials which require this hard, firm technique. With us very little is practised or known of handweaving of furnishing stuffs. In countries like Sweden and Germany, where the tradition has been based on close woven peasant techniques, weaving has inevitably developed with cottons, linens, and hard-spun wools suitable for furnishings. The knowledge of wools, their various characteristics and qualities is hardly yet found in Europe outside England. Therefore it is in this country that wool-weaving may be studied in all its details starting from the special breeding of sheep for fleece, on to the production of various types of fleece for different purposes, and, finally, to the making of the light-weight modern tweeds whose fundamental qualities are determined from the sheep itself.

England was developing during the nineteenth century the use of machinery before other countries had thought of it. We had the leisure and money to do this; not having been torn to pieces by wars (as in Germany, France, and America); we were experiencing a long period of quiet in which industrial enterprise could prosper. The textile trade, more than any other, responded to these conditions and was stimulated by such inventive geniuses as Arkwright, Cartwright, and others. There was an immense increase in mechanical interests; more complicated became the looms, swifter their working appliances, enormously greater their output, which was absorbed in an expansion of European markets as well as by India and America. This expansion was also due to the great discoveries in iron and steel and the consequent development of the shipping industry.[1]

During this period the English peasant completely disappeared. There were landowners and farm labourers, and, in the towns and cities, the heads of industries and industrial slave workers. The independent peasant, farming his own piece of land, became unknown. He disappeared with the beginning of industrialization, and the industries that are indispensable to a peasant class disappeared with him. There is no peasant dress or household textile tradition left in England, no peasant class remaining with a tradition attached to the land. By the middle of the last century men, women, and children had been absorbed into the factories or gone to the colonies, which at that time were wanting all the people they could get. The transition between hand- and machine-work was one of the most tragic moments in English history. The machine was the Victorian god and the fascination of the new worship, of accumulating vast wealth out of it (at the expense of the workers), is a chapter of history that does not bear looking into. Badly planned towns, back-to-back houses, factories built anyhow and wherever possible, no planning with an idea of the future, producing dirt and squalor indescribable (and there are south Wales and Lancashire to prove it). This state of things is not inherent in the use of machinery. It was only the result of not being willing or clever enough to control its marvellous powers. The overdriven hand-worker of an exhausted tradition was still fighting for his existence, even to the end of the last century.

1.See The Rise of Modern Industry.

The first craftsman who realized how important it was that handwork

12

should be saved from extinction was William Morris. He was artist, poet, writer, craftsman, and he understood the indissoluble unity of the art of an age with its social system. He reacted in a practical and vital way against the bad, insincere, so-called art that was everywhere to be seen in the nineteenth century. He saw how art was divorced from the life of the people – of the rich as well as of the poor – and his struggle to get beauty back into ordinary things made him realize that living conditions must also be changed. 'What business have we with art at all, unless all can share it?' he says in one of his lectures. 'Morris is the true prophet of the twentieth century, the father of the modern movement. We owe it to him that an ordinary man's dwelling-house has once more become a worthy object of the architect's thought, and a chair, a wallpaper, or a vase a worthy object of the artist's imagination.'[2] His influence extended all over Europe. Although the Arts and Crafts movement which he started had the disastrous effect of isolating the individual craftsman and separating him from the trend of industrial development, it did save him from extinction. But the craftsman was still a unit fighting for his existence as something apart from the industrial life of his age, and so remained until the post-War attitude to life required a fresh conception of the crafts in relation to the new architecture and industry. The change is happening slowly and painfully. 'The battle has to be fought on all fronts. Not one of the subjects is less essential, not one can be neglected; neither slum clearance, nor the renovation of school buildings; neither the levelling of class contrasts, nor the raising of standards of design.'[3] It is not possible to go back to the days when hand-weaving supplied the needs of the people. A new orientation of the crafts must be found – a new idea of where they stand in relation to machinery. Not the age of machinery of the nineteenth century, which had no aesthetic conception and trampled everything under its money-making feet – human beings as well as ideas – but the new self-conscious age of the post-War twentieth century, which knows that machine-made things can be good and beautiful, that machine technique need not necessarily be soul and body destroying. So far, machine use and the actual making of machines themselves have gone ahead faster than the ideas of the men who use them. We have the machines, but we have not known yet what to do with them; except to make profits. We have produced and are still producing, aesthetically speaking, the most hideous and terrible things. But that is not the necessary product of the machine. It means that we have not understood it, that we have let it run away with us. But we are now at the start of a post-War consciousness, a post-War art and life, entirely different from that at the beginning of the century. The idea of controlling the machine and making out of it something beautiful, is gradually developing. We are at least beginning to feel that our own age has something to express. It does not now seem fitting to copy eighteenth-century or Gothic furniture, buildings, textiles, to look upon design, or to worship the antique, as we did even a few years ago. There is something new to be said, though we are still feeling how difficult it is to say it. It requires great creative effort to deal with the mass of new possibilities and new materials which are being poured out by the machine.

The problem is still too new but the power and the understanding will come; the new art of the machine age will eventually be born. One of the foundations of this art – perhaps its main foundation – is the understanding of all materials, the understanding of their intrinsic values, what they can do, or be made to do. This fundamental axiom of all living art has been forgotten since the great Gothic Middle Ages. Since then, artists, architects, and industrialists have skimmed the surface of past civilizations for their inspiration; instead of expressing the biotechnics of the materials of their own

2. Nikolaus Pevsner, An Enquiry into Industrial Art in England, 1937.

3. Pevsner, ibid.

age as they arose. Buildings were made to look like Grecian temples, or were deliberately copied from Gothic and other styles. The insincerity of the last two or three centuries has been stupendous, and still is in textiles. The new synthetic raw materials have mostly been used for copying the natural raw materials. This is as much a setback in the development of the textile art as the copying of Gothic is to architecture. New conditions require a new expression and we still have to find this new textile expression. As Herbert Read says in Art and Industry: 'The real problem is not to adapt production to the aesthetic standards of handicraft, but to think out new aesthetic standards for methods of production.'

## POST-WAR WEAVING
## AS PART OF THE NEW ARCHITECTURE

All European countries are developing a new expression of architecture, based on the new building materials – steel, concrete, glass. These materials are capable of great flexibility in design and a style is gradually evolving, making full use of their possibilities – possibilities that were unknown to the builders in brick, stone, and wood. There is very little that cannot be done in this new technique and the change-over from the old tradition will be long and very difficult – not only from the point of view of a new style, involved in the experience of dealing with entirely new materials; but in persuading the general public that this is a new material which of necessity requires a new expression in architecture. It is the natural evolution of the machine age. It is the style required by great factories, by the growth of cities, by the need for sunlight and air which the old way of building did not take sufficiently into account, because it could not. And also for the need for a new expression of design. Artists cannot satisfactorily fall back on architecture such as neo-Gothic, eighteenth century, Baroque, in a twentieth-century mechanical age. The new building materials have arrived; with them has come a need for a new synthesis of the arts and a re-orientation of the crafts in relation to the whole. The real expression of machine technique has not yet arrived. The machine is still copying old worn-out traditions, not creating a new one. It is still working in individual units instead of creating a modern synthesis – a synthesis of the crafts taking part in producing beautiful and satisfactory buildings – a synthesis of the artist, craftsman, and architect. It is becoming more and more recognized that the artist has a vision which should be accepted as part of the whole of modern development. The artist can only be of use to his civilization by accepting the machine; and the machine must work with the artist as its brain. There is at this moment the struggle between the two extremes – the unliving unimaginative money-making machine technique, and the alive imaginative artist. Neither can live without the other. Out of this struggle will be born the new expression of the future which is neither one nor the other, but evolved from both.

Some of the most beautiful buildings in Europe are the result of this close collaboration between the artist and the machine. (A gem of modern building is a small library at Viipuri in Finland, built by Alvar Aalto in 1935, exquisite in its proportions and conception of colour and finish and practicability. The Diet House of Helsingfors is another practical illustration of the collaboration of the craftsman and architect using handwork and modern machine technique.)

The weaving being carried on now in modern workshops all over Europe is a creative movement, involving experimentation with new techniques, with new raw materials – involving the constant recognition of the needs of the movement – the recognition of the requirements of modern building and of modern life, which in its turn is expressing the needs of post-War youth. It is flexible, alive for new ideas, experimental, building up a modern weaving technique which will fit in with the new architecture. It has the whole world to draw upon, not only the tradition of its own country. Perhaps in Finland this new expression is to be seen to most advantage. Here and there appears an entirely new idea in textile; some piece of stuff that could not have been made in any other period of time.; expressing new material in a new way. In German also, the line of development is with new ideas in synthetic materials. The lack of the natural raw materials is forcing weavers in Germany to use synthetic yarns in a most vital and interesting way. The new yarns and the new materials made from them are creating a new tradition in woven stuff which is not a mere copy of silks and woollens such as the development has tended to be so far. The synthetic materials can be made to do anything, just as the new building materials can. Their development is only just starting.

## SPINNING

*The essence of all the old crafts was in their vitality, their response to the natural conditions and the psychology of their times.*
Lethaby: *Form in Civilization*, 1922

Hand-spinning is the foundation of weaving. It is creating the yarn from the raw material upon which all the best weaving of every civilization has been and is still being built. A large proportion of the yarn for weaving at the present day is produced by hand, on spindles or wheels.

Spindle-spinning has been known from the earliest time. Spindle whorls (the weight at the end of the spindle) are found even in Stone Age remains. In the early Egyptian dynasties (5000-4000 BC) fine spinning was a highly developed craft. The earliest remains of a spun thread date from those remote years.

Professor Flinders Petrie records a find of thread, coloured blue and red, from a tomb of the XIIth dynasty (3500-2000 BC), although the earliest woven cloth discovered is of later date.

The spinning-wheel is a comparatively late development, although very early and extremely simple spinning-wheels have been found in China and India. Generally speaking, spindle-spinning at the present time belongs to the nomad and pastoral peoples, as the freedom and smallness of the implement makes it possible to spin while moving and walking. On the other hand, spinning by spindle can also be a sedentary occupation. The cotton-spinners of Upper Egypt, West Africa or India, for example, sit on the ground to spin, resting the end of their spindle in a cup-shaped receptacle.

There are many methods of using the spindle. There is the free swinging or suspended spindle. This is the most usual of all methods and for speed by hand has never been surpassed. The distaff is sometimes used with this method of spinning, especially in Europe; this makes easier the handling of a quantity of raw material. The carded fleece or flax is bound on to a rod or flat board, varying in length and size, and this is fastened into the belt of the spinner. Examples of beautifully-carved and painted distaffs are to be found in all the Folk Museums; and in the markets of southern Europe and elsewhere, where spindle-spinning is carried on, are still to be bought finely carved and interesting distaffs. A method of winding the carded fleece round the left arm is also practised. With cotton-spinning the distaff is rarely used. The traditional method is to deal direct with the cotton on the seed. This is pulled off from the seed in such a way as to leave the fibres more or less parallel. It is then rolled into an elongated ball or pulled out into a long sliver. This is the method practised in the Sudan. The Indian method is different; the seeds are usually ginned out and small rolls made from which to spin.

There is another method of the suspended-spindle type practised in the Caucasus and elsewhere, in which the spindle is held with the whorl upwards and the stick is rolled quickly against the thigh, thus setting up a considerable spin, while the left hand determines the amount of material from the distaff or from the fleece held in the hand.

The third important method of spindle-spinning is that of the continuous twirling of the spindle in the right hand while the left hand releases the raw material according to the size of the thread required. The spindle is held upright and does not leave the hand. This method is difficult to acquire, but it has its obvious advantages over the free swinging spindle types as it makes it possible to spin while sitting and walking.

But for the most delicate spinning such as the incredible fineness of the Dacca muslins (India) there is a fourth method, that of the spindle resting in a saucer-shaped receptacle and being twirled by the right hand. This obviously is more satisfactory for the making of very fine thread, as the weight of the spindle is relieved from the thread itself. The twirling of the spindle in this case is sometimes done by rolling the stick on the thigh, or by continuous spin of the spindle by the right hand.

All these methods are still in operation in various parts of the world, with slight variations in the way of handling the raw material in relation to the spindle.

The development from spindle-spinning to the wheel probably started in Asia and the Far East, and the wheel may have been introduced into Europe in the Middle Ages about the time of the introduction of silk. In an early fourteenth-century manuscript there are several illustrations of spinning-wheels; and it is certain they were in use in Europe before the sixteenth century. The earliest type is the hand wheel. In Wales it is called the 'Great Wheel', in Ireland the 'Long Wheel', and in Scotland the 'Muckle Wheel'. This is still in use in remote districts (though more often now used for bobbin making). It is also found in the Faroe Islands and all the northern countries. These wheels are large single-banded wheels without a flyer, turned by the right hand while the left hand manipulates the fleece. It is really an elaborate extension of the spindle motion, the spinning and the winding on to the bobbin being two separate operations.

The spindle with the flyer was the next step in the evolution of the wheel. This was invented by a German, Johann Jürgen in 1530.[4] It was an important step forward in the history of spinning. The addition of the treadle to the wheel was a later introduction still; but this must have made an immense difference to the speed of spinning, as it left both hands free to attend to the thread. The pulling-out process and the regulating of the size of the thread now changes from the left hand to the right, the left hand helping to determine the amount of spin required for the thread. This still remains the characteristic difference between the two types of spinning – between spindle-spinning and the treadle-wheel spinning. The bobbin with the flyer has remained the type of wheel used up to the present day. The flyer determines the amount of spin required for the thread which is being wound on to the bobbin, which again is regulated by the tension of the continuous

4. This same idea was also invented earlier by Leonardo da Vinci, who made elaborate and beautiful drawings of a spinning-wheel with a flyer. His idea, however, never materialised, but it was undoubtedly the first idea of the modern spinning machinery.

double band connecting the wheel with the flyer and bobbin. This tension is the sensitive keynote to all spinning and has to be continually adjusted according to the type of yarn required.

At present the hand-spun thread is more flexibly interesting than that of the highly developed machine-spinners produce, and also of a better quality, both aesthetically and practically. This is not necessarily so, as the machine properly under control is capable of producing beautiful and interesting threads.

Every raw material has its own definite expression, its biotechnic quality. This can even be found in the various types of fleece. Each kind of fleece has its own perfect expression – the ideal thread which expresses its special quality. For instance, the Lincoln fleece produces a thread, bringing out its essential qualities, which is a very fine smooth yarn, almost identical with linen, and should behave more or less in the same way when used with other yarns, with no elasticity and capable of the smooth hard fineness of linen. On the other hand, the Southdown fleece could not possibly be spun into such a thread; its type is a softly spun yarn keeping to the full the characteristic elasticity. Other excellent threads can of course be made from each type, but in each fleece and for every kind of raw material, there is the type of thread which belongs to it, and is inherent in it. It is the work of the hand-spinner to find out these types, and build on them, singly and in combination with other raw materials. At present trade yarns are superbly clever copies of the old type of yarns. The whole trade outlook up to now is affected by what has been done – synthetic yarns made to look like silk or wool, cotton yarns made to look like linen or silk. But no yarn has been produced by the machine spinners which can surpass the beauty and quality of – for example – early Peruvian cotton thread or Indian even to the present day, or the fineness and quality of some of the woollen yarns of Asia, and the fineness and flexibility of the early Egyptian linen. They remain still supreme examples of the spinner's skill and art. New yarns will ultimately be born out of experiments with synthetic fibres, which offer an entirely new field of expression in the making of yarns.

---

One could not come away from the basket-maker without feeling, in a serious and unusual way, that what is meant by grit and English character has not nearly so much to do with Cabinet Ministers and their slogans as with such men as this: who really have never admitted defeat, who still persist in the thankless, inglorious task of making something of common use rather better, and all the time with less profit to themselves out of it, than those who rule or those who patronize them.

T. Hennell, 'The Basket-Maker', in *Architectural Review*, January 1941

# Bernard Leach

1887-1979

Throughout his long, busy life Leach restlessly sought balance among conflicting qualities and ideas in craft, art, philosophy and religion. Excited by the complex relations between aesthetics, ethics, and cultural history he proposed a synthesis of cultural values based upon his own experience of East and West. His hopes grew from a rich blend of reference: he could admire a Chinese pot as a Greek form after its modification by Buddhist ideology, and relish the Japanese aesthetic which helped to guide his admiration. As descriptive draughtsman, eclectic potter, and anecdotal commentator he tirelessly illustrated his own pilgrim's progress with the physical gusto of an Edwardian explorer.

*A Potter's Book* is his credo. If the seven technical chapters are the maps of Leach's progress, then 'Towards a Standard' explains the reasons for setting out on the journey.

FROM

A POTTER'S BOOK

## 1940

### TOWARDS A STANDARD

'Towards a Standard'. 1940. This is the whole of Chapter 1 from *A Potter's Book*, Faber & Faber, London 1940. This has remained in print ever since its second edition in 1945.

Very few people in this country think of the making of pottery as an art, and amongst those few the great majority have no criterion of aesthetic values which would enable them to distinguish between the genuinely good and the meretricious. Even more fortunate is the position of the average potter, who without some standard of fitness and beauty derived from tradition cannot be expected to produce, not necessarily masterpieces, but even intrinsically sound work.

The potter is no longer a peasant or journeyman as in the past, nor can he be any longer described as an industrial worker: he is by force of circumstances an artist-craftsman, working for the most part alone or with a few assistants. Factories have practically driven folk-art out or England; it survives only in out of the way corners even in Europe, and the artist-craftsman, since the day of William Morris, has been the chief means of defence against the materialism of industry and its insensibility to beauty.

Here at the very beginning it should be made clear that the work of the individual potter or potter-artist, who performs all or nearly all the processes of production with his own hands, belongs to one aesthetic category, and the finished result of the operations of industrialized manufacture, or mass-production, to another and quite different category. In the work of the potter-artist, who throws his own pots, there is a unity of design and execution, a co-operation of hand and undivided personality, for designer and craftsman are one, that has no counterpart in the work of the designer for mass-production, whose office is to make drawings or models of utensils, often to be cast or moulded in parts and subsequently assembled. The art of the craftsman, to use Herbert Read's terminology, is intuitive and humanistic (one hand one brain); that of the designer for re-duplication, rational, abstract and tectonic, the work of the engineer or constructor rather than that of the 'artist'. Each method has its own aesthetic significance. Examples of both can be good or bad. The distinction between them lies in the relegation of the actual making not merely to other hands than those of the designer but to power driven machines. The products of the latter can never possess the same intimate qualities as the former, but to deny them the possibility of excellence of design in terms of what mechanical reproduction can do is both blind and obstinate. A motor car such as a Rolls Royce Phantom achieves a kind of perfection although its appeal is mainly intellectual and material. There I think we come to the crux of the matter: good hand craftsmanship is directly subject to the prime source of human activity, whereas machine crafts, even at their best, are activated at one remove – by the intellect. No doubt the work of the intuitive craftsman would be considered by most people to be of a higher, more personal, order of beauty; nevertheless, industrial pottery at its best, done from the drawings of a constructor who is an artist, can certainly have an intuitive element.[1] The trouble, however, is that at a conservative estimate about nine-tenths of the industrial pottery produced in England no less than in other countries is hopelessly bad in both form and decoration. With the exception of a few traditional shapes and patterns for table-ware, and others designed by the best designers available today and painted by the best available artists (none of whom is a potter), turned out notably by the Wedgwood and Royal Worcester and Minton factories and by the Makin and Gray firms in Hanley, and excluding also a few purely functional and utilitarian designs, some of which are also traditional, such as Doulton's acid-jars, we meet elsewhere with bad forms and banal, debased, pretentious decoration – qualities that are perhaps most conspicuous in 'fancy vases', flower-pots and other ornamental pieces, in which we find a crudity of colour combined with cheapness and inappropriateness of decoration and tawdriness of form that must be seen to be believed. And although the mechanical processes are indeed marvellous, as for example the automatic glazing, cleaning, measuring and stamping of many millions per month of bathroom tiles, fired in a single non-stop tunnel kiln, the mere fact of their being mass-produced is no reason why these tiles should be as cheaply designed and as dull and miserable in colour as it is possible for tiles to be; nor in the case of hollow-ware is the casting of shapes so exactly and so quickly and with such perfect pastes an adequate excuse for dead shapes, dead clay, dead lithographed printing or the laboured painting of dead patterns. Indeed the more elaborate and expensive the decoration the more niggling and lifeless it is, and the nearer it approaches the long deceased fashion of naturalism of the nineteenth century, when close attention to detail and the careful painting of pictures upon porcelain in enamel colours was considered the summit of ceramic art – 'applied' art with a vengeance! On the other hand, if the bulk of the pottery turned out in England today is mass-produced and of inferior form and decoration, its inferiority is not so much due to the manner of its production – for mass-produced wares can not only be of fine quality of body[2] and beautiful in form, if designed by the right men – but for various extrinsic reasons, chief of which is the failure of the manufacturer to interest himself in good design. The want of artistic initiative on the part of the manufacturers must be ascribed to the general lowering of taste under conditions of competitive industrialism. The public is ever increasingly out of touch with the making of articles of everyday use, and although its entrepreneurs, the buyers and salesmen of trade, are continually caught out in their under-estimation of what people like they cannot be entirely blamed for catering to safe markets. Even if, as Pevsner says, 'one cannot condemn an industrialist too severely because he does not jump at every suggested artistic improvement', and it 'would be absurd to suggest to the producer

1. 'Whenever the final product of the machine is designed or determined by anyone sensitive to formal values, that product can and does become an abstract work of art in the subtler sense of the term.' Herbert Read, *Art and Industry*, p.37.

2. '... pottery manufacturers know that mass production can in ceramics, at least as regards the quality of the body, help greatly towards improvements. The reason is that more efficient kilns can be used and better conditions of firing attained.' – Comp. Nikolaus Pevsner, *An Enquiry into Industrial Art in England*, 1937, p.191 and p.83.

that he ought to ruin himself for the community', there is nevertheless no reason why he should not work as far as possible towards replacing bad forms and decorations with good, and realize, in spite of the cheerful assurances of buyers and travellers, that he must cater to bad taste, that one of the chief reasons why 'the public (apart from a few hopelessly insensitive individuals) likes' tawdry utensils, is because as a rule it can get no others. Apart from the initial expense of new moulds, and provided a competent designer is available, there is no apparent ground for believing that good commercial pottery should be any more expensive to make than bad.

Sung dynasty
stoneware bottle

It is obvious that the standards of the world's best pottery, for example, those of the T'ang and Sung periods in China and the best of the Ming, Korean celadons and Ri-cho, early Japanese tea-master's wares[3], early Persian, Syrian, Hispano-Moresque, German Bellarmines, some Delft and English slipware, cannot well be applied to industrial work, for such pottery was a completely unified human expression. It had not been mechanized. Yet there is no doubt that much can be learned by the industrial potter or designer from the wares especially of the Sung and early Ming dynasties. The Chinese potters' use of natural colours and textures in clays, the quality of their glazes (e.g. the Ying-ching and Tz'ou Chou families), the beauty and vitality of their well-balanced and proportioned forms, could be a constant source of inspiration to the designer for mass-production no less than to the craftsman.

3. i.e. pottery approved of by the Japanese tea-masters, adepts in the Cha-no-yu or tea-ceremony, who have for several centuries been the foremost art critics in Japan and have counted among their numbers many creative artists of the first rank. For an account of the spirit of the Cha-no-yu, see Okakura Kakuzo, The Book of Tea, also A.L. Sadler, Cha-no-yu, London 1934.

It is no discredit to the scientific and utilitarian advances of the English pottery industry to say that the beauty to which the Sung potters attained was far beyond the highest that from its beginnings in Josiah Wedgwood the English factories ever aimed at. The two traditions and methods of production are radically different, and the intuitive, organic qualities of Sung pottery can never be completely expressed by the rational and tectonic methods of big industry. Concentration upon mechanical production and utilitarian and functional qualities is today necessary and justified, and as already said there is no reason to suppose that factory-made utilitarian wares may not by reason of their precision, their pleasing lines and perfection of technique, added to complete adaptation to use, have a great beauty of their own. Even during the course of the last two centuries moulded English tea ware of admirable design has been made, and often its decoration, especially the 'Japan' and other conventionalized set patterns of the late eighteenth and early nineteenth centuries, has been, if not great art, at least possessed of much charm. It would be surprising if equally good patterns could not be turned out by able designers today.

4. There has never been a European stoneware tradition except that of the Rhenish salt-glazed wares. 'Accepting the Sung standard' is a very different thing from imitating particular Sung pieces. It means the use so far as possible of natural materials in the endeavour to obtain the best quality of body and glaze; in throwing and in a striving towards unity, spontaneity, and simplicity of form, and in general the subordination of all attempts at technical cleverness to straightforward, un-selfconscious workmanship. A strict adherence to Chinese standards, howsoever fine, cannot be advocated, for no matter what the source and power of a stimulus, what we make of it is the only thing that counts. We are not the Chinese of a thousand years ago, and the underlying racial and social and economic conditions which produced the Sung traditions in art will never be repeated; but that is no reason why we should not draw all the inspiration we can from the Sung potters.

It is quite otherwise with the studio potter. He is indeed constrained to look to the best of the earlier periods for inspiration and may, so far as stoneware and porcelain are concerned, accept the Sung standard without hesitation. As it is, there are a few English craftsman potters today who do accept it, and their work is incomparably the best that is now being turned out.[4] Others go back to an outmoded 'arts and crafts' tradition, which seems to have had its origin in France in the last quarter of the nineteenth century and to have been largely influenced by modern Japanese designs, which became fashionable soon after the Paris Exhibition of 1867. Its characteristic features are weakness of form, especially of lip and foot, and, except in the case of the salt-glazed wares of the Martin Brothers (much of which was also influenced by Japanese design), crudely coloured glazes in which all aesthetic quality is lost in technique, as always happens when the means are mistaken for the end. It is easy to understand the impression made on potters by the discovery, first in France by Chaplet and later in England by William Burton, of how to make the brilliant high-temperature single colour and flambé glazes of the Ching period in China; but in the absence of tradition, again technique triumphed over art and eccentricity and weakness over strength. The attempted revival of lustre painting under pre-Raphaelite influence by William de Morgan led as one might expect to nothing fresh and vital in form, or for that matter in decoration. Nor does the example of the Doulton company in preserving the English salt-glazed tradition seem to have had any influence on studio potters, beyond the Martins' and, possibly, William Gordon, who was recently making good salted porcelain at Chesterfield.

In the absence of some agreement, however inarticulate, as to a common standard, one may hope to find an occasional work of genius in the free, or so-called fine arts (frequently then only the outcome of pain and poverty and lifelong obscurity); but in applied art, which depends upon collaboration in the workshop and constant sales to a public, there is even less hope. Indeed, amongst some at least of the free arts there does exist what one may call a classic standard, according to which the work of today, especially in literature and music, is compared with the great work of the past. That the criterion of beauty is a living thing and constantly in flux, is true, but here at least there is a continuous if ever changing consensus of opinion as to what may be called great achievement. In regard to pottery such a criterion can hardly be said ever to have entered the consciousness of Western man. In the East it has long been in existence, especially in Japan, where the aesthetic sensibility of educated people has been stimulated by the ablest of critics for some three hundred or more years. As space will only allow me to speak briefly of this great aesthetic cult and its unrivalled standard of artistic appreciation, I cannot do better than give a more or less condensed and paraphrased extract from an essay on popular, or folk, arts and crafts by Soetsu Yanagi, the intellectual leader of the Japanese craft movement today:

*I have many occasions to call at the residences of well-known art collectors, but I find too often that the articles of everyday use in their homes are far from being artistic, to say the least. They often leave me with a sad suspicion as to how much these collectors really appreciate beauty.*

*To me the greatest thing is to live beauty in our daily life and to crown every moment with things of beauty. It is then, and then only, that the art of the people as a whole is endowed with its richest significance. For its products are those made by a great many craftsmen for the mass of the people, and the moment this art declines the life of the nation is removed far away from beauty. So long as beauty abides in only a few articles created by a few geniuses, the Kingdom of Beauty is nowhere near realization.*

*Fortunately, in Japan, handicraft objects have been treasured through the channel of ceremonial tea. Cha-no-yu in the last analysis is a means of harmonizing life and beauty. . . . It may be thought of as an aesthetics of the practical arts. In all its appurtenances, whether it be in the architecture, the garden, or the utensils, the first principle is utility and the adornment of life with refinement. Not beauty for beauty's own sake, but beauty answering all immediate needs of life – that is the essence of ceremonial tea. . . .*

*One may ask, what then is the nature of the beauty which has been discovered by these tea-masters? . . . In the first place it is non-indivudalistic. . . . As in medieval Europe art meant adherence to tradition, so in the East all works of arts or crafts were governed equally by common principles. . . . Some of the most famous tea-bowls were originally the simplest of utensils in popular use in Korea or China; many of them were the rice bowls of Korean peasants. But the amazingly keen eye of the Cha-no-yu master has discovered in these odd, neglected pieces a unique beauty; for what most appeals to him are the things originally made for everyday use. In* brief, Cha-no-yu may be defined as an aesthetics of actual living, in which utility is the first principle of beauty. And that is why such great significance has been given to certain articles necessary for everyday life. . . .

The next important aspect of the works of people's art is that they are simple and unassuming. Here the quality of extravagance that is always associated with expensive art objects is wholly absent, and any surplus of decorativeness is objectionable. . . . Simplicity may be thought of as characteristic of cheap things, but it must be remembered that it is a quality that harmonizes well with beauty. That which is truly beautiful is often simple and restrained. . . . I am told that St Francis of Assisi advocated what he called 'Holy Poverty'. A thing possessed in some manner of the virtue of poverty has an indescribable beauty. Indeed, Beauty and Humility border upon each other. What is so appealing in the art of the people is this very quality . . . beauty accompanied by the nobleness of poverty. The Japanese people have a special word shibui to express this ideal beauty. . . . It is impossible to translate it satisfactorily into one English term, 'austere', 'subdued', 'restrained', these words come nearest. Etymologically, shibui means 'astringent', and is used to describe profound, unassuming and quiet feeling. The mere fact that we have such an adjective would not call for second thought, but what does call for special note is the fact that this adjective is the final criterion for the highest form of beauty. It is, moreover, an ordinary word, and is repeated continually in our casual conversation. It is in itself unusual that a whole nation should share a standard word for our aesthetic apprasial. Here in this criterion of ours for the best and most beautiful may be observed the fundamental principle of the aesthetic tastes of the Japanese people. . . . If you have travelled much in rural Japan you must have come across one of these stone monuments, with the inscription Sangai Banrei To, at a crossroad or in a deserted corner. This inscription means 'a monument to the unknown, departed souls of the million people of the world.' This monument is an expression of the Buddhist's compassion for the countless number of forgotten and uncared-for souls. I am one of those whose prayer it is to erect such monuments in the Kingdom of Beauty.

Thus from a Buddhist background, ethically much akin to the medieval Christianity on which the neo-Thomists have based their attitude towards art, Mr Yanagi seems to me in these arresting and moving sentences to have thrown down a challenge not only to his Japanese contemporaries but to us as well – a challenge to our over-accentuated individualism. For one may indeed look back with an acute sense of loss to those periods when the communal element, with its native religious, psychologial and aesthetic basis, was all-powerful as an ennobling and transmuting influence and source of life.

A potter's traditions are part of a nation's cultural inheritance and in our time we are faced with the breakdown of the Christian inspiration in art. We live in dire need of a unifying culture out of which fresh traditions grow. The potter's problem is at root the universal problem and it is difficult to see how any solution aiming at less than the full interplay of East and West can provide either humanity, or the individual potter, with a sound foundation for a world-wide culture. Liberal democracy, which served as a basis for the development of industrialism, provides us today with a vague humanism as insufficient to inspire art as either the economics of Karl Marx or the totalitarian conception of national life, but at least it continues to supply an environment in which the individual is left comparatively free.

Our need of a criterion in pottery is apparent and seems to be provided by the work of the T'ang and Sung potters which during the last twenty years has been widely accepted as the noblest achievement in ceramics. But the successful assimilation of strange stimuli requires a healthy organism, and it remains to be seen whether there is enough vitality in Europe to absorb from early Chinese pottery even more than we did during the eighteenth and nineteenth centuries from late Chinese porcelain. At the moment it is difficult to believe that the general arrogance of our materialism and the particular self-sufficiency of the pottery trade will permit the subtler scale of early oriental values to be perceived, except by artists and some sensitive people of leisure. Influences from alien cultures either upon art or industry must pass through an organic assimilation before they can become part and parcel of our growth. This happens, moreover, only when they supply an inherent need, and is usually inaugurated by the enthusiasm and profound conviction of men who have themselves succeeded in making the synthesis. The superficial imitation of early Chinese shapes, patterns, colours and technique signify nothing unless new life emerges from the fresh combination. The temptation for the individual potter is to stand back with the paralysis of frustration in face of such a sea of change, but we cannot afford to wait until the tide of a new culture rises.

The necessity for a psychological and aesthetic common foundation in any workshop group of craftsmen cannot be exaggerated, if the resulting crafts are to have any vitality. That vitality is the expression of the spirit and culture of the workers. In factories the principal objectives are bound to be sales and dividends and aesthetic considerations must remain secondary. The class of goods may be high, and the management considerate and even humanitarian, but neither the creative side of the lives of the workers nor the character of their products as human expressions of perfection can be given the same degree of freedom which we rightly expect in hand work. The essential activity in a factory is the mass-production of the sheer necessities of life and the function of the hand worker on the other hand is more generally human.

The problem is made increasingly difficult for the reason that the people who are attracted today by the hand crafts are no longer the simple-minded peasantry, who from generation to generation worked on in the protective unconsciousness of tradition, but mainly self-conscious art students. They come to me year after year from the Royal College, or the Central School, or Camberwell, for longer or shorter, usually shorter, periods of apprenticeship. As soon as they have picked up enough knowledge, or what they think is enough, off they go to start potting on a studio scale for themselves. Very few have proved themselves to be artists. And what of others, those thousands who pass through these schools and then either disappear from sight or continue to produce bad work. Again, in the past tradition would have developed and used their more moderate talents; in our own one cannot escape the sense of a great wastage.

In crafts the age-old traditions of hand work, which enabled humble English artisans to take their part in such truly human activities as the making of medieval tiles and pitchers and culminated in magnificent co-operations like Chartres Cathedral, have long since crumbled away. The small establishments of the Tofts and other slipware potters were succeeded by the factories of Wedgwoods and the Spodes, and in a short space of time the standard of craftsmanship, which had been built up by the labour of centuries, the intimate feeling for material and form, and the common, homely, almost family workshop life had given way to specialization and the inevitable development of mass production. For that no individual can be praised or blamed: like many another institution it arose in response to a human need, moving parallel on the one hand with the slow progress of economic democracy, and on the other with an unprecendented rise in the population. But although we have now reached a point where for the first time in history we are able to produce enough and more than enough for all, the trouble from the artist's or craftsman's, or for that matter any sane person's point of view, is not only that the problem of equitable distribution is still unsolved, but that so many of the things we have thus contrived to make are inhuman.

In the field of ceramics the responsibility for the all-pervading bad taste of the last century and the very probable ninety per cent bad taste of today lies mainly with machine production and the accompanying indifference to aesthetic considerations of individual industrialists and their influence on the sensibility of the public.[5] Yet although industrialists will as time goes on become more and more conscious of the desirability of, if not the necessity for good form and decoration, it is also plain that during the last twenty-five years a far reaching change in aesthetic judgment has come about, not only in England, but literally all over the civilized world. A new type of craftsman, called individual, studio, or creative, has emerged, and a new idea of pottery is being worked out by him as a result of an immensely broadened outlook. Another wave of inspiration has come to us from the Far East, and out of the tomb-moulds of long dead Koreans and Chinese, looted and disturbed by the encroachment of Western commercialism, has arisen a new appreciation of ceramic beauty.

It is just about fifty years ago that Carriès, a young French sculptor, began to make stoneware based upon old Japanese models. He has been followed by a number of potters in Paris, such as Delaherche, Decoeur, Cazin and many others, whose work has been inspired by the simplicity and restraint of the Sung potters. In Holland, Germany, Austria, Scandinavia, America, Japan and England there has been a similar response to the same stimulus, and factory products are being more and more influenced by them. One need only mention Sèvres and Copenhagen. Amongst all these individual efforts to my mind the Japanese and English are the best.

Pots, like all other forms or art, are human expressions: pleasure, pain or indifference before them depends upon their natures, and their natures are inevitably projections of the minds of their creators. It is unfortunate that as a consequence of its divorce from life, the 'applied' no less than the 'fine' art of our time, more than in any other age, suffers from excessive self-consciousness, or what is often called pose, a very different thing from the unconscious, inherent, personal and race character which has distinguished all the great periods of creative art. It is also important to remember that, although pottery is made to be used, this fact in no way simplifies the problem of artistic expression; there can be no fulness or complete realization of utility without beauty, refinement and charm, for the simple reason that their absence must in the long run be intolerable to both maker and consumer. We desire not only food but also the enjoyment and zest of eating. The continued production of utilities without delight in making and using is bound to produce not only boredom and to end in sterility. And the greater part of what passes for pleasure in the form and decoration and colour of pottery for the people today is so banal, so false and ridiculous in the confusion of mechanical perfection with beauty, as to be in itself an indictment of our popular half-culture.

The art forms of a community are the crystallizations of its culture (which may indeed be a very different thing from its civilization), and pottery traditions are no exception to the rule. In the T'ang period it is not difficult to recognize the Chinese genius for synthesis, here reinterpreting Greek and

5. This is not to say that any better taste was shown in the work of the late nineteenth and early twentieth century hand-potters in England up to fifteen or twenty years ago, or by many of them even now; but it is probable that the example set by industrialism and the strain of getting away from it was largely responsible even for their demoralization.

Buddhist ideology in terms of contemporary need, and combining these elements within the native framework of Taoist and Confucian concepts, thus fundamentally modifying and extending the boundaries of their ideas of beauty and truth. In the greatest period, that of the Sung dynasty, all these different influences are welded together in one, for unification was then supreme. Until the beginning of the industrial era analogous processes of synthesis had always been at work amongst themselves, but since that time the cultural background has lost much of its assimilating force, and the ideas we have adopted and used have been moulded into conformity with a conception of life in which imagination has been subordinated to invention and beauty to the requirements of the trade. In our time technique, the means to an end, has become an end in itself, and has thus justified Chinese criticism of us as a civilization 'outside in'.

Since the last quarter of the nineteenth century, the reaction started by William Morris has been taking place mainly outside industry and has culminated in what I have called the individual, or artist, craftsman. Beginning in protest against the irresponsible use of power, it came to an end in pseudo-medieval crafts little related to national work and life. Thence has arisen the affirmation of the mechanical age in art – functionalism. This, through let us say, Picasso,[6] Le Corbusier and Gropius of the Bauhaus, is having its effect on all crafts. A movement which however based by its initiators on a new and dynamic concept of three-dimensional form, tends amongst those who attempt to carry the idea into industry to an over-intellectual effort to discover norms of orderliness and utility. Such a process limits the enjoyment of work to the designer, and overlooks the irregular and irrational element in all fine activity including the making of pottery. Herein lies the significance of the artist-craftsman as distinct from the factory designer. Almost alone amongst workmen does he exercise the responsibility of making things for full human use – objects which are the projections of men – alive in themselves. To him the question of standard is of vital importance, and through his work to industry, and through industry to everyone. He is faced with a broken tradition, and, what is even more serious, with a culture in rapid process of change. Our sensibility to beauty is ministered to for the most part only by the work of a handful of men of genius, for the history of all nations with a developing industrialism shows that the unconscious, intuitive craftsman breaks down under the strain of transition from hand and tool to industrial machinery. His horse-sense and creative vigour, his capacity to assimilate new methods and new ideas became perverted. Only the artist and craftsman of unusual perception and strength of character stands a chance of selecting what is best from the welter of ideas which rolls in upon him today. As soon as the craftsman becomes individual and detached from his tradition he stands on the same footing as the artist. This may not signify much when one thinks of the number of artists in relation to the number of paintings done each year which will appeal with any conviction to men a century hence! But the important question is how in our disintegrating times individual potters are to discover their particular kind of truth, in other words, their highest standard, and further, by what means it can be passed on to other artist-potters to the end that humanistic work of true merit, especially for domestic use, may be produced.

I can still remember vividly how twenty-five years ago I stood before the magnificent examples of the pottery of the Sung dynasty in the Tokyo Museum wondering how an individual potter of today could possibly appropriate to himself a beauty so impersonal, so inevitable – the patient unassuming outcome of centuries of tradition gradually developing through

6. It is worth recording that Picasso himself, perhaps the most creative artist alive, has written, 'decorative art bears no resemblance to easel painting, to the production of a picture. One is utilitarian, the other a noble play. An armchair means the back against which one leans. It is a utensil. It is not art.' *Creative Art*, June 1930.

the experience of material and increasing complexity of need, and the sublimated emotion of a long succession of Chinese or Korean workers. I was abashed. I know now that it is a task beyond the power of any one man, and what makes the matter still worse, far from there being any unity of purpose and faith, at the present moment there is such an obsession with the individual point of view among English craftsmen, that one often hears them ridicule the very idea of a new communal standard. Independence once achieved is very precious, but an exaggerated pride in its possession stands bluntly in the way of concurrence in either aim or action, and the pride is only too often merely that of an artist on a dunghill. Since the Great War, however, there have been at least some signs of change, in science, in philosophy, in politics, even in the world-wide acceptance by the younger artists of a more or less common geometric abstract. But even this new common factor has been accompanied by a growing awareness of emptiness and sterility.

We craftsmen, who have been called artist, have the whole world to draw upon for incentive beauty. It is difficult enough to keep one's head above water in this maelstrom, to live truly and work sanely without that sustaining and steadying power of tradition, which guided all applied art in the past. In my own particular case the problem has been conditioned by my having been born in China and educated in England. I have had for this reason the two extremes of culture to draw upon, and it was this which caused me to return to Japan, where the synthesis of East and West has gone farthest. Living there among the younger men, I have with them learned to press forward in the hope of binding together those elements from the ends of the earth which are now giving form to the art of the coming age. I may tend to overstress the significance of East and West to one another, yet if we consider how much we owe to the East in the field of ceramics alone, and how recent a thing is Western recognition of the supreme beauty of the work of the early Chinese, perhaps I may be forgiven for the sake of the first-hand knowledge which I have been able to gather both of the spirit and manner in which that work was produced.

The manner, or technique, will be dealt with in the following chapters: here at the outset I am endeavouring to lay hold of a spirit and a standard which applies to both East and West. What we want to know is how to recognize the good or bad qualities in any given pot, and we are at least able to say that one should look first for the nature of the pot and know it for an expression of the potter in the background. He may be an unknown peasant or he may be a Staite Murray. In the former case his period and its culture and his national characteristics will play a more important role than his personality; in the latter, the chances are that personality will predominate. In either case sincerity is what matters, and according to the degree in which the vital force of the potter and that of his culture behind him flow through the processes of making, the resulting pot will have life in it or not.

I have often sought for some method of suggesting to people who have not had the experience of making pottery a means of approach to the recognition of what is good, based upon common human experience rather than upon aesthetic hairsplitting. A distinguished Japanese potter, Mr Kawai of Kyoto, when asked how people are to recognize good work, answered simply, 'With their bodies'; by which he meant, with the mind acting directly through the senses, taking in form, texture, pattern and colour, and referring the sharp immediate impressions to personal experience of use and beauty combined. But as pottery is made for uses with which we are all too familiar, the difficulty probably lies less in one's ability to recognize proper adaptation of form to function than in other directions, primarily perhaps in unfamiliarity with the nature of the raw material, clay, and its natural possibilities and limitations, and also in uncertainty as to the more imponderable qualities of vitality and relative excellence of form, both of which are indispensable constituents of beauty. It must always be remembered that the dissociation of use and beauty is a purely arbitrary thing. It is true that pots exist which are useful and not beautiful, and others that are beautiful and impractical; but neither of these extremes can be considered normal: the normal is a balanced combination of the two. Thus in looking for the best approach to pottery it seems reasonable to expect that beauty will emerge from a fusion of the individual character and culture of the potter with the nature of his materials – clay, pigment, glaze – and his management of fire, and that consequently we may hope to find in good pots those innate qualities which we most admire in people. It is for this reason that I consider the mood, or nature, of a pot to be of first importance. It represents our instinctive total reaction to either man or pot, and although there is no guarantee that our judgment is true for others, it is at least essentially honest and as likely to be true as any judgment we are capable of making at that particular phase of our development. It is far better to run the risk of making an occasional blunder than to attempt cold-blooded analyses based upon other people's theories. Judgment in art cannot be other than intuitive and founded upon sense experience, on what Kawai calls 'the body'. No process of reasoning can be a substitute for or widen the range of our intuitive knowledge.

This does not mean that we cannot use our common sense in examining the qualities in a pot which give us its character, such as form, texture, decoration and glaze, for analytic reasoning is important enough as a support to intuition. Beginning with the colour and texture of the clay, one must ask, apart from its technical suitability, whether it is well related to the thrown or moulded shape created by the potter and to the purpose for which the pot is intended – what, for example, is appropriate for a porous unglazed water jug is utterly unsuitable for an acid jar. Does its fired character give pleasure to the eye as well as to the touch; its texture contrast pleasingly with the glaze? Has it where exposed to the flame turned to a dull brick red which contrasts happily with the heavy jade green of a celadon? Does it show an interesting granular surface under an otherwise lifeless porcelain glaze? Has its plasticity been such as to encourage the thrower to his best efforts, for the form cannot be dissociated from its material. The shape of a pot cannot be dissociated from the way it has been made, one may throw fifty pots in an hour, on the same model, which only vary in fractions of an inch, and yet only half a dozen of them may possess that right relationship of parts which gives vitality – life flowing for a few moments perfectly through the hands of the potter.

Apart from the basic clay, the form of the pot is of the first importance, and the first thing we must look for is, as already indicated, proper adaptation to use and suitability to material. Without these we cannot expect to find beauty in any of its modes, nobility, austerity, strength, breadth, subtlety, warmth – qualities which apply equally to our judgments of human and ceramic values. Nor do these qualities arise from human characteristics alone, but from a common recognition of forms whether man-made or natural, which we associate with them. Of all forms we know best our own and attach to it the greatest degree of evocative emotion; next come animal, plant and mineral forms; lastly, and mainly in our own time, geometric abstracts, largely the inventions of man's brain. It is not without reason that important parts of pots should be known as foot, belly, shoulder, neck and lip, or that curve and angle should often be thought of as male or female. Beauty of ceramic form, which is at once subjective and objective, (rather than representational) sculpture. It is subjective in that the innate character of the potter, his stock and his tradition live afresh in his work; objective in so far as his selection is drawn from the background of universal human experience.

Subordinate to form but intimately connected with it is the problem of decoration, and the question arises whether the increased orchestration adds to the total effect or not. Decoration will be treated more fully later on, here it is enough to say that, although some of the very finest pots are quite plain, it is nevertheless of the greatest significance. Many a good piece has been spoiled by a weak or tasteless design, printed or applied in one way or another: not only must the pattern be good in itself and freely executed, but it must combine with and improve the form and harmonize with the natural variations of both colour and texture of body and glaze.

The upshot of the argument is that a pot in order to be good should be a genuine expression of life. It implies sincerity on the part of the potter and truth in the conception and execution of the work. By this reasoning we are thrown back upon the oldest of questions, but there is no escaping fundamental issues in discussing problems of art at a period of break-up and change. Art is an epitome of life experience and in searching for a standard in pottery elastic enough to cover both past and present we are compelled to look far afield and to examine the principles upon which the best pots of East and West have been based. In a broad way the difference between the old potters and the new is between unconsciousness within a single culture and individual consciousness of all cultures. And to this one can only add that until a life synthesis is reached by humanity the individual potter can only hope to deepen and widen his consciousness in anticipation and contribution towards that end.

The method by which a pot is formed determines its general character, whether hand modelled or built up out of coils or slices, or freely thrown on the wheel, or thrown in a mould, or cast entirely in a mould – each process conditions the interpretation of the original idea, and each has a limited range of right usage, from the easy flowing application of which follows the sense of satisfaction and adequacy of technique. It is for this reason that the industrial practice of rigidly separating designer on paper from maker in clay is responsible for much of the deadness of commercial pottery, for it is a waste of opportunity as well as a straining of technique to make moulded pots as like thrown pots as possible. The beauty of each method lies in using that method honestly, for what it is worth, not in imitating other quite different processes.[7]

The range of plastic beauty achieved in primitive pottery made chiefly by the hands of women without a wheel and with tools only of wood or stone, basketry, textiles, leaves of trees or stitched animal hides, is immense. The whole world seems to have contributed to it during thousands of prehistoric years: Minoan, archaic Greek, African, North and South American, pots of the Black Earth Region and neolithic China, pigmented but unglazed, often so fine that one might be tempted to surrender all claim for the supremacy of eleventh and twelfth century China, were it not for the fact that the general cultural and technical achievements of the Sung Chinese were so much greater. For this reason I shall deal in this book for the most part with wheel-thrown forms, which reached their greatest perfection round about that period.

A pot thrown on a good wheel with responsive clay, but not too soapy in texture, is impressed and expressed, urged and pulled and coaxed through a series of rhythmic movements, which like those of a dance are all related and interdependent. The spinning wet clay must be kept dead true to the

Stoneware pot, brushed white slip under pattern in iron, Korea, Ri dynasty

7. Every designer either on paper or of model parts should have first-hand experience not only of the processes of manufacture, but also of the limitations no less than the potentialities of his materials. What is obviously needed is a new type of designer who knows both approaches to pottery and can therefore keep industry in touch with fresh artistic expression in the studio. Without such an alliance in the near future between artist-craftsman and factory, it is difficult to conceive how pots could be made in Staffordshire which would be even respectable in the scale of beauty the world has known. The tendency to employ sculptors and painters of reputation to make designs for the industry is useful up to a point, but it gives no guarantee that these artists know and feel their medium, nor that the factories and their reduplicating processes will do justice to the designs. The link is not close enough.

28

centre of the wheel while it is being hollowed and drawn up, expanded and contracted into a living embodiment of the potter's intention. The preconceived shape will include the mark of each part of the process of throwing, the ribs left by the fingers, the upward thrust of the cylinder from the wheel-head to the major curve of the belly, the fulness or leanness of that curve, the pause and turn on the shoulder, often accentuated with ridge or collar, where convex movement changes to concave, the neck tapering to the lip with a concluding accent and conciseness of finish. Many of the noblest and most spontaneous pots are complete at this point, but others, especially such as are to have a foot-ring or bevelled lip, need to be pared on the wheel when half dry. This cutting off of shavings gives a different and sharper quality of finish: the difference between modelling and carving; and the two surfaces must be brought into harmony with one another.

The foot, upon which the pot stands, should be reasonably wide for stability, but over and beyond that its angles and proportion should relate to the lip, to which the eye instinctively leaps. The cutting of the foot does not end with the profile; the inside of the ring is nearly always hollowed out in the East. Stoneware pots are seldom glazed over the bottom, and the exposed clay tells how thoroughly the potter felt the contrast between the profile with its necessary concluding foot and the perfect curve of the pot through it.

There are many types of foot-cutting well understood by Oriental potters and often associated with certain kinds of vessel or with certain localities, in which refinement has been worked out by a long process of trial and error into a fixed tradition.

It is interesting to see an Oriental pick up a pot for examination, and presently carefully turn it over to look at the clay and the form and cutting of the foot. He inspects it as carefully as a banker a doubtful signature – in fact, he is looking for the bona fides of the author. There in the most naked but hidden part of the work he expects to come into closest touch with the character and perception of its maker. He looks to see how far and how well the pot has been dipped, in what relation the texture and colour of the clay stand to the glaze, whether the foot has the right width, depth, angle, undercut, bevels and general feeling to carry and complete the form above it. Nothing can be concealed there, and much of his final pleasure lies in the satisfaction of knowing that this last examination and scrutiny has been passed with honour.

As for the shapes of pots and good proportions in different types, it is impossible to do more than offer a few general suggestions in the footnotes to the illustrations of particular examples. Artists of many races have believed that there are fundamental laws of proportion and composition, and I too believe it; for what we call laws are no more than generalizations founded on our sense experience, but when the attempt is made to reduce such generalizations to mathematical formulae, it is difficult to believe that they can be applied in practice without robbing the craftsman's work of its vitality. No formula, however accurate, can take the place of direct perception.

Here, for example, are a few of the constructional ideas that I have found useful:
1. The ends of lines are important; the middles take care of themselves.
2. Lines are forces, and the points at which they change or cross are significant and call for emphasis.
3. Vertical lines are of growth, horizontal lines are of rest, diagonal lines are of change.
4. Straight line and curve, square and circle, cube and sphere are the potter's polarities, which he works into a rhythm of form under one clear concept.

5. Curves for beauty, angles for strength.

6. A small foot for grace, a broad one for stability.

7. Enduring forms are full of quiet assurance. Overstatement is worse than understatement.

8. Technique is a means to an end. It is no end in itself. If the end is achieved, and a fine pot comes out of the kiln, let us not be hypercritical about fortuitous blemishes. Some of the most beautiful pots in the world are full of technical imperfections. On the other hand, the Japanese have often gone too far and made pots with deliberate imperfections and overstatements of technical characteristics. This is nothing more than a kind of intellectual snobbery, rather to be expected from groups of second-rate tea-masters, and a very different thing from the sanded foot of Ming porcelains or the Korean foot-ring, spur-marked with quartz, whose virtue was the virtue of necessity. There was no question of pose about it. But there comes a time when the accidentals of potting have to be considered consciously as such, and that it the position today.

Round the question of accidentals and incidentals in pottery making revolve some of the chief difficulties we encounter in reaching a new idea of standard. After the symmetries and microscopic precision of mass production these two words seem such mouthfuls to swallow. But if T'ang or Sung pottery is accepted as the highest achievement in ceramics they will have to be swallowed. Eastern and Western thought alike regard man and his work as very inadequate and variable affairs, and an Oriental art lover eyes any perfect piece of technique with the suspicion that it contains little depth of meaning. In all the greatest pottery of the world the natural limitations of both the material and the maker are accepted without question. In China the clays are often coarse and usually exposed, the glazes are thick, and crackled, and run, and occasionally skip, the brushwork is vigorous and calligraphic, not realistic and 'finished', the throwing and moulding are frank, and accidental kiln effects are frequent.

Apologies for these 'imperfections' by authorities like the late Mr Joseph Burton on the ground that they were incidental to primitive handwork amuse Oriental writers on art, who feel that such expressions of opinion merely expose the critic's lack of insight. The Far Eastern point of view is that all these qualities can be used and that they are incidental to nature rather than accidental to man.

A more recent dictum occasionally heard is to the effect that where irregularities occur the potter 'has not realized his intentions'. It should not be forgotten, however, that within the potter's intentions are included all sorts of variations depending on the nature and manner of use of his materials and ranging from the fortuitous and often highly effective skipping of a glaze to wide differences in its colour and quality, and that so long as they do not involve structural weaknesses or by their eccentricity detract from the beauty of the pot, they are acceptable to him. It is the uniformity of perfection that kills. On the other hand, if a pot is spoiled by blistering or cracking, it is spoiled, and there is no doubt about it.

During the long Victorian period 'perfect finish' came to mean two things, either great realistic detail and meticulous surface finish or a concealing of the means by which the end had been achieved. Even so great a rebel as Whistler proclaimed the latter idea in print if not in paint. An unprejudiced survey of pre-industrial pottery, especially Far Eastern, must lead to the conclusion either that its makers were first class bunglers or that we have got our values upside down. But at the same time, if feeling in this matter is indeed changing, in spite of the emphasis on technical precision necessitated by mechanically made products, nevertheless, the way in which craftsmen rightly make use of 'accidentals' and 'incidentals' has inevitably been lost sight of. Technique has become so complex and so hidden away from common sight that we no longer know good clay, good throwing, turning or brushwork, or good firing when we see them. Nor are we constantly reminded through doing things by hand, now from each part of a craftsman's job of any real interest variations emerge, which must be dealt with on the spur of the moment. The closest analogy is that of the kitchen, with which a pottery has so much in common. Many of the problems touched on in this chapter will appear more familiar if translated into terms of good home cooking, for despite individual preferences we all know something from experience about good and bad food. But today the average man or woman judges pots by a Victorian trade standard and food apparently by none at all. And although a few people turn to books, museums and collectors for enlightenment, there are few good books save technical,[8] and the acquisitive impulse of the collector is responsible for many false values. Rarity is no guarantee of beauty, and the cunning search for it is only a hindrance to appreciation of beauty as normality.

The extent to which quite ordinary people react to the changing beauty of a shape on the potter's wheel has been a continual revelation to me of their latent desire, and often capacity, to make good things, to use them or at the very least to learn to know them. To make a thing oneself is the nearest way to understanding; but although our newer education is insistent upon this counterpoise to theoretic learning, there are hardly any schools or teachers in this country who are introducing boys and girls to the kind of making which involves real beauty. The sort of thing that goes by the name of Art and Craft in most schools, including many art schools, the next generation could very well do without.

So far as pottery is concerned, school training is a doubtful method in any case. It does not bring students into contact with the actual conditions of the craft either as hand or machine work. At best they receive no more than a half training as individual potters. The number who have come to me from well-known schools without even an elementary knowledge of clays, of throwing, of glazes and their composition, of kilns and their construction and use – the very foundations of the craft – reveals a state of affairs which could not be tolerated in any other subject.

In childhood a natural process of rehearsal and growth through experience is constant, but educationalists do not take this sufficiently into account in the teaching of pottery. I often see electric kilns and power wheels installed in schools, and clay, pigments and glazes bought ready made. This is beginning at the end, and is a loss of opportunity and a waste of money. Children and students learn far more by re-experiencing, as far as possible, the evolution of the potter's craft from its primitive origins. They enjoy finding and digging their own clay, building their own kilns and making their own colours and glazes as potters used to do before the machine age. Shoji Hamada recounted to me once how when he was a boy in a Japanese village he took part as a matter of course in making half the things

8. Exceptions must be made in the case of Dora Billington's short but informative volume, The Art of the Potter, Oxford University Press, 1937, and as a handbook for the student, Geo. T. Cox's Pottery for Artists, Craftsmen and Teachers, Macmillan.

used by the villagers with the consequence that he grew up knowing out of his body the nature of wood, of cotton and silk, of metal and clay and foodstuffs. Local tradition was still pure enough to provide a standard of form, pattern and colour which embodied that deeper wisdom of beauty in articles of daily use which we have almost lost. Such a child could never be entirely deadened by mechanical and monetary values. Only with the enthusiasm engendered by such personal experience is there any likelihood of a generation growing up capable of appreciating and demanding beauty in our domestic pottery. Until that time comes the individual potter, together with other artist craftsmen, is bound to remain outside the normal flow of a healthy national life.

A revival must essentially be the work of individuals, finding for themselves the thing they seek. It cannot be imposed from without. One cannot endow a revival; except to the extent of providing open opportunities for the individual. Craftsmen cannot be recruited by public advertisement nor by asking men about to be demobilised to write their names on a list; for if so the standard of work will not be high enough to make the revival succeed.

T.Hennell: *British Craftsmen*, 1943

We believe that much can be done to restore a pride in craftsmanship by the revival or creation of guilds of craftsmen, and we recommend that the appropriate bodies review the whole question of apprenticeship to such crafts.

Ministry of Works and Planning: *Report on Land Utilisation in Rural Areas*, 1944

In this post-war world, in which it is to be hoped that jerry-built bungalows – vilest of all desecrations in the countryside – and chromium-plated furniture will be quickly succeeded by the building of a greater number of houses with grace and dignity . . . and by the making of furniture a little more worthy of our great masters, the hand-weaver and cabinet-maker will certainly play an important part.

Norman Wymer:*English Country Crafts*, 1946

The potter
Michael Cardew
at Winchcombe,
drawing by
Thomas Hennell,
*Architectural Review*,
1941

# Arthur Lane

1909-1963

Forty years on, this soberly illustrated 80-page book has become a classic. *Style in Pottery* is a primer for the enjoyment of pottery by those who can also enjoy the benevolent magisterial summation, quite free from academic jargon, of 'some constant principles'.

FROM

STYLE IN POTTERY

# 1948

## [INTRODUCTION]

Extracts from *Style in Pottery*, 1948: the whole of the introduction and first section: 'The Potter's Means and Aims'; and the whole of Chapter 5: 'Modern Wares'.

Quite apart from the needs that make it a part of their everyday lives, most people regard pottery with friendly feelings, gladly including quite a lot of it among the not strictly useful objects that help to turn a dwelling into a home. But on the whole they are indulgently uncritical about the aesthetic qualities of these possessions. Pictures and furniture are readily defended as the expression of personal taste, but 'china' is something that just happens. It may acquire a special sanctity if identified (by an 'expert') as Worcester, Wedgwood, or Dresden; yet even the experts, the collectors, tend to sharpen their appreciation only so far as to distinguish between the work of different factories. If asked to explain the value of their favourite pieces, considered purely as works of art, most collectors would treat the question as unfair and irrelevant.

But the potters who for thousands of years have served the human race have for the most part been intelligent craftsmen, consciously exercising a complicated ritual to turn out a decent job. Many have possessed an intuitive gift that enabled them to go farther, to impose on serviceable vessels that element of willed fantasy that we describe as 'style'; these have in fact been artists. Not necessarily artists in the modern individualistic sense, for the finest pottery has often been the product less of an individual than a team, a whole workshop whose collective experience took more than a generation or two to ripen. Pottery, whether regarded as art or craft, has limits to its range of expression; it is naturally measured by the grasp of a pair of hands; it is dominated by the circular section of the wheel; even when purely ornamental, it tends to preserve the convention of being an utensil. Surely, then, within these limits it must be possible to discover some constant principles, to which the imaginative vagaries of pottery style must in varying degree conform.

This book attempts to discover such principles. But it remains for the reader to test them by first-hand knowledge of actual specimens. No photographic illustrations, however good, can do more than suggest the delights of colour, texture, and volume through which pottery makes its most direct appeal. And though there is pottery of some kind always around us, most of it is confined within the modern idiom of industrial white porcelain or earthenware, and we may be confused by the innumerable modern reproductions in earlier styles. A widely critical judgement is best formed by study of the selected pieces in museums, where alone we are likely to see wares of all periods and civilizations. Even within the range of a single period or factory we may need to see several vessels together before we become fully conscious of their common 'style'.

## THE POTTER'S MEANS AND AIMS

By 'pottery' let us here mean vessels of baked clay, complete in themselves, and not images of living things. We thus rule out decorated tilework, which is part of architecture, and pottery or porcelain figures, which could be considered as sculpture. 'Style' will mean good handling of potter's material – not necessarily the 'style' of a particular epoch in art-history, such as we understand by Gothic, Renaissance, and so on. For though potters in every age share some ideas of form and decoration with workers in other materials, they can express those ideas only so far as their control over their pottery medium allows. Coarse pottery is easy enough to make; but refinements of texture, surface, and ornament call for a fund of technical knowledge that can only be acquired by long experiment or by learning from other potters who have already mastered the problem. Knowledge of this kind may be handed down through generations, and transmitted from one country to another either by wandering potters or by examples of their work. An instance familiar to all is the painted porcelain of China, which reached Europe in such quantities during the seventeenth and eighteenth centuries. European potters took a long time to discover how true porcelain was made, but both before and after the discovery they successfully imitated the shapes and decoration of the Chinese wares, though these were completely at variance with the idiom of European art. Nothing could illustrate more clearly the working of the potter's mind. He is absorbed first and foremost with the technical mysteries of his craft, and is prepared to accept as incidentals whatever forms and decoration are proposed by his teacher, who may live at the opposite end of the world. The novelty of the new technique must wear off before he can regard it simply as a means for expressing the artistic ideas of his own society.

We as laymen are naturally most interested in the appearance of the finished pot. When we begin to analyse our reasons for liking it or not, we think first of its shape, then of the skill evident in arranging and carrying out the decoration. These are, so to speak, intellectual qualities, not too hard to explain in words. But when we come to such things as colour, roughness or smoothness of surface, and solidity or flimsiness of the clay material, then words are harder to find. For these are sensuous qualities; they ruffle the surface of our emotions in the most pleasing way; but how can we describe their value to people who have not undergone the same experience? Western writers on ceramics borrow homely metaphors from cookery; the Chinese more poetically compare the appearance of a glaze to phenomena in nature, such as 'blue of the sky after rain'. However indescribable, the sensuous qualities are more important in pottery than in almost any other minor art. The very material of which a pot is made is part of its 'style'.

Not all clays are suitable material for the potter. Some are not stiff enough to bear modelling; others crack or melt in the fire. It is usually necessary to mix two or more kinds of clay, sand, or powdered rock, after each has been thoroughly cleansed. The kinds of clay used, and the carefully regulated ascending degree of heat in the kiln, both help to determine the texture of the finished pots; whether they are to be earthenware, relatively soft and loosely knit; stoneware, dense, hard, and heavy; or porcelain, which is harder than stoneware, brilliantly white, and translucent where the walls of the pot are thin. Porcelain is one of the most beautiful artificial substances that man can make, and stoneware has a ringing integrity that sets it high above soft earthenware.

Liquids will soak through earthenware unless it is protected by glaze, which is in effect a thin surface coat of glass. Glazes for earthenware are usually made of finely ground sand or quartz mixed in water with a 'flux' – potash, soda, oxide of lead; the flux cause the mixture to melt and fuse itself on to the clay while the temperature in the kiln is comparitively low. Stoneware and porcelain are impervious to liquids, but gain a pleasanter surface when glazed. A peculiar glaze can be formed on stoneware by throwing common salt into the kiln when the heat is greatest; this causes the surface of the pot itself to vitrify, but also disintegrates it into a pebbled texture like that of an orange-skin. Other laid-on glazes for stoneware can be made of clay or powdered stones mixed with a flux. On porcelain the glaze is of flux and china-stone, the felspathic rock that with china clay forms the composition of the porcelain itself; here the physical union of glaze and pot is complete.

Colour is the most potent magic the potter can command. Allied with glaze, it may have a freshness and luminosity unattainable in any other medium of art, and this freshness does not fade with time. All potter's colours have to pass through fire, and for that reason they must be of mineral origin – oxides of iron, copper, cobalt, and so on. Dyes from plants or insects (madder or cochineal, for example) will not do. It is the action of the fire itself that transmutes these drab-looking minerals into the bright colours on the finished pot. Sometimes coluring matter is mixed with glaze; or a clear glaze may allow colours underneath to show through; or painting in colours may be added over the fired glaze, in which case the pot must be sent to the kiln once again. Some of the potter's finest effects are those of broken colour, caused by the interaction of fire, molten glaze, and underlying clay.

Such then, in bare outline, are the potter's materials – clay 'body', glaze, and colours. They are hardly 'raw' materials, for they must be so carefully worked on before they are fit to use. The uninstructed layman sees nothing of the immense labour in applied chemistry and physics by which a glaze or body is prepared. But he will often recognize traces of the ordeal the pots have gone through in the fire. The body may have sagged slightly out of shape; the glaze may have run unevenly in waves or drops, leaving parts of the clay exposed; colours, too, may be uneven in tone, and painted decoration may have blurred in the swimming glaze. Should we condemn these accidents as flaws? Not without asking what the potter was aiming at, and to what extent he claimed to control them. A defect in pottery made with the mechanical resources of modern industry cannot be excused. And a high standard of technical perfection is demanded of any potter who seeks the refined effects proper to such an exquisite material as porcelain. But to many other kinds of pottery a casual roughness gives the breath of life. Fire is an awe-inspiring, unaccountable element, and it is good that this wild partner should at times assert his share in the potter's work. But then the human contribution, the shape and ornament of the pot, must be correspondingly robust. When the two forces act in harmony, as they did so often in China and the Near East, the resulting wares have a power to stir the imagination seldom encountered in European pottery.

A potter can give shape to his wet clay in various ways. He can pinch out a small bowl or build up a large vase with his unaided hands. To save walking round the vase he could turn it on a pivoted disk, or slow wheel. But this primitive instrument was replaced as soon as might be by the fast-revolving potter's wheel, which caused the clay to spring up inside the potter's hands under its own power. The wheel to this day dominates pottery shape. It is true that in Roman times, in the eighteenth century, and in our modern industrial potteries clay vessels have commonly been shaped by pressing in moulds. But at some stage these moulded pieces are almost invariably transferred to the wheel or lathe, either for trimming or for decoration. And in consequence the horizontal section of most pots is a circle. The potter may indent the circle with fluting or draw it out into lobes while the clay is still soft but he usually expresses his sense of form through the vertical curves, angles, and straight lines of the vessel seen in profile. These admit of astonishing variety. They are affected by the texture and the plastic strength of the wet clay. Delicate mouldings would be inappropriate if the clay were coarse-grained, and with some clays extravagant curves would invite collapse. There is a direct relationship between the curves of a vase, the thickness of its walls, and the strength of the clay; and 'good potting' allows the clay to reveal its strength by making the walls no thicker than they need be to support the shape.

Soft clay on the wheel seems of itself to suggest certain shapes to the potter's hand. All are based on the sphere, the ovoid, the cone, and the cylinder. Some pots even when finished record each intuitive gesture of their maker. But usually the potter's spontaneity must yield something to the material demand for use, or the spiritual demand for elaboration. A storage jar need only be rough, but vessels to eat and drink from should be smooth for cleanliness and comfort in handling. Smoothness, a primary aim of potters from the earliest times, draws attention away from the volume and substance of the vase to concentrate on its profile outlines. The handles and spouts so often necessary to household wares yet further detract from the roundness of the shape; one is almost compelled to look at the pot from one or other of two opposite sides. Now nothing could be more insipid than a pot in which we are aware of the two-dimensional outlines alone, with an uninteresting neutral area in the middle. The very first problem the potter as artist has to solve is how to reaffirm the third dimension, the bulge of the shape between the two profiles to right and left. He can do it in the simplest way by modifying the shape. Let us at this point observe the crucial part played in pottery form by horizontal lines. From the way our bodies are constructed, the most reassuring sight in nature, the orientation by which we gauge space and form in relation to ourselves, is the horizontal line – the line of our two eyes, of the horizon. We have an exact and immediate perception of length when the lines are cut short – we measure them from the centre outwards. As any dress designer knows, such lines are best avoided in fashions for the fuller figure. But they are very serviceable to the potter. For if in turning the pot he makes ridges or grooves, these will become horizontal lines bridging the space between the profiles and tying them together. A sharp kink in the profile will have almost the same effect. And our eyes cannot help but measure these lines; they explore out from the centre and back again, with a subconscious muscular action that at once makes us aware of the receding curves of the pot. It is a favourite trick to concentrate these measurable horizontal lines round the narrower parts of the pot, towards the neck or foot; they there give a sense of constriction that emphasizes the free escape of the curves between them. One might go so far to say that no pot shape appears really stable unless it has at least one strongly defined horizontal accent. Most often its place is the foot or lip (or both). . . .

In using such words as lip, neck, shoulder, belly to describe the shape of a pot we acknowledge its likeness to a living thing. Potters have at various

Vase,
Chelsea,
18th century

times emphasized the idea by giving animal or vegetable shape to part of a vessel, if not the whole. In the Chelsea vase (a swollen urn on a wriggling plinth, all larded with rococo scrolls) the suggestion of life is the more disturbing because not explicit; a metamorphosis appears to have been arrested just before reaching the shape of any animal we know. But beyond this point pottery begins to encroach upon sculpture. Its true genius, like that of architecture, is closely bound up with abstract geometrical form.

The potter can suggest volume in ways other than by modifying the shape. He can do it through ornament on the surface of the pot. It hardly matters whether the ornament is carved, moulded or painted, though each technique has its own problems, its own possibilities for delight. Nor can we say that some subjects are suitable for pottery-decoration and others not; the mythological figure painting on early Greek vases is just as legitimate as the casually ornamental abstracts from nature so dear to the Chinese. Everything depends on the way the decoration is spaced, on the extent to which it emphasizes the shape and roundness of the pot. We may distinguish three principal rhythms in pottery ornament; the single punctuation mark that first seizes our attention; the continuous frieze that leads our eye in imagination right round the pot; and the all-over repeating pattern, which again suggests continuity where the motives narrow out in perspective to right and left. A tall Bernard Leach vase of 1930 shows with classic simplicity the leaping fish as punctuation, the painted horizontal bands below and above as continuous frieze. The potter has here so reduced the importance of lip and foot that we first apprehend the shape and volume of the pot through following the suggestions offered by the painting. . . . It fails if through over-elaboration or over-emphasis it prevents us from noticing anything else.

Very often the surface to be decorated is that of a shallow plate or dish. Here there is no third dimension to think of, the decorator has greater scope. Dishes have often been designed as show-pieces, to stand on edge against a wall. Some have a very definite 'right way up' for the picture on them. But even so one cannot help feeling that the most satisfactory designs are those which emphasize the circularity of the shape, whether by a continuous border, by radiating or 'all-over' patterns, or by a 'punctuation-mark' arrangement comprehensible from any point of view.

We have now considered material, shapes, and ornament, leaving a less obvious but still important point till last. At all times the main bulk of the pottery has been made for household use. This in itself imposes conditions on style — we have noticed smoothness, handles, and spouts. Now pottery, like other utensils, can be perfectly adapted for use and at the same time hideous to look at. Before the Second World War there was much talk of 'functional-ism' in the useful arts. Its promoters used this catchword to discredit the fripperies of their predecessors and open the way for new fripperies of their own. But many simple people were deceived: at last, they thought, this incomprehensible nonsense called art can be explained away: usefulness and beauty are the same thing. Years of shabby living may now have taught them to think again. Usefulness is no more than a condition to be fulfilled. Grace in fulfilment is an extra, properly called art. In pottery it may go no farther than a choice of certain proportions in shape, backed by good material competently used. But usually men's imagination has craved for something more, and potters have been able and willing to give it them. How far ornament or elaboration should go depends on appetite. A point is reached where usefulness and elaboration begin to conflict; the pottery has to be used with special care, perhaps only on special occasions; it becomes an instrument of ceremony. The care may be worth while; people consent to wear special uncomfortable clothes for parties, because this heightens their sense of importance. The fine porcelain of the eighteenth century would have spiritual advantages over the canteen mug, even if one had to wash up oneself. Finally, pottery may reach a point where it is of no 'use' at all, except to be looked at, like a painting or sculpture. And why not, if we like looking at pottery? Feeding, ceremony, and contemplation are all legitimate human activities, and in each the potter can serve us well.

## MODERN WARES

In the countries of western civilization we seem to have stabilized the kinds of pottery we need for daily use. For the table we have either white earthenware of the Wedgwood type (and the Wedgwood factory is still one of the most progressive in England); or else the more expensive and durable white porcelain. Both are produced in great quantity, with all the resources of the modern chemist and engineer. And though, as anyone can see who visits an up-to-date factory, a surprising number of operations remain to be performed by the skilful human hand, this skill must conform with a pattern worked out by a master-designer on his drawing-board. As a result we have wares whose technical perfection is virtually complete. It is in shapes and decoration, where style should be most eloquent, that we now seem tongue-tied. The nineteenth century revived the ornament of all previous ages. In table-wares, its especial delight was to reproduce by mechnical means the showy effects of eighteenth-century rococo porcelain. Since the First World War most people of taste have come to despise these ostentatious shams, and after a brief but disastrous flirtation with 'modernistic' post-cubist art in the nineteen-twenties, have tried to re-establish a link with the style of the late eighteenth century. We now find the economy and elegance of late Georgian architecture very sympathetic, and our useful pottery often recalls, if it does not actually reproduce, the forms created by the first Josiah Wedgwood. But his slightly sentimental grace escapes us. Even the simplest border-pattern painted on old 'Queen's ware' had a fragile life, hardly to be revived in a generation where everyone can write but few can draw. Hand-painting is at a discount with the modern industrialist, a brake on speed in production. Apart from shapes, our chief hope for aesthetic satisfaction lies in the use of new glazes, in new combinations of coloured materials, and in transfer-printing of contemporary design. Only in a few places on the European continent does 'porcelain-painting' still mean something in everyday speech.

A reaction against the mechanical and monotonous efficiency of modern industrial pottery began before the end of the nineteenth century, and in recent years a small number of 'studio-potters', working precariously as experimental craftsmen, have tried to broaden contemporary appreciation of pottery as an art. In England, they have drawn inspiration from early Chinese stonewares, Japanese peasant-pottery, and old English slipware. So long as we continue to use polished wooden furniture and metal cutlery their productions cannot compete economically with our flimsy but convenient white crockery. They might at most grace the table in the country cottage where the weary seek refuge from urban civilization. But as objects of contemplation, the best 'studio' pots have a dignity and character that stand outside time and place; they are true works of art; and the imagination and skill of their making may even rouse an echo among the industrialists. It is significant that in some factory-made ornamental pottery we should now find matt, soft-toned glazes, and forms suggested by ancient bronze vessels from China.

# John Farleigh

1900–65

In *Beyond East and West* (1978) Bernard Leach recalls War-time meetings about the crafts:

*At the Government's request but at our own expense a committee gathered monthly in the National Gallery in Trafalgar Square to do what it could for the remaining craftsmen of England, for the sake of the future. The present Crafts Centre is the residue of those efforts – originally under John Farleigh, C.B.E., and later Sir Charles Tennyson.*

Farleigh's collection of his wartime notes and essays *It Never Dies* (1946) states the need for a permanent centre for the crafts; 'Such a project must be aided by the state and it must be prepared to give independence of action to a responsible body of craftsmen.' A constitution, designed to unify the members of the various founding crafts societies, was agreed in 1948, and the Centre probably opened in 1950. Its history remains to be written, but the Centre did not receive direct state aid, although it was given the power to decide if certain artefacts were 'works of art' and therefore free from the heavy purchase tax. But by the early 1960s the membership of the Centre was under attack from within and without. In May 1964 The Crafts Council of Great Britain was formed, with very ambitious plans to take the crafts to a much wider public.

In this book the story continues with Gordon Russell's foreword to the Council's *Craftsmanship Today* exhibition of 1965.

## THE CRAFTS CENTRE OF GREAT BRITAIN

# 1950

'The Crafts Centre of Great Britain' a brief illustrated notice in The Studio, August 1950.

After many years of planning the Crafts Centre of Great Britain has established, in Hay Hill, a permanent exhibition of the work of the fine craftsmen – perhaps the first thing of its kind in our history.

Fine craftsmanship as a term is used by the Centre to define the work of the man who designs as well as makes, and excels at both. This is not so common as it may seem. Figures show that of the crafts represented there, namely gold- and silversmithing, jewelry, furniture and musical instruments, pottery, iron work, woven and printed textiles, embroidery, bookbinding, calligraphy, glass, lithography and wood engraving, only 500 or less make up the membership of the five societies that have co-operated to form the Centre.

As the Centre succeeds in its purpose it will, no doubt, attract a number of craftsmen who so far have refused to join a society of any kind. Even so it is doubtful whether exhibiting members will increase to more than 1,000 during the next ten years.

If, however, the standard of work is maintained at sufficiently high level, 500 is a number to be reckoned with and the influence of the work can be considerable. It has already proved effective. Scattered as they are over the whole of the British Isles, these craftsmen have held together the threads of good workmanship and design since the last century, when the origins of the craft movement can be traced back to Ruskin and Morris. They have created their own pockets of influence, while some have made reputations that are fast becoming international.

The Crafts Centre is, in a sense, a shop window for five of the major craft societies. Most of the world passes through London at some time, and to the question 'where can we see the work of the designer-craftsman of to-day?' we now have the answer.

This may seem a simple objective, yet we must remember that neither the British public nor the visitor from abroad knew of or had seen the best of this kind of work. It must have seemed that we no longer produced finely designed hand-made articles and that our great tradition had in the nine-teenth century become submerged.

Visitors from abroad could not hope to discover more than one or two of our craftsmen; and heaven help us if they judged our work by the 'Arte and Crafte Shoppes' and the 'Craft Corners' in the big stores. The fog of sentimentality and good-hearted voluntary labour had to be cleared up some time.

With the help of our architect Sergei Kadleigh we have attempted to provide a background of restrained elegance and taste that will prove the crafts capable of holding their own in an urban background.

The great craftsmen of the past made for patrons of taste and discernment – they also made with unconscious ease objects of daily use that were without question lovely and of their own time.

There are still people of taste and discernment who will find at the Centre that the work of the fine craftsman of to-day is surprisingly cheap. If these craftsmen are no longer unselfconscious it is because they have had to make the desperate struggle to preserve and, in some cases, to rediscover the arts of designing and making over these last seventy years. A tradition has been rebuilt, not only from the desire to make beautiful the objects of daily use but also to find a satisfactory way of life. Long ago Ruskin pointed out that the machine was not enough.

Industry is now recognizing the need for designers; and who better than the craftsman can tell the qualities inherent in good design, for he uses the actual materials and follows the process of the design from the first rough sketch on paper to the last touch of the tool?

Design is the evolution of the shape in the right material for a given purpose plus the personality of the craftsman and in some cases the client. At the Centre the commissioned work will be seen before it goes to the client; thus the practical and experimental will be combined.

The future policy will cover a number of special exhibitions arranged to bring out different aspects of the crafts.

I hope I may be forgiven if at this point I emphasize the need for generous financial support. The Centre is a non-trading, non-profit-making body dependent almost entirely on public support for its finances. If the Centre succeeds it will be because the British public still cherishes the work of its craftsmen and believes in the importance of the crafts and their contribution towards civilization. With sufficient support our craftsmen can continue to lead the world in workmanship and design – but only if the public takes its full share of responsibility.

---

On the whole, I feel that a designer who is going to be too rigid about the interpretation of his design should find a man who is nothing more than a supercraftsman and prepared to carry out his designs to the last detail.

Leslie Durbin, interviewed by John Farleigh in *The Creative Craftsman*, 1950

# Bernard Leach

1887 - 1979

The success of *A Potter's Book* (1940; 2nd edition 1945, and frequent reprints) gave Leach an audience for his judgements about pots. He followed his exhibitions abroad: to Sweden, Norway and Denmark in 1949; to Canada and the USA in 1950 for four months of teaching, lecturing and judging competitive exhibitions. *A Potter's Portfolio* may be seen as the condensed version of those lively, sometimes combative, teaching tours. It is certainly the most polished of his writings, perhaps because it is so condensed, and contains several classic statements, such as the phrase that begins: 'A potter on his wheel is doing two things at the same time'.

FROM
## 'A POTTER'S PORTFOLIO'
# 1955

Two extracts from *A Potter's Portfolio*, Faber & Faber, London, 1951, a large format book with many big illustrations suitable for use as teaching aids.

The basic process of composition in pottery, as in other forms of art, appears to depend upon an intuitive perception of the way in which similar and dissimilar elements can be coordinated in a new whole. The actual coordinating or creative faculty defies analysis; it exists – it knows that this speaks to that in such and such a way. It employs catalysis, thereby relating the seemingly unrelatable. Repetition and contrast, symmetry and asymmetry, major and minor, dark against light, convex and concave – these and many other dualisms have to be resolved in every pot by the catalytic effect of the neutrals. By a neutral I mean a line, shape or colour in which opposites have already come to an equilibrium. The difference is that between primaries and secondaries in colour. For example, in a painting, or a woven fabric, there may be a grey, made up of red and blue primaries, in which the red speaks to a red area, and the blue to a blue, producing a sudden harmony where there was discord before. Or in a pot a tenuous neutral area may be the link which successfully relates two otherwise ambiguous statements of form. Or in a pattern one slowly discovers that the unpainted part is, so to speak, of an acoustical importance better understood in the Far East. In pattern, as in melody, proverb or dance, irreducible components are united in a relationship of complete rhythmic simplicity. Some pots are enhanced by decoration, others are not. The application of pattern, singly or in repetition, should be strictly determined by the need of the shape for further orchestration. Generally speaking, decoration should be subordinate to form but not at the price of dull uniformity. Certain areas of pots call for an accent by banding the articulation of their movement or growth, for example at the neck, shoulder, or just below the major curve. Then the horizontal spaces so formed seem to demand further content. An almost universal potter's answer has been the wave movement, fast or slow, abrupt or tranquil in the rise and fall of which repetitive niches are provided for every variety of motif. But no matter what one writes about the complex relationships of shape, pattern and colour-texture, ultimately it is the manner in which such abstract ideas are applied which will determine the vitality of the work, for the pot is indeed the projection of the man who makes it and of the culture, or cultures, upon which he draws. . . .

Aesthetically a pot may be analyzed for its abstract content or a humanistic expression; subjectively or objectively; for its relationships of pure form; or for its manner or handwriting and suggestion of source of emotional content. It may be coolly intellectual, or warmly emotional, or any combination of such opposite tendencies. Whatever school it belongs to, however, the shape and pattern must, I believe, conform to inner principles of growth which can be felt even if they cannot be easily fathomed by intellectual analysis. Every movement hangs like frozen music in delicate but precise tension. Volumes, open spaces and outlines are parts of a living whole; they are thoughts, controlled forces in counterpoise of rhythm. A single intuitive pressure on the spinning wet clay and the whole pot comes to life; a false touch and the expression is lost. Of twenty similar pots on a board – all made to weight and measure in the same number of minutes – only one may have that life.

A potter on his wheel is doing two things at the same time: he is making hollow wares to stand upon a level surface for the common usage of the home, and he is exploring space. His endeavour is determined in one respect by use, but in other ways by a never-ending search for perfection of form. Between the subtle opposition and interplay of centrifugal and gravitational force, between straight and curve (ultimately of sphere and cylinder, the hints of which can be seen between the foot and lip of every pot), are hidden all the potter's experience of beauty. Under his hands the clay responds to emotion and thought from a long past, to his own intuition of the lovely and the true, accurately recording the stages of his own inward development. The pot is the man: his virtues and his vices are shown therein – no disguise is possible.

The virtues of a pot are derived from the familiar virtues of life. They can be seen by the naked eye of anyone sensitive to form, colour and texture who is reasonably experienced in the language of clay. That language has its construction and even rules which the innate sense of fitness has extracted from experience in every quarter of the globe. . . . Rules ask to be broken if they are not of our own making, but principles if they are deep and wide enough can be suggestive and helpful. Whether we verbalize them or not we are aware of them, and from this angle or that, individually as well as historically, they form the invisible core of standard and tradition. The pot is the man, he a focal point in his race, and it in turn is held together by traditions embedded in a culture. In our day, the threads have been loosened and a creative mind finds itself alone with the responsibility of discovering its own meaning and pattern out of the warp and weft of all traditions and all cultures. Without achieving integration or wholeness he cannot encompass the extended vision and extract from it a true synthesis.

To repeat an earlier belief that for me is central, the quality which appears to me fundamental in all pots is life in one or more of its modes: inner harmony, nobility, purity, strength, breadth and generosity, or even exquisiteness and charm. But it is one thing to make a list of virtues in man and pot and another to interpret them in the counterpoint of convex and concave, hard and soft, growth and rest – for this is the breathing of the universal in the particular.

# Patrick Heron

BORN 1920

Heron was already an important figure as painter and critic (for the *New Statesman*, 1947-50). He had (and has) a close connection with the arts community in St Ives, partly formed in 1944-45 when he had worked at Bernard Leach's pottery. His talk seeks common ground for painting and ceramics and finds it in an organic, rhythmical abstraction.

The Dartington conference was attended by 122 delegates from seventeen countries. The lectures, discussions and demonstrations dealt with techniques, education and aesthetics. For Bernard Leach it was a dream come true: 'The interchange of two hemispheres' – East and West sharing each other's thoughts once again. His old friends Yanagi and Hamada were there, expressing that philosophy of craftsmanship at the centre of Leach's efforts to persuade others about the unifying nature of the healthy crafts. Dr Soetsu Yanagi, the philosopher-critic, was Leach's mentor; Shoji Hamada, who had helped Leach create the St Ives pottery in 1920, was an embodiment of all their hopes for the crafts. After Dartington the three of them travelled slowly across the USA telling the story of the conference to craftsmen and students. The tour continued in Japan where Leach spent a further eighteen months: a time of work and travel described in this book's excerpts from *A Potter in Japan*, 1952-54, published in Britain in 1960.

Yanagi, Leach
and Hamada
at the Dartington
Conference,
1952

THE CRAFTS IN RELATION
TO CONTEMPORARY ART

# 1952

The whole of his talk
delivered at the
International Conference of
Craftsmen in Pottery and
Textiles held at Dartington
Hall, Totnes, Devon, 17-27
July 1952.

I've often wondered to what extent I have myself been influenced, as a painter, by the 14 months I spent at the Leach Pottery at St Ives in 1944 and 1945. Until fairly recently the idiom which I made my own was the idiom of still life: that is to say, the sort of spatial organisation which I most habitually constructed in my canvases was an organisation involving the limited spatial sequence typical of still-life painting. It is possible to argue that all painters are *primarily* concerned with the definition of space: it is possible to believe that all painters – whether they are representational or avowedly 'abstract' (or 'non-figurative', as I prefer to say) – it is possible to believe that they are all more vitally concerned with giving concrete, tangible reality to certain abstract rhythms, certain patterns or formal configurations, than to specific, individual forms. The actual single forms which a painter uses to create that characteristic rhythm of spatial definition which is typical of his work – which, indeed *is* his work – the individual forms he uses are of less significance, considered separately, than the total configuration in which they are set. In the final analysis, of course, it is impossible to separate the two. Individual forms in a canvas are not individual: they have already suffered a transformation as the result, simply, of various kinds of pressure which the total composition, the total design, inflicts upon all its components. Incidentally, this is one major cause of what is popularly known as *distortion* in figurative painting. A pictorial image of, say, a candlestick may lurch to the left at its base, to the right at its middle, and to the left again at the top. All this may be attributable to the various horizontal thrusts exerted upon the vertical candlestick by adjacent objects or forms in the composition. However, what I am trying to lead up to at this point is not some conclusions on the nature of space-relationships in modern painting. I am hoping to suggest certain parallels which exist between contemporary pictorial and ceramic aesthetic. In my own early post-war pictures – if I may refer for a moment to my own experience – there appeared a number of still-life objects amongst which were some jugs, coffee pots and vases. These pots looked remarkably like Leach pots. They also bore some resemblance to jugs in pictures by Braque. Crititics of my paintings have been very conscious of this second influence – but, I think, not of the first. Nor have I ever heard *anyone* speak of the extraordinary similarity which exists between the actual jugs of Bernard Leach and the pictorial jug-image which Braque has slowly evolved since about 1924, and in which, in a famous picture painted in 1942, was almost identical with the waisted stoneware 'lemonade jug' which features in the Leach Pottery's catalogue.

But this example of an actual and a pictorial pottery sharing many of the same qualities does not point, I am convinced, to the simple case of a direct influence (at any rate where Leach and Braque are concerned). Leach's significance is not merely that of an individual artist: he is typical of a whole movement, a movement, of course, which he has done more than anyone else in England to establish. Braque, on the other hand – though so personal a painter that his direct artistic descendants are a mere handful – Braque is one of the great pioneers of modern painting. Potter and painter, each in his own sphere, has created, or released, a new rhythm. Perhaps that sounds simple or easy. Let me say, then, that I do not believe any achievement in the visual arts to be greater than this. One may think up a new subject for painting, one may concoct a new formal synthesis out of familiar components, or one may replace identifiable forms by unidentifiable ones (that is all that a good abstract painter has done – he has stripped his forms of their recognisable, identifiable 'faces' and presented them in a faceless guise: what a bad abstract painter does – and there are thousands of them about now – does not concern us. But what one cannot do, without drawing on the deepest and most unexpected resources of human feeling or consciousness, is to create a rhythm which is a new rhythm. I am not claiming that Leach or Hamada or Cardew or

Staite Murray is comparable, as an aesthetic *innovator*, to Braque. What I do claim is that these potters have re-established an ancient valid formal rhythm which precisely coincides with the formal rhythm of certain modern painters, and notably of Braque. Now rhythm cannot be pin-pointed. It pervades a picture, or a pot, dominating its forms, dictating its character and, above all, determining its intervals. Rhythm in painting is that logical force which suddenly gives the subject – whether still life, landscape or figure – its new identity as a pictorial image. On the one hand, the artist may be in love with his subject and want to paint it. And, on the other, the artist may only have at his disposal certain habitual, if not exactly mechanical, rhythms, certain reflexes of eye, arm and hand; certain rhythmic gestures of the brush. While this is his condition the sort of marks he makes on his canvas will be one thing and the sort of picture he is trying to paint will be quite another. This state of affairs will persist unless, and until, that sudden experience arises in which he surprises himself by seeing, for the first time, a new rhythmical statement (in terms of his medium) which *embodies* his beloved subject-matter. Personally I believe that we shall not be deluding ourselves if we insist on the *physical* nature of this whole experience. Speaking as a painter, I can testify to the following sequence of sensations: the sudden apprehension of the form of a new picture is first registered, in my own case at any rate, as a distinct feeling of hollowness somewhere in the region of the diaphragm. I am noting possible subjects all day long, every day, quite involuntarily. Thus it is not a question of painting *when* I see a subject: it is a question of calling up a subject ( or to be more precise of calling up an immense variety of remembered subjects simultaneously) *when* I am ready for action with my brush and palette. So I begin with the hollow feeling. Next, this uncomfortable sensation in one's middle grows into a sort of palpitation, which, in turn, seems rapidly to spread upwards and outwards until the muscles of one's right arm (if one is right-handed) become agitated by a sort of electric energy. This energy in one's arm is the prelude to painting because it can only be released by grabbing a brush and starting to paint.

This means allowing one's arm and hand free rein to weave upon the canvas a complex of forms which will, as likely as not, be decidedly problematical and surprising to oneself. Conscious thought about design or form or structure simply does not enter into it at this stage. One's arm has been given its freedom and it discharges its twitching energy upon the unfortunate canvas: one's conscious mind, at such a moment, is probably doing no more than observe the swiftly changing tangle on the canvas. What time it can spare from doing this is taken up in contemplating – not design – but the subject of the picture. When I work I am *thinking* of one thing, but *feeling* and *doing* something else. My mind, when I am painting, is completely engrossed – not by the painting itself but by something *beyond* my painting: something I will call the subject, though I do not mean that in quite the ordinary sense of the term. I might be in London, and the subject of my picture might be a room in St Ives, Cornwall. It is a room with a view: a room with a huge window overlooking the harbour; and beyond, the harbour, the bay: and beyond the bay – infinity (plus an island with a lighthouse). Now while I work away, there in London, I cannot *think* – with my conscious mind – of anything but my St Ives room, with its window. While I paint I *am* in St Ives. Meanwhile, however, the picture is being constructed very rapidly by my right hand: my hand hardly pauses to consult *me*, because I am lost in an intense reverie of a remembered place.

From all this I conclude that, if one focuses the whole of one's conscious mind on one aspect of a creative problem, one's natural instinct will thus be freed to resolve things on another level and in its own terms. And I think this means, in relation to painting, that if the artist concentrates his mind upon vision, his hand will take care of all those complex matters of design of which the finished painting primarily consists. One cannot consider a question of pictorial architecture in cold blood – and cannot measure one form against another, as a cold calculation of mere design. The result will always be a dead design. One can only record the pictorial configuration from the standpoint of one's vision, one's deepest feeling. And, as I've tried to suggest, one's vision may be felt before it is seen. The unborn image, which is one's new picture, is something which first announces itself to one – as I've said – as a sudden access of energy in the pit of one's stomach, in one's arm, in one's fingers. It is felt before it is seen – for the simple reason that it cannot be seen until one's hand has created it on canvas. Even then the painter is incapable of seeing what he has done – at least, for a week or two. One thus has this sensation, as Picasso has noticed, that one's picture goes on changing of its own accord, long after one has ceased to interfere with its anatomy or have a hand in its constitution.

I have subjected you to all this talk about the painter's processes because I believe that the painter and the potter or weaver have one thing in common, above all else. We are all dedicated to perpetuating the *creative act* in an age which is increasingly dominated by inhuman mechanistic processes. Our civilisation depends of course for its continued existence upon its science, its technical skills and its brilliantly impersonal power to manipulate matter. No one I imagine really proposes that we should jettison science – not even such cranks and lunatics as the modern painters or the hand potters would advocate total withdrawal from the present position of advanced techniques for dealing with physical problems.

Yet the fact remains that potter, weaver, painter – are all equally aware of immense dangers inherent in the very nature of our civilization. Our potting, weaving, painting is not only an affirmation – an affirmation of our deepest, instinctive awareness that the very texture of life is dependent rather upon organism than upon mechanism – it is also a protest. Our work is at one and the same instant, therefore, an affirmation of faith and a protest against an encroaching enemy. What is the enemy – precisely? I think we all recognise that techniques are capable of dominating men – rather than the other way about. I think we feel that technology is turning, on every hand, into technocracy. Man is becoming increasingly subject to more processes. He is thus losing both responsibility, personality and his chances of happiness and fulfilment. So the 'cranky' potters and weavers and the 'red' painters all protest. And of course it may be said that even the crankiest, wobbliest of pots, the lumpiest cloth and the dottiest pictures are all effective in one single respect: that they register protest. Even bad individual work is at any rate individual, a projection of organic values of some sort into a scene that is streamlined by impersonal mechanistic forces.

But now I want to return to aesthetics. Bad hand pottery may succeed in registering a protest – but it can do little more. In order to perform the infinitely more important of the two functions, vis à vis society, which I have mentioned – in order to affirm positive values – craft must achieve the intensity of communication of art. Craft that is not art is not craft either. Nor is there, in my opinion, a separable, distinct entity called technique. If the word 'technique' is not to be defined, simply, as *the power to materialise a concept*, the power to give concrete material form to what was previously an invisible complex (within the artist) of thought and feeling, of intellectual abstraction and emotion – then I do not believe the word possesses any valid usefulness as applied to art. In the context of the applied sciences, of course 'technique' has quite a different connotation. In such a connection 'technique' implies a practitioner's capacity to execute certain movements in the manipulation either of materials or of abstract ideas. In this sphere, technique can be measured – as it can, possibly, in the case of musical executants. One knows in advance how a given action can be performed: one knows, therefore, how to measure the comparative success of the performer, whether he be among the first violins, on the field at Lord's cricket ground or in the chemistry lab.

But in the arts – which include, in my view, what are known as the crafts – technique means something much subtler. We commonly complain that a painter's technique is faulty, or non-existent, when what we really mean is that the artist's aims are so unfamiliar to us that we are unconsciously assuming that they were something other than they in fact are. Technique in art cannot be meaured in the abstract. It has to be considered in relation to each artist's unique aims. But once we know or can recognise these aims, we have already passed, at a bound, from a consideration of means to a consideration of ends. So I repeat – technique is simply the power to bestow visible, concrete, particular form upon what hitherto remained an abstract, invisible, unknowable entity. When we say an artist's technique is faulty we are giving him the benefit of the doubt to a quite unwarranted degree: we are making him a present of a conception which he has shown no signs of entertaining himself: in saying 'what he is trying to do is alright, but he doesn't know how to set about it' the 'what he is trying to do' is really a figment of our own imaginations. The artist does not exist whose so-called vision is finer that his so-called technique: everyone does the utmost he is capable of doing: no one has a vision in excess of his power to materialise that vision. To suppose that an artist may get better is, however, quite permissible. Everyone gets better or worse all the time. But if what we mean is that such-and-such an artist may improve – we should say this, rather than suggest that his hand lags behind his mind and sensibility. In that instant in which a finer, bolder, more sensitive vision is granted to an artist – in that instant he knows the exact means for realising his vision.

I have laboured this point because I think it is vital for a proper conception of the creative process. But I hope I haven't given the impression that I believe all creative processes in the arts to be quite automatic, and thus devoid of intense and sustained intellectual effort. If I am not wrong, the nature of intellectual effort itself is that it proceeds on the pattern I have already suggested. The rational faculty itself is not mechanistic and smoothly inevitable in its operations. In moments of the purest mental concentration we still experience, I should have said, a process of leaps and bounds. We jump to conclusions quite literally. If 2 x 2 = 4 is demonstrated to me – I either leap to an appreciation of this mathematical fact – or I remain in the dark about it. I *do not* proceed smoothly and at an even pace along the railway line of logic, reaching conclusions as regularly as stations.

It seems to me that the arts of pottery and weaving will only remain arts so long as this intuitive apprehension of *life* is conveyed through the pot or the textile. A work of art consists in an arrangement of material factors being so ordered that they exist for evermore in a state of tension in relation to one another. The subtle asymmetry of a pot by Leach or Hamada is the asymmetry of life itself. You can analyse the construction of a pot by either in terms of geometry – but it will not get you very far. Geometry is there: the component members of the pot are describable, up to a point, in terms of arcs, straight lines and angles. But the pot lives and breathes and – to quote

T.S.Eliot for the second day running —

> ... as a Chinese jar still
> Moves perpetually in its stillness.

How Leach and Hamada transcend the geometry of mechnical form and achieve the asymmetry of organic form is, in the final analysis, a mystery perhaps. But one can say a thing or two about their formal characteristics — their habits of formal composition.

The whole emphasis in the work of Hamada, Leach, Cardew and others is, it seems to me, upon what I call submerged rhythms. The modern tradition which these potters have in common is nourished by Sung, by Korea, by Japanese country pottery, by Medieval English and English slipware. All these have at least one great quality in common: submerged rhythms. By this I mean that what we apprehend most immediately and most powerfully is not a series of sharply precise articulations at the surface of the pot. Pure arcs or sharp angles at the meeting of rigid planes are nowhere in evidence. Indeed rigidity is the quality most opposed to the essence of this whole group. Form is essentially fluid in Hamada or Leach, just as it is always blunted at its sharper extremities. We feel a powerful pulse in their pots: a rhythm that seems at its most emphatic just below the glazed surface. This is also a characteristic of natural forms – legs, boulders that have been washed by the sea, or even in the human figure, where the structural form is below the surface of the flesh – the bone is under the muscle.

I feel very strongly that in this respect precisely – its aspect of submerged form, submerged rhythms, the pottery of Leach or Hamada is utterly contemporary: the exact counterpart, in ceramic terms, of the sculpture of Henry Moore or the painting of Braque. Braque has said that the painter should put himself in rhythmic or formal sympathy with nature: he should not copy it. By doing the first he gets close to that natural reality he loves: by the second he estranges himself from nature. The first involves empathy, intuitive relaxation and the power to absorb nature: its products – whether in the paintings of Braque or the pots we saw this morning by contemporary Japanese – are like natural phenomena, only they are controlled. In those Japanese pots where glaze was spilt over a more regular pattern one witnessed the superb control of a natural energy – an energy which is inherent in the material. The results had the naturalness of lichen growing on rocks – which is also a close parallel with textures in Braque or Picasso. Moore's figures enhance the life of the stone or wood they are carved out of. Leach or Hamada, or the old English Slipware potter, or the country potters in Japan, all enhance clay. Their art does not seek to dominate natural material, but to co-operate with it. In my view the reason why so much that is best in contemporary art and craft today has its power to move us is just this: it provides the contrast with our power-ridden, science-ridden age, which seeks to dominate natural material wherever it encounters it – devitalizing it and ourselves in the process. The art of the contemporary craftsman is of immense importance because it can recall the organic; it announces the truth that the mystery of life itself can still be proclaimed by a piece of cloth or a cup and saucer. The crafts are also, it must always be realised, the most consistent receptacles of abstract art. Man's will to form – and all form as such is abstract – man's will to form is expressed in pottery and weaving no less than in painting and sculpture. If I believe this sense of form is of immeasurable importance to mankind — that may well be because, for me, the moral and the aesthetic have a single identity. Ethics are the aesthetics of behaviour.

# Peter Floud

1911–1960

In 1952 Floud had assembled the exhibition of *Victorian and Edwardian Decorative Arts* at the Victoria and Albert Museum, where he was the Keeper of the Circulation Department. He had identified a pioneering strain of original design that was much broader than Arts and Crafts movement activity. In this article he suggests that present-day crafts ideas have narrowed activity still further by emphasising the value of designer and maker being the same person. He notes a stylistic swing away from the traditions being established in the 1920s (he means by Bernard Leach and Ethel Mairet) and back towards the more ornamental tastes of the late-Victorian pioneers. Floud laments the relative decline of craft furniture, silver, and jewellery. Activity in the last two was still heavily sedated by high levels of purchase tax (the jewellery rate had reached 125 per cent) but a genuine revival was just about to begin, greatly helped by the Worshipful Company of Goldsmiths in the City of London, whose Art Director, Graham Hughes, was instrumental in promoting, exhibiting, and stimulating commissions for almost thirty years.

## THE CRAFTS THEN AND NOW

# 1953

The Studio, April 1953.

A comparison between the position of the crafts in 1953 and in 1893 is not so arbitrary as at first appears, for the latter year saw not only the founding of *The Studio*, but also the first full flowering of the Arts and Crafts Exhibition Society, which then held its Fourth Exhibition and issued its influential 'Arts and Crafts Essays'. A comparison between the two years should, therefore, enable us to judge to what extent the original aims of the Arts and Crafts movement have been fulfilled, modified, or abandoned during the last 60 years.

Perhaps the most unexpected fact to emerge from such a comparison is that the main pivot of current Arts and Crafts doctrine, and indeed the main criterion normally employed today in defining craft-work – namely the identity of designer and craftsman – received little attention in 1893. The founders of the Society – men such as Walter Crane, Lewis Day, and Heywood Sumner – never executed their own designs, but invariably turned them over to commercial firms (in the case of furniture, textiles, wallpaper and pottery) or to professional craftsmen or women in the case of embroidery or woodcarving.) It is, of course, true that William Morris (in contradistinction from his fellow-designers) himself mastered the practice of many crafts, but even he (having once discovered the technical secrets of the craft) rarely executed his own designs or would have thought the result any better had he done so.

The present-day emphasis on this point derives, in fact, not direct from Morris or early Arts and Crafts teaching, but rather from the second-generation collaboration of doctrine worked out in the first decade of this century by men such as W.R.Lethaby, who were preoccupied with the application of craft principles to the training of art-students and to education generally. It was this later generation which – by first stressing the didactic and therapeutic value of craftwork – paved the way for the present-day belief that craft products have a special value in that they express the individual personality of the maker in a direct unmediated way that is impossible in the case of work – even handwork – undertaken at second-hand. The most striking result of this shift in emphasis is that whereas the highlights of the 1893 exhibition were the woven hangings, the printed velveteens, the silk damasks, and the wallpapers, designed for enterprising firms such as Alexander Morton, A.H.Lee, Thomas Wardle, John Wilson and Jeffrey & Co, the staple exhibits at all present-day craft shows are the studio pots and the individually executed hand-weavings – two categories which did not so much as exist in 1893.

Craft pottery in 1893 meant the painted and lustred wares designed by William de Morgan at his Sands End Pottery, Fulham, or else the vegetable vases and fantastic modelled figures and birds produced by the Martin brothers at Southall. De Morgan's products, with their brilliant colours based on Persian models, their glossy finish and their carefully delineated animals and fishes, have no discernible influence on any of our contemporary potters, and his system of designing on paper and entrusting the painting to assistants such as the two Passengers or Joe Juster is quite out of tune with modern studio practice.

As is well known, the modern school of British studio-potters dates its birth not from the establishment of the indigenous Arts and Crafts movement, but from Bernard Leach's return from Japan in 1920, and bases its practice on two traditions – the early Chinese and the English medieval – both of which were almost unrecognized in the 1890s. Between the wars its standards gradually came to dominate all English studio pottery, till by 1939 it could be said that all serious potters recognized and accepted its influence.

However, since 1945, a number of new potters have come forward whose work represents, in varying degrees, a revulsion from the generation-long dominance of the Leach, Staite Murray, Cardew school. Lucie Rie, with her continental training, her experiments with thinly-potted porcelain, and her liking for dry, gritty textures and scratched decoration, represents a modest reaction, which younger potters such as James Tower have developed by frankly abandoning symmetrical wheel-thrown shapes in favour of elongated, vaguely zoomorphic, hand-modelled forms. A more extreme reaction is typified by Steven Sykes and the potters who have gained inspiration from his experiments with stylized figures and impressed decoration. Strangely enough some of his work bears a curious resemblance to that of the Martin brothers, particularly in his use of detachable parts, his tendency to a certain deliberate whimsicality, and his readiness to produce frankly unusable decorative objects. His debt to them is, no doubt, unconscious, but nevertheless serves to remind us that such cases of the wheel turning full circle will become increasingly frequent as we now begin to see the development of new trends which are reactions against early twentieth-century movements which were themselves reactions against late-Victorian taste.

Steven Sykes:
Gabriel, tile
in low relief,
pale blue glaze
over red clay

The contrast between 1893 and 1953 is particularly clear in the case of hand-weaving. Almost all hand-weavers today – and there are many thousands – work in the tradition established by the late Ethel Mairet after her return to this country in 1910 – a tradition based on Indian and Scandinavian peasant weaving, relying for its appeal on variety of texture rather than complexity of weave or pattern, and involving in a particularly intense form the mystique of the individual worker expressing his personality through the medium of cloth dyed, spun, and woven by himself to his own design. Nothing of the sort existed in 1893, and hand-weaving at that time consisted exclusively in the elaborate figured woollen and silk fabrics designed by Morris, Walter Crane, and others for steady production in the hand-loom sheds at Merton Abbey, Carlisle, or Braintree, and drawing their stylistic inspiration from the sophisticated late-Gothic silks of Palermo and Lucca, or the eighteenth century products of the Spitalfields industry.

In the case of tapestry-weaving the contrast is even more striking, for, of all the weaving techniques, tapestry is the one which needs the least equipment and which lends itself most readily to the immediate expression of the individual weaver's personality. One would therefore have expected it to be particularly favoured by the Arts and Crafts movement. In fact, however, the only tapestries produced by the pioneers were the very different arras hangings executed at Merton Abbey by Morris's trained weavers to the designs of Walter Crane, Burne-Jones and others, and it is not till the 1920s that we find individual craftworkers turning to experiments with small individually worked tapesty panels, as a result of the obvious advantages of the technique in the teaching of children. Comparison between the majestic *Angeli Laudantes* tapesty designed by Burne-Jones and Morris (1894) and Gordon Crook's little *Hands* panel – a typical example of the individually conceived tapestry, shown at the 1952 Arts and Crafts Exhibition – makes the contrast between the two approaches quite clear.

The only professionally-woven tapestries on the Morris scale produced in recent years have been those executed on the Edinburgh looms to the design of easel painters. At present this enterprise is more or less in abeyance, but the project for weaving the huge hanging required for Coventry Cathedral will no doubt keep the looms busy for many years. A successful attempt to produce a cheap substitute for tapestry has been Michael O'Connell's lively printed and stencilled hangings, for which no counterpart can be found in the early Arts and Crafts movement.

Gordon Crook:
*Hands*, tapestry
panel, 1952.
Right,
Edward Burne-Jones
and William Morris:
*Angeli Laudantes*,
tapestry, 1894.

In embroidery, if we confine our attention to the original work done by the pioneering spirits of each generation, we see that same curious unconscious rapprochement between 1953 and 1893 that we have noted in the case of pottery. The earlier date marks the apogee of late-Victorian needlework as shown not only at the Arts and Crafts Exhibition but also at the Chicago International Exhibition of that year. Not only were men like Walter Crane regularly designing large panels and portières to be executed by their industrious wives, but embroideresses such as May Morris, Mrs Thackeray Turner, and Mary Newill, were beginning their careers as independent designers. Their work, though varied, mostly depended, at that date, on the effect of heavy crewel wools and bold, broad, often pictorial, designs. A

Frances Richards:
Embroidery after design by
Ceri Richards, 1950

generation later, in the 1920s, we find the emphasis rather on minute and delicate stitchery, employed on carefully elaborated formal patterns, as in the work of needlewomen such as Mrs Christie and Mrs Simmonds. Now, the work done since the war by such embroideresses as Frances Richards and Constance Howard shows, by reaction, a reversion to much bolder and less formal techniques – including a free use of appliqué – and frankly pictorial designs: a movement which is carried to its logical conclusion in the so-called 'fabric collages' of Margaret Kaye and others. The same emphasis on spontaneous designing is naturally to be found equally in the work of those contemporary embroideresses – such as Peggy Thomas – who exploit the infinite possibilities of the modern sewing-machine.

In the case of textile-printing no valid comparison can be made between the two dates, for though a certain amount of original hand-block printing by *individual* designer-craftsmen was being done in the late 1920s and 1930s, nothing, as far as we know, was being produced before that date, and very little of interest has been produced since about 1945. The absence of such individual hand-blocked textiles in the early days of the movement (at a time when Morris and others were producing quantities of superb *workshop*-printed hand-block textiles) is further confirmation of the changed emphasis on the sanctity of the artist-craftsman. On the other hand, the absence of interesting work since about 1945 is simply due to the fact that, with the development of commercial screen-printing and the possibility this gives for economic short runs, artists who in the 1930s had no alternative but to print their own designs, can now confidently hope to sell them to the trade.

Space forbids a detailed comparison of furniture design in 1893 and 1953. The former date is, however, of special significance as marking the year in which Ernest Gimson and the two Barnsleys moved to Gloucestershire and thus established the modern Cotswold School. It may with justice be said that all modern craft-furniture stems directly from their efforts. Even original designers, such as the late Romney Green, who never actually worked in the Cotswolds, could not escape Gimson's influence, and those few craftsmen-designers who valiantly attempt to carry on today in a forlorn effort to compete with architect-designed mass-produced furniture, would hardly claim to have added anything to Gimson's heritage.

The difficulties facing present-day craftsmen-silversmiths are even greater than those facing the furniture makers, for today's prices place their wares beyond the resources of almost all customers except universities, city companies, cathedrals, and the like, whose demands are naturally conservative and circumscribed. A detailed comparison of post-war output with the work of 1893 would therefore be invidious, especially as at the former date such original designers as C.R.Ashbee, Henry Wilson, A.S.Dixon, and Gilbert Marks were already launched on their careers. It is, however, legitimate to ask why it is that there is not today, and has not been for a generation, any designer producing cheap, simple, utilitarian metalwork of the quality popularized by W.A.S.Benson in the 1890s, and why it is that the craft of enamelling has almost entirely died out. In the 1890s remarkable work in champlevé and in painted enamels was being executed by Alexander Fisher, Nelson Dawson and others, and Clement Heaton was experimenting in cloisonné. Today practically nothing is being done, other than the routine production of heraldic enamels for presentation silver.

W.A.S.Benson:
Silver-plated
spun nickel
teapot, c.1895

A comparison of the status of craft jewellery today with the situation in 1893 would be almost as discouraging were it not for the efforts of the Central School and the Royal College. These are as yet too recent to have established

themselves firmly, but it seems that here again there may prove to be an unconscious rapprochement between the late-Victorian and what one must presumably now call the early-Elizabethan. Certainly the approach favoured by the Central School is more in tune with the somewhat barbaric taste of C.R.Ashbee's late-Victorian brooches and clasps than with the refined and elegant pendants of Arthur Gaskin and Paul Cooper which were typical of the period between 1905 and 1925.

It seems then that this comparison of 1953 and 1893 should lead us to two main conclusions: firstly that the original craftwork done today is much closer stylistically to the work of the late-Victorian pioneers than to that of the 1920s; secondly, that present-day Arts and Crafts doctrine, by emphasizing individualistic and subjective criteria, and especially by insisting on the identity of designer and executant, defines the crafts much more narrowly than did the accepted theory of 1893. It would be valuable if the movement took the opportunity of this jubilee to consider the extent, if any, to which the present difficult – and indeed discouraging – position of so many of the crafts is connected within this change.


# Dora Billington

1890-1968

Billington was an admired teacher of pottery at the Central School of Arts and Crafts in London, at a time when the school was considered an adventurous alternative to the pervasive influence of Bernard Leach. She tries to pay Leach his due by aligning his directness with the 'right-making' of Lethaby (the architect, designer, and first Principal of the Central at the turn of the century), but her teacherly enthusiasm is all for the sprightly inventiveness and graphic vivacity of this post-war generation (to which she adds Lucie Rie).


## THE YOUNGER ENGLISH POTTERS

# 1953

Two articles from *The Studio*° 'The Younger English Potters', March 1953; and 'The New Look in British Pottery', January 1955.

Studio pottery, after some years of increasing production and decreasing inspiration, now shows welcome signs of coming to life again, like a bonfire which after dying down suddenly bursts into flame in a different place: from a spark, perhaps, igniting the top of the pile, or from a gradual break-through from its smouldering foundations. In order to understand this particular bonfire it may be useful to inquire what has fed and kept it alight since it first started in the latter half of the last century.

Perhaps the first studio potter in this country was William De Morgan, a friend of William Morris, and the only potter in the band of craftsmen who started the 'Craft Movement' and founded the Arts and Crafts Exhibition Society. De Morgan, however, was more interested in colour and decoration than plastic form, and devoted many years of research and experiment to the problems of the brilliant colours and glazes of Persian and other Near Eastern wares, which he learned to reproduce with remarkable technical fidelity. His designs, although in many cases a deliberate and scholarly pastiche, somehow look unmistakably English nineteenth century and some are rather like Morris textiles; though unlike Morris textiles they didn't inspire others to follow the lead. We must look to France for further experiments in brightly coloured glazes.

The Martin Brothers, stoneware jug, c.1900

The Martin brothers, working also in the latter half of the nineteenth century, used the English technique of salt-glazed stoneware. Their approach was sculptural; shapes were thrown on the wheel and either modelled into grotesque heads or birds – Toby jugs with a difference – or tooled and inlaid with coloured slips to the likeness of fruits and shells. The colour was subdued, chiefly grey and brown; the Martins' great contribution was their feeling for plastic form and for the textures and colours of natural clays, which they used with an unfettered invention and vitality. The Martins also were too individual to attract a direct following, but they had started something – an interest in clay and the potters' wheel – out of which has grown studio pottery as we know it today.

To fall in love with Chinese and other Far Eastern stoneware was a natural result; potters learning to throw looked with newly awakened eyes at these apparently simple and noble shapes with their jade-like glazes. And how well they fitted into the new simplicity of decor in the 1920s and '30s. But how elusive it all was, technically and aesthetically!

Then Bernard Leach appeared on the scene, direct from the Far East, able – and willing – to explain not only the technique, but how this elusive beauty grew out of the direct and straightforward but very sensitive, use of tool and material. This approach to good design through 'right-making' had already been taught by Professor Lethaby and others, and had found ready acceptance in other crafts. (There is something in the English character that responds to that kind of 'common-sense', sometimes, alas to the avoidance of that more troublesome and elusive element, imagination.) It only needed someone to show potters their own 'right-making'. It is easy to over-simplify and be perhaps a little unfair to others who were working in the 1920s, and producing some good work; but it is largely due to Bernard Leach's influence that for some years an ever-increasing number of potters were busily discovering what a well-thrown curve should look like; the right kind of pulled handle, the right balance, top to foot, the marraige of body and glaze, and the fundamental simplicity of this Far Eastern stoneware technique. Also the calligraphic use of a brush for decoration. Another result of this awareness of clay was a revival, by Bernard Leach and his pupil Michael Cardew, of the traditional brown and cream slip wares, which had never quite died out.

In the enthusiasm of these discoveries many beautiful pots were made, beautiful by any standards, the best of which would bear comparison with their Eastern prototypes. And although much has been said about imitation Sung, and, admitting its influence, sometimes to the exclusion all else, there was little attempt at actual copying, or deliberate pastiche; it was much more an affair of 'like methods like results'.

But, as time went on, it became clear that something was wrong; with familiarity came disillusion; stoneware had gone stale and no one seemed able to do anything about it. The critics were bored, the public was bored and complained about drab colours, even potters were bored and went on mechanically improving their technique and refining their aesthetic formula, oblivious of the trends of contemporary design in other crafts and materials. Was it – or, to change the tense, for now we are considering the position today – is it true that Far Eastern stoneware has never really taken root in this country and must wither because it can't grow? Superficially considered, from the point of view of what can be called 'style', it probably will; there are signs of its happening already; but its general influence regarding principles of 'right-making' have become well and truly rooted in the English potter's consciousness; principles which can, and will, be applied to other styles and techniques.

There are signs at last that a few younger potters are beginning to work and think in a more contemporary way. Perhaps the first to break away from Far Eastern influence was the late Sam Haile, whose big rugged shapes and wide thin bowls are clothed in rich primitive patterns, African or aboriginal American in inspiration, and expressed with a fine disregard of 'correct' technique, in a mixture of slip, scratched line and painted pigment. His tragic death a few years ago was a great loss and, although he could hardly be called one of the younger potters, he pointed the way to a new outlook by force of his own originality.

At the other end of the scale are the porcelain bowls made by Lucie Rie, thrown and turned to an exquisite thinness and decorated with bands of colour textured with fine, incised lines. There is T'ing delicacy expressed in a truly contemporary manner; the shapes clear cut and strong for all their apparent fragility. The white translucent paste is beautiful and her colours, black, grey and soft yellow, definite and contemporary. These little bowls are collectors' pieces, but they do suggest what *might* be done for the table. *Must* in fact be done by somebody. Studio potters will sooner or later have to face the problems of tableware – in porcelain! If English potters don't do it, others will.

Having, to some extent at least, mastered the difficult art of throwing, an increasing number of potters are cutting and bending the circular pots into non-circular, even asymmetric, shapes and are discovering how much can be done, if done quickly and deftly, without destroying the spring of the original thrown shape, and without losing their usefulness as pots or bowls; indeed, sometimes they gain in that respect when the curved top can be bent over slightly to form a handle. These bowls by Kenneth Clark have surely gained in interest and vitality by being cut, while losing nothing of their thrown quality. This pedestal bowl by Eleanor Whittall is an interesting experiment in combining squared and rounded forms. Nicholas Vergette has cut his bowl into a completely asymmetric shape and given it three legs to stand on. But that is only the beginning of the fun. Sculptor potters are becoming aware of the possibility of the thrown shape as 'something to work on', following, probably quite unconsciously, the lead of the Martin Brothers, and, dare one say it? – perhaps a little more consciously, Picasso! But the influences, which are in any case unavoidable, are completely submerged in the abundant vitality and originality of three potters, William Newland, Nicholas Vergette and Margaret Hine, all of whom have tackled this interesting problem.

William Newland: *Minoan Bull*, red clay with slip-trailed decoration

William Newland's *Minoan Bull* is fine, strong and masculine; and if it owes inspiration to Minoan Art it owes its strength and simplicity to a very intelligent use of thrown shapes. A potter will observe with interest that the body is a thrown pot, the head another, the legs thrown, while the tail and horns are pulled, like handles. Truly potter's sculpture, the bold slip-trailed decoration tilting the balance slightly over to pottery. The *Bird* with its emphasis on triangular shapes is strong and simple, and any potter would soon discover its component thrown sections, although partly camouflaged by boldly painted pattern. Another Bull with Europa on its back (circus version?) is similar in technique to the *Minoan Bull*, but less 'sculptural' in shape; gayer, and brightly painted in blue on white.

Margaret Hine's *Owl* and *Goat*, especially the *Owl*, are interesting examples of the same technique, expressed with a feminine delicacy. The decoration shows the use of incised glaze, in patterns that, just sufficiently, explain and emphasize the form.

Nicholas Vergette approaches the problem with great versatility and a sense of fun. His *Cats* have lost their figures but are still thrown pots: aggresssively feline, they deserve a place among the less reputable of Old Possum's 'Practical Cats'. More abstract are the 'Drip Pots' and 'Cactus Pots' made up of several thrown shapes with pulled attachments in the way of arms and legs and given a further touch of fantasy with painted and incised pattern, in blue and green and yellow. Gaiety and a sense of fun are creeping back, and about time too. The aura of solemnity and preciousness that has surrounded so much studio pottery is unnatural. A sense of fun was apparent in the pottery of any period that had any vitality: clay is a responsive medium that lends itself to spontaneous wit and fun.

What a delightful book could be written on the comic element in pottery. English pottery is rich in somewhat bucolic humour, and even the eighteenth-century porcelain nymphs and swains had their sly jokes.

In a more serious vein Nicholas Vergette will take a thrown pot and cut away a considerable amount of it, leaving slender forms related outside to the original shape, with an exciting pattern of shadows to be seen through the holes.

Decoration, too, shows signs of new life. William Newland has carried slip decoration a stage further; his slip is used in a very liquid state and poured on to the dishes in big simple masses that are nearly, but never quite, out of control and are given form and definition by a few deft touches with feather or trailer.

James Tower: Leaf-shaped dish with black and white glaze decoration

Both in slip and in painted decoration there is a tendency to use strong contrasts of light and dark, virtually black and white and more or less completely abstract pattern with the emphasis on straight lines rather than curves and hard straight lines at that, much of it incised, into the body or into the glaze. James Tower's sense of scale and placing is most impressive in the long leaf-shaped dish with a design in white on a beautiful black glaze; a black bowl has an exciting network of fine white line spread over the inside, setting up tensions in all directions and strangely satisfying. So satisfying that one feels it unnecessary to travel further. One could gaze and gaze at it, fascinated; but 'What next, Mr Tower?'

Nicholas Vergette has done some quite exciting decoration on moulded boat-shaped dishes (a charming and useful type of shape which we have adopted, gratefully, from Scandinavia). He also uses a great deal of black and white; strong white lines and spots on a black ground and fine white lines providing a half-tone. Almost Persian in its richness of pattern is the design of three fishes in black and white majolica; although in no sense a pastiche, it seems, to the writer at least, to have more in common with thirteenth-century Persian decoration than anything done by De Morgan. A Persian richness is also achieved by Steven Sykes, although in an English technique, by the use of stamps and dies and sprigged ornament on his pots and tiles. Pattern is coming back, and colour will come with it; but it takes time. Time for the potter to decide what he wants to do and is equipped to do. Pottery colour is closely bound up with technique; it is not just a matter of squeezing something out of a tube, or even buying ready-made glazes and colours from the manufacturers. The colour scheme of a pot begins with the clay. These remarks are only intended as a slight explanation of the apparent slowness of potters to rise to the demand for 'more colour'. It is not an attempt to fend off any painters or sculptors who feel they would like to try their hand at pottery. Such experiments may well be most stimulating and very welcome, if only they will take the trouble to learn something about the materials and the potters' ways of using them. English potters on the whole are very conscious of the need for more imaginative experiment, but not at the expense of 'right-making'.

# Dora Billington

## THE NEW LOOK IN BRITISH POTTERY:
## THE WORK OF WILLIAM NEWLAND
## MARGARET HINE AND NICHOLAS VERGETTE

# 1956

To all who saw the work of these three potters so admirably displayed at the Crafts Centre last July, it must have been apparent that English studio pottery is at last acquiring a 'New Look', more in tune with current ideas in house decoration and design generally. Gay, amusing, colourful – within the range of 'good' pottery colour – an exciting mixture of sculpture, painting and potting.

There will always be a place for the austerely beautiful thrown shape, with a fine body and glaze, but in that category only the best has much value; the rest is in danger of being pretentious and dull. On the other hand clay can be used, with sympathy and imagination, in an infinite variety of ways, not always dependant on superlative skill; a fact of which Continental potters are well aware.

But won't this amusing contemporary pottery very quickly date? Of course it will, just as quickly as a pastiche of seventeenth century slipware, or thirteenth century Sung wares; all aspects of twentieth century studio pottery; to be judged, a hundred, or even fifty years hence, by standards probably very different to ours. The standards of good workmanship which we recognise in all good pots of any period, and to which we cling, passionately and a little dogmatically, need to be restated and interpreted afresh by each generation; and each making its own imaginative contribution. Why are we in this country so afraid of imaginative experiment? Even a little breaking of the rules would be a tonic occasionally. Every pottery studio in this country might well have inscribed on its walls, 'Craftsmanship is not enough.' The work of the potters under review is by no means impeccable in technique, a fact which they willingly – but regretfully – admit; only pleading lack of experience in dealing with new problems and the desire to preserve freshness of handling. But there is no lack of imagination, and endless experiment, both in design and technique.

Being twentieth-century potters their outlook is eclectic; travel abroad, museums, and contemporary art of all kinds have had their influence; to Newland primitive art has a compelling fascination, and which he studies, ponders over and discusses endlessly. His is the more reasoned approach, the others working more intuitively. But at the back of it all is the Mediterranean influence which is creeping into studio pottery; once again the wheel has turned, the influence of the Far East is slowly but surely giving place to, possibly, another Classic revival, with a difference. A little intangible at present, but even among stoneware potters is appearing a feeling for shapes and proportions very different from those of a few years ago. Picasso may have had something to do with it; many of his pots are Greek in shape and decoration, if not in refinement. There were one or two magnificent 'Greek' pots in his recent exhibition at the Marlborough Gallery; but it goes deeper than that. One result, or symptom, of this Greek influence is the increasing use of terra cotta in all sorts of natural clay colours, not only for sculpture but for pots, and for the combinations of both in which potters are today experimenting. It is this experimental attitude of mind which is bringing new life to pottery; no longer sheltering behind well established standards and techniques, anything can be tried, and judged on its merits.

Sharing as they do the same workshop and the results of many experiments, the work of these three potters is bound to have certain things in common, but the real differences are not far to seek. Newland's work is bold, 'big' in form even when not big in size, and masculine. There is a clear cut difference between his painted decoration which is essentially flat, and his developing sculptural sense. His *Minoan Bull* has given place to a *Cow* less massive but more interesting in form (inspired by the cow in the dairy shop window?) His *Sitting Figure* in unglazed terra cotta made from thrown shapes is nearer to representational sculpture than pot form, and the movement is emphasised with a few brush strokes in black that have a life of their own. A *Horse* not yet complete, but the subject of much thought and experiment, may be his best yet. Newland is a most capable thrower of big bold shapes. One of the biggest bowls made recently came to an untimely end on its way to the Crafts Centre, but in spite of difficulties of firing and transport it is to be hoped he will continue to make these fine pots, and decorate them, not with cut out patterns, please, but with a big brush.

William Newland: stoneware bowl, rust, black and grey

Margaret Hine's work is delightfully feminine. Her *Pigeons*, by now a considerable flock, and all different, still proclaim their thrown origin, and yet are very real birds. Elegant in shape, with delicate patterns incised in the glaze that fit admirably the smooth pigeon-like contours. This technique of using one incised glaze over another these potters discovered for themselves, and they use it a great deal. Margaret Hine further emphasises with it the long lines of her *Two Standing Figures with a Child*, dramatic in its contrasts of black and white. But her colour is by no means confined to black and white; some of the more toylike models of clowns and circus riders glow with colour, as do some of the painted dishes: with clear yellows, greens, blues and purples used with elusive good taste. Her painted designs have Persian richness.

Margaret Hine *Horse and Rider*, Black and yellow glaze

Nicholas Vergette's work, though much of it is in the round, somehow suggests a painter's approach. His best work is evocative, always suggesting more than is actually stated. His disreputable cats have multiplied since the previous exhibition, and they readily find homes, but my cat is a more dignified creature. The *Goatherds* have strayed from some Mediterranean pasture; in the same spirit, too, are the cactus gardens, queer evocative shapes that might have been some primitive children's toys. Nicholas Vergette also throws pots, simple shapes with interesting texture patternings. But charming as are the figure groups, cactus gardens and other amusing fantasies, it is good to see him turning seriously to tiles – Architects please note. In his tile panels the painter's concepts can have their fullest expression.

Nicholas Vergette: Three *Fishes*, black and white majolica

A wall panel of two standing figures in black incised on white, arresting in its main shapes is a little confused by too many lines; clearer and admirably flat are the fishes, and mermaid, on the black and white table top. But his coloured wall panels employ all the resources of the painter. His *Feeding the Birds* evokes St Francis by some Italian master. The Italian landscape is there, perspective in line and tone, a colour scheme of soft greys, blues and pale gold, figures moving within the picture; but look again, it's still a flat tile pattern of films of colour incised and painted line. What couldn't be done with such tile murals given the opportunity.

Vergette is also experimenting in pottery mosaic and has solved the problem of making flat glazed tesserae, thus avoiding the glitter which has been the chief drawback of this technique. A panel of *Birds* in soft broken colour points to unlimited possiblities, both for walls and for table tops.

Here is a very brief account of the work of three potters who are producing things which are neither 'pot-boilers', nor precious collectors' pieces, but made to fit into the contemporary scene, already decorating a number of shops and cafés in London.

---

What have been dismissed as the decorative crafts  – the producers of elegant trifles – are in reality the focus of all the determination and creative thinking directed to the development and perpetuation of the craftsman's way of living and working . . . This group does not comprise mere opportunists: they are the people who are slowly building up a modern tradition of the crafts. Their sphere of influence will grow. More and more people are realising that progress, based on science and invention, is a myth, and are eagerly searching for a more human way of living and working and the crafts provide it.

Harry Norris, furniture maker and former chairman of the Red Rose Guild of Craftsmen, interviewed by

John Farleigh in *The Creative Craftsman*, 1950

No art can exist without sincerity and conviction. The artist, the craftsman, working as individuals become channels for the expression of the totality of their experience and intuitive knowledge of their life and times. Anything extraneous – an over-preoccupation with technique, tongue-in-cheek playing to the gallery, decoration added for decoration's sake – adulterates and corrupts the result.

Sam Smith: '30 Years a Toyman', in *Crafts Review* 1, 1959

---

Compared to the cohorts of weavers and potters,    toymen form no more than a guerrilla band. They have a sense of honour and rightness but avoid the square-bashing and discipline which fall to the enlisted man. Perhaps in time more will come to savour their liberty . . . The thing that makes me mad (and as a guerrilla, want to snipe at it), is craft snobbism, which though ready to concede that all crafts are art, adds that some are more art than others.

Sam Smith: '30 Years a Toyman', in *Crafts Review* 1, 1959

---

*Dave:*    What do you think I am, Ronnie? You think I'm an artist-craftsman? Nothing of that sort. A designer? Not even that. Designers are ten a penny. I don't mind, Ronnie – believe me I don't. (*But he does.*) I've reached the point where I can face the fact that I'm not a prophet . . . Did you expect anything else? You wanted us to grow to be giants, didn't you? The mighty artist craftsman!

Arnold Wesker: *I'm Talking About Jerusalem*, 1960; Act 3, Scene III, set in 1959

# Bernard Leach

1887-1979

This was Leach's third trip to Japan as an adult. He had lived there from 1909-20, returned in 1934-35 at the invitation of the National Craft Society, travelling with Yanagi and Hamada all over Japan in search of country crafts. This time he had travelled with the same two friends back from the Dartington conference, with all of them visiting craftspeople and students across the USA and back in Japan. Leach's life in Japan was filled with writing and drawing, lecturing and advising, making pots and travelling. Although sometimes exhausted and ill he records theory and practice with equal relish. It is this book and *Hamada: Potter* (1975) that expose Leach's affections most eloquently and sympathetically. There are some real disappointments – not of a craft versus industry nature, but new craft versus old – because he is revisiting, and reliving, scenes from the 1930s in which all the participants have subtly changed.

FROM

## A POTTER IN JAPAN 1952-54

# 1960

[6 JULY 1953]

Extracts from *A Potter in Japan 1952-54* (1960) based on his diaries and the round-robin letters he sent back to England: 'Hamada'sa Mashiko'; 'Back in Tokyo and Kyoto'; 'Onda'; 'Conclusions and Farewells'.

At 6pm I called for the first dip in the bath which is, in these parts, an iron cauldron set in concrete, large enough to sit in comfortably up to the neck, squatting on a protective wooden board tethered (not always) to the bottom. A maid comes and calls from outside 'how is it Leachsan?' If I answer, 'rather hot' she pumps and a flow of cold water rushes through a bamboo pipe until I cry 'stop'. If it is not hot enough, I soon hear the crackle of more wood underneath my stewpot. Of course one washes before getting in, sitting on an upturned tub and splashing ad lib. One washes more thoroughly after the first dip and then sits and simmers and all the worries and strains of the day float away with the steam. Then at last the household, usually the men, gather around the long table on benches to a hearty meal in the central farmhouse kitchen whence the wood smoke rises to the rafters and a vent in the thatch 30 feet overhead.

### HAMADA'S MASHIKO

I have watched Hamada throw and turn this curious soft, sandy clay. The local subsoil appears sandy but when pinched most of the granules smooth out between thumb and forefinger. Nevertheless, the various mixtures which he favours as the years pass contain a high proportion of siliceous grit which yield the broken, bready, textures which he likes to contrast with heavy wood-ash glazes. He throws boldly and fast and turns great strips of shavings off when the clay is only just sufficiently dry to keep its shape on the chuck. A special technique of coiling is employed for the upper parts of large pots, the lower portion having been thrown normally and half-hardened. The freedom and ease with which he does this is a marvel. But the more one watches, the more one realizes that it is the result of a balance in Hamada himself. Clear and quiet conceptual thought proceeding spontaneously into equally clarified, articulated actions. People come and talk to him about practical matters, visitors arrive and have to be looked after, the old carpenter who has been working for years on the new house wants to consult with him; he gives directions, chats, etc., and most of the time he does so sitting eyeing his pot, or goes on throwing, talking over his shoulder, undisturbed in himself. Yes, his pots are articulated like the bones of a human arm, movement following movement with joints in between, unlike the smooth carvature of Greek pots or German Bellarmines. Actually the pots themselves, whether being thrown or turned, are rarely perfectly centred. Not that Hamada tries to keep them out of centre, he simply is unattached to mechanical accuracy for its own sake. If the pot functions and feels and looks good – that is enough. Our Western judgment as to whether it does these things is radically different. We, speaking broadly, start off with an expectation derived from the machine and its deadly accurate precision and we have built a way of life and an evaluation around that conception of labour and its productions. Until recently the East has not done so, consequently Eastern expectation of both use and pleasure from pots, and other things of course, is fresh with the vitality of irregularity innate in handwork and natural raw materials. Not only may the clays be rough for many usages, and the shapes of only approximate symmetry, but, more significantly, a far greater scale of human expression is allowed the potter in play of texture, colour, brushwork and form. Their inner life has a chance to come out. Watching Hamada, one sees this taking place.

Bernard Leach: stoneware jug made at Mashiko

[9 JULY 1953]

Second earthquake jolt. The bushes are festooned with spider webs this morning, beaded with dew. Some prudent hens are high-stepping in the shade beneath looking for the early worm with one-eyed, head cocked vision: A power-saw whines across the paddy fields in the village; mist wreathes slowly across the mountain.

Our anxiety has been to get the pots dried in time so that our plans may carry through. It has rained and rained and everything is damp and mouldy. Yanagi sent some brown bread from Tokyo and it arrived green. Yesterday about 1,000 pots were carried in and out, three times for sun and shower. Today the pots stayed out until 4pm, then the whole lot, 2,000, were carried on boards down the muddy, slippery path to the smaller kiln beyond the lower house, 250 yards away, and massed around the long shed on the ground. After tea, the biscuit-firing kiln-packing was started and was nearly complete by supper time. Finished afterwards by candlelight and the fire started. I have never seen anything like it. Everybody, except Richard and I, knew their jobs and had a deft control of their bodies. The four chamber doors are only four feet high and one packer was in each compartment, standing with a bent back, or kneeling on the soft sand floor, packing the fragile pots on shelves like ours, but much rougher, and at a speed which would have shaken our St Ives folk. Outside there was a running, skipping, high stepping flow of pots to the kiln – nobody flustered or irritated and there were not more breakages than with us. Hamada took no hand, he was throwing a late order of small winecups and they too were turned and dried and squeezed in at the last! A slow stoking went on all through the night with big wood at the main firemouth with all the vents open. Progress next day as at St Ives – the first chamber done by 3pm. Then side stoking with very small wood and all four chambers finished by 8pm. The height of the kiln is lower and the width is a little less than ours and there is much more space left at the tops of the bungs of saggers and above the shelves. Also there is a porthole for stoking to right and left of the main lower firemouth. No chimney.

---

In the train Yanagi told me the history of the 'Kichizaemon Edo' Tea-bowl – the most famous of the classic Corean Tea-bowls made in the Ri Dynasty as common-or-garden rice bowls. This one belonged to Fumaiko, the Feudal Lord of Matsue who died about 100 years ago. His son placed it in the great Zen monastery of Diatokuji in Kyoto and it has not been used since. The Tea Masters of today say it has gone dry from lack of use, for tea soaks into crackle and leaves a slight deposit on the surface which adds quality and a friendly warmth to the glaze and exposed clay. When the bowl is exhibited thousands come to see it from far and near; after a week it is turned upside down and thousands come again to see its foot-ring. Yanagi added that there are better bowls. But the really strange and interesting thing is that the perceptive eyes of the early Tea Masters not only selected what two or three hundred years of highly critical aestheticism has continued to rank on the highest plane, from out of a background of quite ordinary country craftsmanship, but furthermore built up a new background, centred in the Tea Room, where these masterpieces of the unknown craftsman became the classics of a new culture.

[20 NOVEMBER 1953]

Kyoto. I have been taking stock of all of last month's travel and discussion, searching for roots and meanings and directions, and back beyond, right to my first coming to Japan forty-five years ago. Something has happened to me almost below the level of consciousness – Dr Suzuki's 'jirikido' and 'tarikido', the mystic paths – 'Tat quam asi' and Manifestation, or the Great Prophets – Buddhism and Christianity – latterly the conviction that without the matrix of religious faith, and today the need for an overall World Faith, the artist-craftsman cannot become the real leader of any craftsman's team, only the conductor of his own compositions, keeping the orchestra in its place as purveyors of his thoughts, save for the exceptional personality who breaks out to form another orchestra, or to walk the tight-rope of personal expression. This does not liberate art in ordinary work and is an insufficient solution. It becomes inescapable to me that until the sweeping compulsion of a great inclusive belief from the deep core to the outer circumference blows through the world once again, all we can do is to tinker, art cannot bring salvation to the many, nor can the solitary road of the mystic; it needs the vision of the individual without individuality.

## ONDA

Every so often since my return to Japan I have been in receipt of invitations and messages from the potters of a remote village called Onda, in the southern island of Kyushu. They seemed to be most earnest that I should go and work with them for a time and they offered to make me a foreign bed, to prepare foreign food and to build a special bathroom. Yanagi told me of his first visit after hours of walking over mountain tracks many years ago, of the simple unspoiled life which they led and of the good pots which they made. He and Hamada were most anxious that I should go there and finally it

Bernard Leach:
The Onda jug

was arranged, but not before I had done all I could to discourage special preparations.

After three winter months of study and writing in Tokyo I eventually started out on this journey alone, on 1 April, taking the 'Tsubame' (Swallow) express, once more, to Kyoto, where I was met by Kawai and his nephew, Takeishi Kawai. We changed into a fast tram and were met at Kobe an hour later by a group of 'Mingei' supporters who entertained us royally at the craft restaurant, 'Chikuyotei'. We had the best 'Tai Sashimi' (raw fillets of sea-bream) which I have yet eaten. At 10pm we boarded a steamer bound for the port of Beppu at the other end of the Inland Sea. At dawn we picked Hamada up on the coast of the big island of Shikohu. He came aboard loaded with some excellent cakes called 'Tarto'. They resembled good swiss rolls, only instead of jam they were filled with a dark sweet bean paste. About 300 years ago the local Daimyo imported this new foreign food from Nagasaki where it had been introduced either by the Dutch or Portuguese traders. We reached Beppu about 8am. This is a famous hot-spring centre and bulges with Japanese Inns. Visitors were strolling the streets in 'yukatta' (cotton kimono provided by hotels). From miles out at sea we had seen the spumes of steam rising against hills as we skimmed over a calm sea. During the night hours we had missed the most exciting scenery when the ship threaded its way with or against fast tidal currents, yet it was a beautiful dream yesterday morning with the ever-changing outlines of the myriad islands and the little dark fishing boats hung in transparency.

On arrival at our Japanese hotel we were met by Mr Hosoda, the governor of Oita Prefecture, and his officials, and entertained to dinner followed by a long and warm discussion about the preservation of crafts in the province. Then we went for a stroll in the busy and unbombed town. Spring festival, cherry blossom, crowds and all shops open until midnight. First we visited antique shops and saw some good things and I bought a Seto oil lamp plate, about 150 years old, for a friend in the British Museum for £2. The prices were lower than in Tokyo where nothing is cheap any more. We were recognized by the dealers, because of the evening papers, I suppose, and proper prices were quoted. I was given a further third reduction 'because I had come to help local crafts'. The others then got busy with bamboo productions, very debased and fussy and finicky, catering as in all places where they is a 'memento trade' to the lowest taste. The other contents of the shops were enervating as well, the awful mannequins, textiles, dolls and pots too, and the everlasting radio turned on like forgotten taps.

Over the mountains by car to the island town of Hiuta to the Sanyokwan Hotel and another large dinner party with local officials. More discussion, the meaning of traditional crafts; why have I come to Kyushu, why to Onda of all places. Some twenty years ago when the late Prince Chichibu, who had read what Yanagi had written, wished to visit it, even the officials did not know just where it was.

Journalists and photographers morning and night, but we got out for a stroll in the evening and I bought another dish with a pattern called 'horse-eye'; we have a slip-ware dish in England with a pattern called the 'boney pie' dish made about the same period by corresponding folk-craftsmen. Hamada possesses an example. The town was much nicer than Beppu, there were good rows of shops and houses – more conservative – more genuine. Next day we called upon a bright and decisive old doctor who wanted us to see his ancient and beautiful house. The earlier portion was built in the Genroku period when the First Kenzan (my landmark of history) was alive. The little pocket gardens were lovely, gentle with the touch of time and an exquisite maple flamed in a quiet enclosure. Indoors everything was in 'Sen Cha' taste and carefully kept. He begged me to come and spend a night on the way back. Then we drove some miles and entered a long valley where the road got narrower and rougher and rougher and the slopes came down to us steep and dark with tall evergreen cryptomeria. At last on a bend we caught a glimpse of fine bark-thatched roofs and men standing, 'Onda no sarayama' (Onda of the mountain plates). We were late for lunch by an hour or more so they must have waited long. All along the winding stream people were waiting in front of their beautiful homes with tall bamboo plumes overhead and flashes of pink cherry in the abrupt slopes. After a light meal we went the round of workshops and were introduced to some of the 180 villagers. Long communal kilns reached down to the rough roadway, but the thing which astonished me most was the potter's clay and its preparation. It is hewn from the hillside as a half-decomposed ferruginous rock and then pounded by wooden stamps of the most primitive kind, a great baulk of wood some 18in square and perhaps 15ft long with a heavy wooden pestle right angled at one end, a pivot towards the other which is hollowed out into a bath holding say 30 gallons of water fed through bamboo pipes until the weight of the water raises the pestle end 6ft or more, causing the water to empty and the pestle to come down every half minute with a heavy thump into the hollowed earth where the soft rock is heaped. Twice a day it is reshovelled and that is all the attention it requires. Each workshop has a pair of these 'Kara usu' (Chinese stamps) as they are called (with a small one alongside for hulling rice), and that makes just enough powdered rock which when mixed with water, and sieved, provides sufficient fairly plastic clay for throwing the year through at practically no cost. A few years ago visiting officials decided that this was all too primitive and installed up-to-date electric machinery in a concrete building, but very soon the villagers had more clay than they knew what to do with, they forgot to oil the unfamiliar bearings (they do not even have to do that with their wooden pivots), and the machinery went to rack and ruin.

We came in for a bath in a tiled bathroom, neat and clean and specially built despite my protestations. Supper followed; butter, cheese, cocoa, meat, fish and even crisp toast away up here in the remote mountains – and somehow they have found out how to prepare them. I hardly like to think of the trouble which has been taken. There is a table for me and a soft chair which they wanted me to sit in whilst they all, twenty-five of them, gathered for a grand meal on the matting. I thanked them, but refused to sit above their level and we put the chair by the desk in the next room where I can sit comfortably and write and draw when I am tired. Old Mr Sakamoto, our host, made a short welcoming speech to which I replied, stumblingly, saying that I had come to learn, but that if in any way I could help them in return, nothing would give me more pleasure. After the food and sake and beer, Hamada and Kawai and everybody else warmed up and talk became free and funny and when Kawai selected a bed-pan for special praise, the conversation became Shakespearian and uproarious, but never nasty. Kawai and Hamada sat most of the next day directing the young throwers who were making Tea-bowls and covered water-pots for them. The pots flowed out so naturally and the

64

suggestions of one or another of us were taken up and incorporated with ease. But on the following day when the bowls were being turned, I fell silent as I simply could not agree with the foot-rings which Kawai favours and I felt that they contradicted the impersonality which he had so warmly advocated only the night before.

[8 APRIL 1954]

Hamada and Kawai have gone, Takeishi and I remained. He looks after me with such thoughtfulness and foresight and acts out of his good nature as a kindly solvent all round. Early this morning, as I lay abed, sounds of water gushing and periodic thumps of the stamps pounding the clay fell upon my ears and the sweet low notes of the Japanese nightingale coming in from the tickets. It is cold before breakfast and I must go and warm up in the 'Kotatsu', which is a low table covered with a rug under which there is a well in the floor with charcoal in the middle. People sit all round and plunge their legs into the warm dug-out. Very friendly. Today I started with my big pots, plates, jars and bread-pans as they take longer to dry. I did not attempt to throw, myself, there wasn't the necessity and I have not got a comparable skill nor familiarity with these tools and clay. Young Sakanoto carried out most of my wishes without difficulty and with a breadth of easy traditional handling which I could not hope to match.

[10 APRIL 1954]

A long day's work. Up at 7am, cold wash, diary, selection of drawings of pots, breakfast at 8am. Back and forth decorating the big pots with brushes and slips, with comb and gravers, keeping an eye on new pots growing on the wheel and yesterday's drying in the sun. Pots everywhere strewn upon the ground amongst playing children and scratching chickens and yet they rarely got broken; potter's children and presumably potter's hens too! I put one pot on its side with its bottom towards the sun and a toddler came in to tell her father that one of the pots had fallen over. During the morning a Press photographer interrupted our work to take this charming photograph of the Sakamotos and myself drinking a cup of tea, spring in the air and the mountain cherry a-bloom. An interval from 12.30pm to 1.30pm for a light lunch, then work until dark interrupted by an interview with a representative of the Mainichi Press who arrived unannounced after a long journey across the island. Bath and supper. Half a dozen brush drawings on the prepared cardboard-backed forms called 'Shikishi' to give to various people who have been kind.

[11 APRIL 1954]

Today half a dozen young potters turned up after walking four hours over the mountains from Koishibara which is the nearest potters village. In fact, Onda's tradition derived from Koishibara 240 years ago. The origin of both, as is so frequently the case in Japan, was in Korea, ravaged by Toyotomi Hideoyashi about sixty years before that. Pottery was a passport, then as now, and the Korean potter-prisoners were settled by the feudal Daimyo in their provinces and usually treated well. These young artisans, for the owners in Koishibara are a clan apart, watched me decorate and 'pull' handles all afternoon and then were persuaded by the Onda potters to stay for a warm-hearted sake supper and a discussion with me afterwards on shape and vitality in pots. Incidentally, they asked the invariable question,

Bernard Leach:
Fishing in
the Inland Sea,
plate design

65

'What did I think of Picasso as a potter?' I gave my usual reply that, however gifted as an artist, he simply was not a potter. Potters start from clay up, he starts from painting down. His pots are often vital and interesting as creative design, but the 'Picassiettes' of his thousand imitators, without his birthright, are an international disaster. They were keen and intelligent in a countrified way and we carried on until bedtime. At four in the morning they set off homeward over the hills.

[12 APRIL 1954]

Today the village has got up an hour earlier than usual to prepare for its Spring Festival in the afternoon. Each of the sixteen households takes bottles of sake and a great dish of special food to a meetingplace, out-of-doors if possible, but today it is raining and so it is to the village hall. Conch shells are blown from household to household to gather the clan and I am seated in the middle of a throng of men, women and children, and toasted, and I toast them back, and reports and speeches are made, and all are merry, and when we cannot eat any more, an entertainment begins. Song and dance and mimicry, broad and very local. I was glad to get to bed, however, as I was not feeling well.

[13 APRIL 1954]

Yes, I have picked up what threatens to be a nasty cold. But I cannot afford to break the rhythm of work and the time-table. So all day I pulled handles for pitchers and jugs, medieval and English in general character, and enjoyed doing it as much as anything connected with the making of pots, the feel of the tongue of wet clay slipping through the palm of one's hand, the ribs and indentations which the pressure of one's fingers makes, the clean nip-off with a spade movement of the right thumb. Then the ramming home of the butt-end at the right point in the profile of the pot, the new bridge with perfect tensions and suitability for easy grasp, and finally the attachment at the other end of the span, with its grace note of wipe off and clean finish. This is very English and nothing more true and beautiful exists than the handles of our old slip-ware. In making handles something other than myself is at work and that, no doubt, is why these remote Japanese mountain potters were attracted, even as I have been attracted by the impersonal rightness of their traditions. In fact, I knew more clearly on this day the underlying motive which has drawn me back to the East once again. It is to rediscover the unknown craftsman in his lair, and to try to learn from living and working with him what we have lost since the Industrial Revolution of wholeness and humility.

Strange to relate, they do make a traditional pitcher with a handle here, and here only, in all Japan. Something like this and with rather a hard handle. Definitely un-Japanese in shape. We concluded that it must be yet another residue of old Dutch or Portuguese influence. I have learned two methods of decoration, one of which was employed in Sung China and which has intrigued and puzzled me for years. They call this one 'Tobe gane' or 'jumping iron'. Instead of a normal right-angled tool for paring the half-dry shapes, they use a springy curved one which, when applied at right-angles to the slowly spinning, slip-covered pot, chatters on the surface, removing a touch of the engobe at each jump, and so exposing the colour of the clay body below. So simple, so quick and so effective. The other process, also with slip, is softer. Slip is basted on to the pot with a broad straight-edged brush, smoothly, and

The jumping iron

the surface is dabbed rhythmically, as it turns slowly, with the loaded brush.

I don't think any European craftsman can have had such an experience as these weeks with these delightful, unspoiled hill-potters, in the remote mountains of Kyushu, has given me. I keep wishing that this one or that of my friends in the West could share it. It has not been the kindness and courtesy alone, extended day after day not only to us, but also to the many visitors, often from far afield, who have been fed and wined and often given beds for the night. What impresses me most is the spontaneous community action with its basic unity of heart. Long may it beat and the 'Karu usu' thump in the stream below. Evening after evening, bath and supper over, the young men, or the old men, or the women, come in groups and talk and ask questions. They want to know about our customs and feelings and I want to know about theirs. They know so much more about us than any corresponding group of villagers in the British Isles knows about them! Am I a dreamer if I think that in some ways they are more prepared for world citizenship? They own their land and homes, there is no dire poverty or great wealth, they grow their staple foods on little terraced fields and paddies between the steeps; clay, water and wood cost but the labour and now they are mentally free from the bondage of tradition. That, however, is where the danger lies. Suddenly take away the props and the resulting stresses and strains may be too much for the old building.

I have been around with some camera men taking a movie of the village and I was rather horrified to find, despite all that we have discussed of an evening, that my shapes and even patterns have been copied in every workshop. I found my children everywhere dressed in ill-fitting garments! That means to say that instead of a ten per cent absorption of outside influence, which I have suggested as normal and healthy, this is at least a 75 per cent invasion without any resistance. And that as I see it is what is happening to Japan, in general, now. This problem of imitation, which appears to the Western mind, at first sight, as commercial dishonestly, requires study and open understanding. Here at Onda the usual superficial interpretation would be wide of the mark. As far as feeling towards me is concerned, the intention is a compliment; I am positive that nothing contrary crossed their minds. To them it was simply the obvious thing to do, and my warnings they read as springing from personal modesty. I lack the training with which to probe the subtleties of group psychology and social evolution involved but it seems fairly obvious that the sense of proprietary rights in design grew with the industrialism and individualism of the nineteenth century. In Japan, and especially in this outlying remnant of old Japan, we run into another set of communal values. In Onda or in some good old country pottery, like Fremington in North Devon, let us say, a good handle, or a good shape, were just good, wherever they came from, without any of this new nonsense about copyright. Craft Guilds existed to preserve standards and protect livelihoods, it is true, but it is only with the entry of the machine, on the one hand, and the separation of artistry from life, upon the other, that this high sense of proprietorship has developed. But it is equally obvious that the assimilative capacity of the far less articulate communities like Onda and Fremington has waned and requires new props. In Japan these are the leaders of the 'Mingei' or craft movement, with their philosophy of humility, and a subordination of over-stressed individualism to a co-operative and social proportion. My anxiety, even before I came here, was that the effect would be just so much more of the alien and indigestible. Yet Onda cannot be kept as an artificial enclave, it must swing with the national tide and one can take comfort by remembering that this, or a very similar process, took place in

Japan when Buddhism brought over Chinese culture and about 300 years were required for assimilation.

As for my own pots, I am far from pleased with their too carefully planned decorations – how different from the carefree, birthright flow of the large traditional jars and bowls and bed-warmers and sake and Shoyu containers, just made to serve requirement in the most straightforward way possible without any art-anxieties. They come out of the life of these hill-farmers, and that is why we replied to Governor Hosoda and his officials, when they suggested that it would be a good thing if the Onda potters were freed from the labours of cultivating the soil, that we could not agree. Theirs is a farmer's art and is as true to nature as the rice they grow and nearly as unconscious of beauty. They like and dislike and possess the broad practical 'know-how', just as with their sowing and reaping and rotation of crops – it is all the same, and unity is the keynote – but ours is in fragments and we cannot pretend to such innocence. For us the hard road of re-integration, either by self-culture, of which I am heartily sick, or by self-forgetfulness. My pots do need a fresh and more naked impulse, less planning, less reliance on the past and more openness to immediate intuition.

## CONCLUSIONS AND FAREWELLS
### [2 SEPTEMBER 1954]

August gone, another three months and all this experience will have sunk into time past.

During these last weeks our long daily discussions, resumed from last summer, for the book on the way of the potter, East and West, have ranged over territory which concerns life as a whole. The more we gathered of means of making pots the more meanings have forced our attention to essential underlying problems. Means are but consequences of meanings, both change almost imperceptibly, thus the meanings of the present as the outcome of what has gone before is our point of departure: the character of art today, the evolution which has led up to it from the anonymous craftsman, through the designer for the machine to the artist-craftsman of our time, the nature and interplay of pottery in East and West as reflecting the cultures of the two hemispheres; thence to the cultures themselves and to the cultural roots in race, climate, aesthetics, morals and philosophies, and ultimately to religious beliefs. Out of all this has emerged a considerable degree of common agreement on fundamentals.

For me the greatest gain has been in appreciation of the meaning of 'Mu', or unattachment, deeply imbedded in Taoism, Buddhism and ever present in Zen-inspired arts and crafts. It is from this Eastern source that I believe that the Western world can draw sustenance and fresh inspiration. This is the ground out of which Oriental art has grown: this is the source of Shibusa, of nothingness, of emptiness, of non-action, of Nirvana. But Western interpretations of this antithetical thought have hitherto been altogether too impregnated with overtones of rational thinking. 'Mu' is no mere negative but a state of undifferentiated being unattached to either negative or positive. It is the quality we most admire in pots and it is that rare condition of which we catch glimpses in men and women when the Spirit of Life blows through them as wind through an open window. Then action flows easily and naturally and without over-stress. This is the antidote to a 'universal grey' but it is not the outcome of individualism or of intellect. It is the treasure of the humble craftsman and the haven of the greatest artist.

Dr Yanagi's aesthetic philosophy, consistently supported by Shoji Hamada and Kanjiro Kawai, is rooted in a belief in the 'unknown craftsman'. In the kind of people I found at Onda and in the kind of work which sprang from life nurtured in the framework of an old and wholesome culture. The twin foundations of such life and such work are belief and humility, two virtues of which we have become sadly bereft in the Western world. Dr Yanagi's opponents accuse him, and the movement, of being retrogressive, they say that an attempt is being made in the teeth of progress to manufacture folk-art. I do not believe that he is so foolish as to think that such a thing is possible. The challenge in his doctrine is more radical than that for it is directed at the modern artist, the artist craftsman and the Tea Master alike. He does not suggest that they should pretend to become unconscious but, for the lack of a better term, what I shall call super-conscious. He states that the artists and the craftsmen, whether they be Bachs or Beethovens, Koyetsus or Cellinis, produced less significant art than the unknown writers of Plain Song, and the unknown weavers of Coptic or Peruvian tapestry, or all the hosts of unknown artisans who humbly in clay and stone and metal and fibre in the protective unconsciousness of great belief all over the world. This is a drastic revaluation which leaves the modern artist stripped and naked on a dunghill of over-stressed individualism. It is an attack upon our current social values, but it is not an attack upon the function of the genuine artist in his proper unobtrusive place in a healthy society. What Yanagi proposes is an abandonment of ego-centricity and pride, which is both good Buddhism and good Christianity. Losing oneself in art in order to find oneself whether by the simple way of belief in tradition and hard repetitive work, let us say as a journeyman potter, or by the intense search and self-discipline of 'satori', or reintegration, of the more conscious artist or craftsman.

It may be that I personally would place more emphasis upon this process of reintegration, or attainment of wholeness, in the individual artist, because I am one, but it is also because, as Western man, we are disintegrated. But this has also become true of modern, and particularly urban, Japanese. Which is illustrated by the fact that forty years ago in Tokyo artists and craftsmen were closer together than they are today, and also by the imitation and indigestion to which I have drawn attention on many pages. The process in Japan has been hastened by an increase in an already powerful national inferiority complex which was the inevitable result of the first defeat of a proud race. Therefore Dr Yanagi's meaning to us Westerners and to Westernized Japanese is reintegration, whereas to the Japanese artisan, as distinguished from artist, and to those of a conservative turn of mind, it is the preservation of integration.

So much for the people and their life; with regard to the works which they produce, these may be judged upon their merits and defects, but we can rest assured that if they are good there must be truth of being behind them, though that may be, and often is, only a private truth of life in comparison to the congregate truth of good traditional periods of society. The best of these appear to me to lie not in those periods when we are accustomed to look for them, such as the High Renaissance, but earlier, even perhaps in what for centuries we have called the Dark Ages. These incubating or smouldering periods burst into first flame in China in the fifth or sixth centuries, in Japan in the seventh to eighth and in Europe between the tenth and twelfth and never was the light so bright again, although there may have been more of it. Then it was that 'men of abounding energy', those whom we later called geniuses, themselves enflamed, worked in the common cause like Prince Shotoku or the great monks of East and West.

If I read Yanagi right, and he says I do, this is what he means. The only difference between us is that he, however he may feel the desirability of the sweeping unifying power of a great inclusive wind of religion, does not see its likelihood, but as a Japanese with the characteristic 'seeing eye', knows that art is an unarguing language of communication between one man's heart and another in his 'Kingdom of Beauty'. I, as the reader may have already sensed, believe that the Great Wind is already on the way.

Another form of the same kind of criticism which is levelled against Yanagi and his followers is that he, and they, talk and write so much about 'Gete' (the ordinary) and so little about 'Johin' (the refined). Taking the former to mean the plains and the latter to mean the hills, it appears to me that the landscape is incomplete without both and that the one calls for the other. If, as I am told, it is true that Yanagi writes little about the mountains, it is surely because they are mole hills and not real mountains. Koyetsu not a hill? Bach not a mountain? That certainly is looking gift horses in the mouth! And yet I am with Yanagi for wanting to look every gift horse in the mouth in this age of ours, for if we don't we'll never get out of the rut we've got into. It has taken us long enough to discover that we are in one and most people, including artists, complain, but won't admit the fact even now. Besides, Yanagi has never said that both of these great men were not mountains in their landscape, what he did say was that there have been bigger ranges formed out of whole peoples over long periods of time. We are at the close of one age and at the commencement of another, that of the maturity of mankind as a whole, and one of the focal points where the greatest experiment in the fusion of the two halves of human culture is painfully taking place is Japan. Our English historian, Arnold Toynbee, explains clearly how Japan has gone headlong into industrialism and lost the ballast of her inheritance. He also states that 'unity is the only alternative to self-destruction in an Atomic Age'. If, as I believe, this is true, we must seek a road towards human unity. Beyond my love of the Japanese people and of the beauty of their land and the warp of its culture, that is why I have come back again and again. It is the excuse for the foregoing pages with all their shortcomings.

This is Dr Yanagi's contribution to the world of art and by reason of his life-long search, persistence and eloquence he has gathered his followers and held together the strongest craft movement of our day. By the examination of art in the light of 'Mu' he has broken the dualistic tensions between the 'I' and the 'not I', between artist and craftsman and between the individual and community. One of the best examples of 'Mu' in pottery is the work of Koreans during the Ri Dynasty, but it shows itself all through Korean crafts to such an extent that it is almost impossible to find any really bad, impure or diseased work. As with the drawings of unspoiled children, no ego obtrudes, never does self-consciousness show its uncomely face.

To a large extent this is true about all folk-art. Such has been the service of the unknown craftsman all over the world. We who have split personalities and split culture are no longer unselfconscious. We have to discover a process of reintegration; the journey from the self back to the whole.

---

We are victims of our own organised violation of the senses. To the humanisation of our daily environment, this journal is faithfully dedicated.

Dedication in first issue of *Crafts Review*, edited by Murray Fieldhouse, potter, 1959

# Bernard Leach

1887 - 1979

A LETTER TO HIS GRANDSON

## 1960

His letter of 26 June 1960 to his twenty-one year old grandson John Leach welcoming his wish to work at the St Ives pottery and setting out the terms of employment – aesthetic and monetary.

My dear Johnnie,

We are delighted to hear from both you and your father that you want to come here for a year at any rate in Nov. next. I have no doubt that you will fit in with the group we shall have & that you will pick up our shapes & methods very quickly & make a good contribution but I want to say at the outset that, necessary as all that is, it is not the real thing for which you should be coming. That is all means to an end, not the end itself.

This is the day of the artist craftsman not of the journeyman potter. That means that any young person taking up a craft today as a vocation only justifies himself (or herself) by finding something to voice or say. That is his life, or true character, extended into his pots. Formerly this was not the case but today it is. We want from the potter the same sort of quality which we expect from a good author, poet, painter or composer. The journeyman potter's place has been taken by the factory.

Thus your main objective should be aesthetic – to know good pot from bad pot & be able to find your way, with your own clear convictions, amidst all the good & bad pots of past & present to making good, sincere & honest pots of your own.

I do not believe that there is any place in Europe where you can get a more helpful background for this endeavour than here and it would be my great pleasure and Janet's to try and give it to you.

After this last journey to America we both feel that a new effort is required of us at St Ives to encourage our group of rather maturer students, & the old hands too, towards freer & more living expression in pots. We think that the standard wares, especially, have become too careful, measured weighed & waxed & calculated. Come & join in the effort to let the streams flow.

Now as to money, we can't pay as your father has. The maximum we have paid a student towards the end of a good two year apprenticeship was £5s-10 to Peter Wood. We could start you at £5 plus overtime @ 2 shillings and ninepence p.h. & bonus which might be guessed at 10 shillings a week. This would yield you net between £6–£7 p.week whilst you are here. Of course we shall keep a look out for a decent & not expensive place for you to stay. This is not a good deal as a living wage but it is as far as we can go on the student apprentice basis.

I doubt myself if one year will be long enough but that we shall see & if, as I expect, you soon master the shapes on our making list we can push your basic wage up a bit. We are busy with visitors already & with pots for coming shows. Just about got our feet on the ground again.

With love to you all

Grandfather

# Gordon Russell

1892-1980

As Chairman of the wartime Utility Furniture Panel and Director of the Council of Industrial Design from 1947 to 1959 Gordon Russell represented the perfect blend of Cotswold commonsense and industrial compatibility for the new Crafts Council. *Craftsmanship Today* tried to stretch its exhibits across this 'wider interpretation' and included traditional items: eel-traps and hand-sewn gloves; craft objects by the disabled; Henry Ford's drawings for his first vehicle, the Quadricycle of 1896. These were the outriders for a good-sounding platoon of craftspeople: for textiles there were Beutlich, Collingwood, Sutton; Barnsley and Peters for furniture; Makepeace and Pye for wooden bowls; Benney, Clements, Durbin and Welch for silver, and another dozen names, equally familiar.

The Crafts Centre of Great Britain still languished in Hay Hill, but in 1965 that body invited Graham Hughes to become its life-saving Chairman. Hughes was the enterprising and influential Art Director of the Worshipful Company of Goldsmiths from 1951 to 1980. In 1966 he moved the Crafts Centre into London's Covent Garden, into the warehouse premises used to show and sell craftwork ever since (but known as Contemporary Applied Arts since 1987).

In the second half of the 1960s Government funds were given to the crafts. Between 1966 and 1970, annual sums varying from £5,000 to £10,000 were divided by the Board of Trade between the Crafts Council of Great Britain, the Crafts Centre of Great Britain, and the Scottish Crafts Centre. In 1971 the Crafts Advisory Committee was set up as a directly funded body with responsibility for administering the government grant to the crafts in England and Wales. The Crafts Council of Great Britain merged with the Crafts Centre of Great Britain to become the British Crafts Centre, with two galleries: the one in Covent Garden, the other, previously the Council gallery, in Waterloo Place, London. In 1972 the CAC, which later became the present Crafts Council, took over the Waterloo Place gallery as its headquarters.

## CRAFTSMANSHIP TODAY

Foreword to *Craftsmanship Today*, an exhibition organised by The Crafts Council of Great Britain at 40 Haymarket, London SW1, from 27 May to 31 July 1965 as it launched a £250,000 appeal for the new Council's aims.

Gentleman-farmer, artist-craftsman, garden-city – all are redolent of an age in which certain occupations become hobbies, very worthy hobbies, but pursued in an amateur, pioneering way, out of the main stream of life.

The insistence of the Arts and Crafts movement in the nineteenth century that designer and maker must be one and the same person assumed that a living tradition, understood by all, still existed or could be recreated. In highly personal crafts such as calligraphy, stained glass or pottery this was possible; but in others, such as smithing or furniture making, which involved extended periods of steady, arduous and highly efficient technical labour, the imaginative designer could seldom command the necessary skill. Nor was the skilled executant necessarily imaginative.

I have always believed that craftsmanship would benefit by a much wider interpretation and by a more sympathetic approach to the complementary method of production by machine. And I could not see why splendid bookbinding should be regarded as artist-craftsman's work whilst

72

splendid saddlemaking was not. Admittedly, no-one knew who had designed the saddle, which had been evolved by countless small improvements over a long period of time. But so to a large extent had the binding of books. No-one expects a highly skilled bricklayer or mason to be an architect. Clocks by master-clockmakers such as Thos. Tompion are accepted as superb pieces of craftsmanship but, from the number which have survived, it is obvious that he could not have made them all himself, nor was he ashamed to use a wheel-cutting machine because it gave him greater accuracy with no loss of quality. That, surely, is the kernel of the matter – quality. So long as the craftsman safeguards quality with devotion he may safely be allowed to call on skills other than his own.

It is with these beliefs in mind that a group of workers have made possible this exhibition of a wider interpretation of craftsmanship. I believe laymen will welcome this approach, which aims to give handwork its right and necesary place in a changing world, in which most of us, men, women and children, have some knowledge of mechanics and, I believe, a growing interest in the arts.

---

A basket-maker who hears a buyer going into raptures about the significant form of a Potato Molly will feel much the same as the cobbler would have felt if he had seen the picture painted by Sir William Nicholson of Gertrude Jekyll's gardening boots. I have yet to meet a studio basket maker. Stanley Bird knows that his fishing baskets are objects of beauty because people from Heal's and Primavera have told him so; and it suits him because it means another market for his ware. His personal judgement would be, more likely, that they are good, well-made baskets, as they have to be to do their job.

Dorothy Wright: 'A Norfolk Craftsman', *Crafts Review* 5, 1960

---

*Dave:* Excitement! You change machines! Big difference! All your life, Sammy, think of it, all your life.

*Sammy:* But you get more money for it.

*Dave:* That I do not have an answer to. (*Pause*) Sammy, remember that chair what you said about it? It looks as though it's sitting down you said . . . Oh Jesus, how do you start explaining this thing. Look Sammy, look at this rack you made for your chisels. Not an ordinary rack, not just bits of wood nailed together but a special one with dove-tail joints here and a mortise and tenon joint there, and look what you put on the side, remember you wanted to decorate it, so you used my carving tools and you worked out a design . . . a whole afternoon you spent on it and you used up three pieces of oak before you were satisfied. Twenty-seven and six you owe me.

*Sammy:* Hell, that were only messing around.

*Dave: Not messing around! Creating!*

Arnold Wesker: *I'm Talking About Jerusalem*, 1960; Act 2, Scene II, set in 1953

# David Kindersley

BORN 1915

David Kindersley's apprenticeship lasted from 1933 to 1936. He then set up his own workshop, but returned to help reorganise Gill's workshop after his death in 1940. His memoir describes life as a craftsman outside the crafts movement – although in full view of its beliefs and practices.

## MY APPRENTICESHIP
## TO MR ERIC GILL

# 1967

*Crafts*, July/August and September/October, 1979, It was first read as a paper at a symposium devoted to Gill's life and work held at the William Andrews Clark Memorial Library at the University of California in 1967.

Arthur Eric Rowton Gill was born on 22 February 1882, the second child in a family of twelve. Throughout his life his energy, particularly his mental energy, enabled him to accomplish considerably more than his fellow men. Moreover, there was that touch of genius, however much he would have denied it, that singled him out as an artist. He refused to think of himself as anything special and, until the last few years of his life, he refused to accept any worldly honours. He was elected an Honorary Associate of the Institute of British Architects, an Associate of the Royal Academy, an Honorary Doctor at Law at Edinburgh University, and his was among the first appointments to the distinction of Designer for Industry.

Mr Gill was an amazing man. Not perhaps a great a great artist in the post-Renaissance sense, he was a complete man whose philosophy fits in best with the anonymity of the Middle Ages. The life he chose to lead was to be subject to the guidance of the Roman Church. He was – some would say – converted to the faith. Other are inclined to the view that he built his religion himself and it fitted that which he saw to be the Church. There is, of course, a great difference between the Roman Catholic Church and a young man's dream of a catholic faith. Although he was to all accounts very correctly instructed before being received into the Church, I don't believe his own personal concept of truth was ever at one with the contemporary Church. This made difficulties for him all his life. He once wrote to a priest, 'the trouble in this matter is partly due to the fact that theologians seldom know what the words mean. They think that work is something like the Breviary, to be got through, and never anything else'. He was visibly hurt by the criticism of priests, because he was too 'true unto himself' to take anything for granted. Everything had to be weighed, judged, worked out, and put into language which, word by word, had to mean reality to him. This process led him to theorise. He loved discussion and what a friend of mine called 'argufying'. The very gifted artist David Jones said of Eric Gill's autobiography, 'I wish it was less about ideas and more about chaps.' This, though, was Gill – he *was* a man of ideas. One must be careful not to miss the point.

John Rothenstein rebukes Mr Gill in the preface to *The First Nudes*, a collection of pencil drawings:

*The light falls from no particular direction; nothing is observed...* *both by his outlook and by his want of early training Gill was unfitted for the direct drawing of the naked model.*

For Mr Gill it was axiomatic that an artist should draw what he thinks and knows. This is, indeed, why his drawings and carvings and engravings are the way they are. He thought images should come out of the head, matured by life and experience. He did, in fact, come to drawing from 'the life' as it is called considerably later than most artists, and he felt this to be a good thing, as he knew already what he was drawing, not as a student striving only to reproduce a facsimile like a camera's.

Mr Gill seems to have been unusually encouraged as a small boy to draw, and he filled exercise books with scenes of the Sussex Downs and the sea. Always he contrived to introduce railway lines, tunnels, stations, and signals. Later he drew the railway engines as an 'engineer child' – accurate working models – with the engine's name and number, already showing his talent for letters. Though he referred to his time in an architect's office as wasted, learning no more than to draw drains, this training – a facility with set-square and compass – made him considerably superior to most sculptors in the obtaining of work. Clear and, indeed, beautiful diagrammatic drawings for client and mason gave his work a greater chance with committees and clients, particularly when these were architects.

Probably the most fortunate relationship he ever had in his early years was with Edward Johnston. Johnston had relearned calligraphy, or writing, as he would rather it were called. Without Johnston's research the calligraphic renaissance in England, Germany and here in America might never have got underway. Certainly Mr Gill would not have found his path as easy with his inscriptional lettering. Edward Johnston taught at South Kensington in what is now called the Royal College of Art. His lectures are still remembered by the older generation of scribes as the most stimulating they ever attended.

Nowadays, calligraphy is no longer taught at the Royal College of Art. Indeed, there are few places in England today where it is considered a part of a student's training. I have heard it derided as 'knitting'. In England today little stands any chance that appears to have no advantage export-wise. The very real need for quality is not pursued to such lengths. Gill and Johnston shared rooms in Lincoln's Inn, and Mr Gill was quick to learn first as a calligrapher and then to apply the pure calligraphic form to stone. His early designs for stone inscriptions were done directly with a large reed or cane pen at full size.

Life was becoming full and exciting for the young Mr Gill. Things were opening up, and he was rubbing shoulders with a group of people, many of whom would have much to give in the next few decades – the Fabians, theosophists, writers, painters, and sculptors. He was beginning to give talks on art, lettering, and sculpture at, amongst other places, the Art Workers Guild – that Morris-oriented craftsmen's forum. Mr Gill took a dim view of the Guild. The membership through his eyes was composed of architects who designed houses in any style you like to name, from Gothic to Georgian, though each style in its time had been the expression of the latest science in building; weavers who produced by hand-loomwork of whose quality most factories would have been ashamed; pottery that leaked, scratched, fell over, and was no use to man or beast; lettering that no one could read: all of it conforming to a spurious idea of beauty or beautification. The crafts movement was one of the first with which he became totally disillusioned.

A.R.Orage, H.G.Wells, Bertrand Russell, Roger Fry, William Rothenstein, Jacob Epstein, and others all met and spoke and influenced Mr Gill in one way or another, but he was to tread a different path altogether. Mr Gill did not feel himself to be an artist but a maker of things that people needed. He felt artists were divorced from society and only existed as hot-house plants unable to survive in a real world. It is true, I think, that Mr Gill was not the stuff of artists, anyway, as we believe them to be today. He liked to know where he was going and he worked best within confined limits: the job commissioned, the drawing well and truly set forth, clearly, and with little

Eric Gill: wood-engraved frontispiece to *The Lord's Song*, a sermon by Gill, 1934

room for mistake; work from the head rather than from the heart. That much of his work had great feeling is no contradiction. He was a very emotional man, and it shows. But above all, he had an excellent brain and he made good use of his talents.

In 1914 Eric married Ethel Moore. Ethel, who took the name of Mary when they both entered the Roman Catholic Church, seemed always to have sensed the greatness of her husband. She planned the safe-keeping of all he did as if knowing that the smallest sketch or letter would be wanted by posterity.

Desperately feeling the need to stand intellectually on his own two feet, he and his wife moved from Hammersmith, London, to Ditchling Common under the Downs in his beloved county of Sussex, to live the simple life as far as possible from things which were false, and to bring up a family in the country on wholesome home-grown food and to wear clothes of their own making. Here they gathered round them, by accident and by choice, a small band of craftsmen and their families. All roads were leading to Rome – it seemed so right for Mr Gill that even atheists and non-Catholics were fostering his interest in the Roman Church.

Frances Cornford, the poet and granddaughter of Charles Darwin, wrote at this time to Mr Gill that her grandfather's views would profoundly alter man's whole outlook and morals. Nevertheless, she, the Raverats, and William Rothenstein were all of the opinion that this was the way for him – writing encouragingly and even disparagingly about their own slothfulness in not thinking the matter out. A visit to Chartres Cathedral had, I think, sown the seed, and from then on the feeling of being 'outside' the true faith gathered momentum. Listening to the purity of plain chant confirmed him in the rightness of the direction he was going. Eric and Mary Gill were received into the Roman Catholic Church on 22 February 1913. The community at Ditchling was named the Guild of St Joseph and St Dominic, and members became tertiaries of the Order of St Dominic, pledged to live the Christian life. Mr Gill was commissioned to carve the Stations of the Cross in the new Catholic cathedral at Westminster. Byzantine in feeling, the cathedral was a pleasant change from the Gothic style. Though still a strange sort of thing to do in the twentieth century, it has a truly noble structure of brick. But when the inside began to be hung with marble veneer to cover up this grand and honest brick structure, it became too much for Mr Gill. Fierce letters appeared in the press, and the battle raged. This time the argument was won and no more marble has appeared. To return to the Stations – these were his first really major works and many people believe them to be his greatest feat. Each is by no means a small task in itself, and the mouldings are worthy of attention, being different for each Station. World War I had just started; this work caused his call-up into the army to be deferred, and he was able to complete the Stations before going to a training camp at Blandford in Dorset. His views on pacifism had not yet begun to mature, but the army instructor who jumped on his feet, every time he failed to brake the lorry in which he was being instructed to drive, did not encourage a benign view of army life.

The fame derived from the Stations at Westminster led to more and more work and, of course, after the war there were the war memorials. Mr Gill had just the right feel for this sort of work – he saw the memorial more often than not in terms of the ancient village crosses whose weathered stumps occupy so many market places and village greens. Fortunately, clients were not slow in appreciating this central position for commemorating the fallen and, as a result, one can today come across these beautiful tall crosses with their delicate and outspoken inscriptions — at Milton Abbas, Trumpington,

South Harting, and Bisham, to mention but a very few of the blessed villages. There were also the private commissions for family inscriptions, surmounted by crested helm, flowing and dagged mantling, and simple shield – once again being sensitively carved, painted in primary colours, and gilded by the hands of a master of commonsense and occasion. Our churches and public buildings are the richer for this man who deigned to carve memorials whilst his fellow sculptors made their academic portrait heads.

As if all this were not enough to keep him and his assistants fully occupied, he was continuously engaged in the work of engraving. Count Kessler of the Cranach Press gave Mr Gill commission after commission, illustrations, initial letters, alphabets, seeking his advice and encouraging him. It was Count Kessler who so much wanted Mr Gill to work with the French sculptor Maillol, and arranged for him to travel to France to meet him. What a disaster! Mr Gill lost courage in Paris. Count Kessler had booked him a suite at a hotel, but the manager became incredulous in view of Mr Gill's bearded appearance and turned him out, believing there must be some mistake!

Mr Gill was now getting more work than he needed. No doubt he had grown somewhat away from the original conception of the Guild at Ditchling. Furthermore, Mr Gill was a tidy businessman and it irked him to see the books of the guild improperly kept. Moreover, he and others were unable to see clearly what was happening with the common purse and where money had gone when it was no longer there! Feelings began to run high and the dream began to slip away.

The position evidently grew unbearable, and the Gill family bought a farm at Capel-y-ffin, high up an almost inaccessible Welsh valley. He described it to a friend:

*Two thousand feet of mountain wall on both sides and to the north of it – no outlet but to the south. Benedictine monastery 400 yards away – Blessed Sacrament and Daily Mass. Good Land – fair price – nice little house and 107 acres with some timber and two rushing streams. Sheep run on mountains, and stone galore – no extra charge. Ten miles to station. Postman on horseback once a day. Doctor on horseback once a week.*

There was a change of outlook at this point. No longer was Mr Gill to consider the Ditchling form of communal living, at least not until the last war, when he gave his moral support to pacifist communities working on the land. The life at Capel-y-ffin proved too cut off and Mr Gill was always away at work. After a few years, once again the Gills were looking for accommodation near or in London – one cannot believe that the womenfolk who had grown so restive in Wales would have been any happier in London. Mary (Mrs Gill) was a keen amateur farmer, and little would ever have persuaded her of the economic impossibility of running a farm along the lines she tried. In London this, at least, would have been impossible.

They settled on a farm about twenty-five miles northwest of London, as inaccessible as possible, on the Chiltern Hills of Buckinghamshire. It was here that I served my apprenticeship.

There are some three hundred listed writings by Mr Gill, and very few if any include the theme of freedom and slavery. I quote:

*That state is a state of slavery in which a man does what he likes to do in his spare time, and in his working time that which is required of him. This state can only exist when what a man likes to do is to please himself. That state is a state of freedom in which a man does what he likes to do in his working time and in his spare time that which is required of him. This state can only exist when what a man likes to do is to please God.*

These words so frequently used by Mr Gill are not his, though I am sure

Eric Gill:
bookplate for
his mentor,
1920

he would have invented them if Ananda Coomaraswamy had not done so. Coomaraswamy can be numbered among his greatest friends. Whilst Mr Gill was discovering for himself that the Dark Ages had chinks of light long ago extinguished by Protestant prejudice, Ananda Coomaraswamy was discovering the common ground between the Christian and the Hindu theology. Here Coomaraswamy and Gill met and remained together in spirit, each casting light on the other's religious heritage. How exciting it must have been to discover in East and West the simple disciplines of craftsmanship and the clear hints of objective reasoning, and to have discovered that the path of man the maker rather than 'man the artist' had once before existed and that the greatest endeavours of men were perhaps derived from such an orientation of mind. Whenever Mr Gill was inclined to confuse art with usefulness, Coomaraswamy reminded him of its sacred foundation. 'The artist is not a special kind of man, but man is a special kind of artist'.

These concepts became a part of the man we know as Eric Gill and all his life they remained his special theme. He worked without ceasing to cast these thoughts into a thousand different aspects, sharpening and chiselling at their significance in religion, society, industrialism, finance and art – in all his work, books, lectures and letters.

No one brought more 'grist to the mill' than Coomaraswamy. Although we are apt to think primarily of Mr Gill as Christian and specifically Roman Catholic in his ideals, the impact of Coomaraswamy's introduction to eastern art was never eclipsed. Indeed, up to a point, Chartres and Ajanta were really not so far apart. Although Chartres led him inevitably into the Catholic faith, his total being, in my opinion, craved the richer and more sensuous approach of the East, where eroticism in art could exist without the private collector of the library strong room, and its possible confusion with pornography. One last quote from Coomaraswamy's book *The Transformation of Nature in Art*:

*Our modern system of thought has substituted for this division of labour a spiritual caste system which divides men into species. Those who have lost most by this are the artist, professionally speaking, on the one hand, and laymen generally on the other. The artist (such as would be so called) loses by his isolation and corresponding price, and by the emasculation of his art, no longer conceived as intellectual, but only as emotional in motivation and significance; the workman (to whom the name of the artist is now denied) loses in that he is not called, but forced to labour unintelligently, goods being valued above men. All alike have lost, in that art being now a luxury, no longer the normal type of all activity, all men are compelled to live in squalor and disorder and have become so inured to this that they are unaware of it. The only surviving artists in the scholastic gothic sense, are scientists, surgeons and engineers, the only ateliers, laboratories.*

I had been working for some months with a firm of Italian marble-carvers. There we put into stone or marble the statuary and portrait heads that were modelled in clay by respectable Royal Academicians. Indeed, there was more of our work in the Royal Academy annual exhibitions than carved by the sculptors themselves. In those days it was the accepted method of work. Sculptors did not carve stone; they modelled in clay for replica in stone or marble by operators skilled in the use of a 'pointing machine'.

I had just begun to read Mr Gill's books, and the basic dishonesty of the above process, both as regards the artist and the material, began, to say the least, to cause me some unease. Here was someone talking about making things in stone and emphasizing that a thing made in stone must be a stone thing – just as a thing made in wood must be a wood thing. It was dishonest to make a thing in clay and then copy it in stone. Things in different materials worked differently. The difference between that which I was doing with the Italians and that which I was now converted to, forced me to seek out an interview with Mr Gill and if possible to be taught by him.

Not infrequently did I overhear my father saying, in hushed tones, 'I apprenticed my son to the sculptor Eric Gill.' It was true, he put down the small premium when the time came. The truth is that people like my father did not come across people such as Mr Gill, and if he had he would certainly not have encouraged me to go to him! My father was a stockbroker in the City of London, and we had a pleasant house in the country where we spent our time playing tennis or golf and having very heated arguments about politics and religion. This background, and that derived from an English public school, created a very sharp contrast when I arrived, aged eighteen, at Mr Gill's workshop.

A letter had been written on my behalf by a mutual acquaintance, but Mr Gill had replied that he could not take on anyone else. Undaunted, I went to Mr Gill's workshop. Fortunately, he was there and would see me.

Of course, the one thing I dared not confess to was the work I was doing with the Italians. Having read his books, I thought this would immediately terminate the interview! He was still unable to take me, as he had all the helpers he needed — indeed, he was expecting another to start work in the coming week. Then the question came. 'What are you doing with yourself now?'

There was a simple straightforward honesty about Mr Gill which I was to realise ever more forcibly later on. But even at this brief first encounter it was impossible not to respond truthfully in reply. I explained, realizing now for certain that all was lost, that I had been trying to learn about masonry and carving and that these Italians had wanted an assistant. At once Mr Gill changed his mind; 'I think if you come back in a month I can take you. You see, the chap that is coming has been to an art school, and I don't think he will last here more than a month.'

My elation knew no bounds. (As the chap obliged, he will remain nameless; indeed I took over his lodgings in the village!)

'What should I do in the coming weeks,' I asked. 'Make something,' he said; 'it doesn't matter what it is, but make something that you know about. Make a wireless set if that is something you understand.'

In fact, I went to Italy, and I suppose I saw the famous Trajan Column and its inscription, but I must confess I did not remember it! On reflection, I think this was a stroke of good luck, as I came to lettering completely fresh when I started work with Mr Gill.

My first job for Mr Gill apart from getting the tea, sweeping up, and lighting fires, was the making of a huge capital L. It was masoned out of a solid block some four feet in height and projected in relief about five inches. Then an S of the same size. These letters were a part of the name 'Bentall's', which was a large shopping centre on the outskirts of London. These letters we carved in the workshop, and we went away to carve Mr Bentall's coat-of-arms on the shop corner in situ, together with various small carvings supporting the windows. The coat-of-arms was very big – one could get one's hands right into the folds of the 'mantling' and still carve away. The crest surmounting the helm was a leopard, and due to the nature of stone it was necessary that the tail of the beast was attached to the torse around the top of the helm. The tail could not possibly be carved curling upwards as was required by Mr Bentall. There was a very violent Mr Bentall accusing Mr Gill of dishonouring his family by making his leopard look like a cur. And Mr Gill offering to add some more spots to his leopard – all this in a busy traffic-ridden street, the only position from which to view the carving.

The building was in the course of construction, and bricklayers, carpenters, plumbers and electricians were everywhere. One morning they had gone. It was a strike. Quite without thinking we had let slip to some bricklayer or other what we were paid by Mr Gill. Now this was very little indeed, and I suppose the attitude was that we were undercutting them. The senior one of us telephoned Mr Gill. By a stroke of luck, Mr Gill was an honorary member of the union that had caused the bother, and soon the trouble was smoothed over.

Those of us who were single never gave money a thought. I think it is true to say that all of us would have worked for Mr Gill without payment, or at the most for our board and lodging. Indeed, on one occasion when money was short, we all immediately offered to work without payment. The work, and the doing of it as well as we could, was our sole aim. There were difficulties for those who were married and had families, and I do think more money should have been found for them. Grumbles were rightly to be heard from the wives, but the work was not affected. We worked all hours, late into the night when necessary.

Mr Gill's method of teaching lettering, if he ever did teach – one must bear in mind that lettering was everywhere and inscriptions were continuously being cut in the workshop – was to ask one to draw an alphabet as one thought letters should be. After this was done, Mr Gill corrected it, saying, in so many words, 'Here we make an A like this' or 'a B like that'. He always spoke quietly, and he never told me not to do anything I was doing, but always said with quiet authority, 'you make it like this', amd more often than not he anchored the thing in your mind with an appropriate and amusing anecdote. In this way, one had before one's very eyes the object made without knowledge and experience and its improved version rendered with the deftest skill. Thus, one could measure the difference and see the virtue in things well done.

The time came for me to cut my first alphabet. This would be in Hopton-Wood stone, an oolitic limestone that is very hard and capable of being polished like marble. Its later widespread use was very largely due to the publicity resulting from its use by Mr Gill. It is, indeed, a great tragedy that this unique stone is no longer available. It is simply crushed and burned to make plaster. It could be very precise and sharp, but its great quality was that perfection of incision could only be procured with difficulty. For Hopton-Wood is made up of minute shell fossils and the stone within the fossil and just outside is soft by comparison with the shell itself. In consequence one must be always on the watch, regulating the angle of cut – steeper if hard, shallower if soft. This inevitably makes for concentration in the letter-cutter, and, providing he has a good letter-form in his mind's eye, the very best work can be done in this stone. One was told in Mr Gill's workshop that if you can carve letters in Hopton-Wood stone, you will be able to carve letters in anything. This type of stone is a constant challenge to the letter-cutter, and I believe it played its own part in Mr Gill's development as a letterer.

After I had finished my alphabet in Hopton-Wood stone and had carefully painted the letters in light red and grey black, I went on to carve a small inscription. Mistakes had always to remain, and Mr Gill never allowed an apprentice to put an error right by any means whatever. For example, if a small piece of stone is chipped out of the edge of a letter, it was a chip for all time. I think he felt that the letter should be a faithful rendering of that which one had in the mind's eye. That the letter suffered damage by accident or carelessness was of little importance compared to cutting a letter that was

Eric Gill:
colophon of
Pigotts Press
1931

ill-conceived. To thicken the stroke of a letter even slightly to do away with the chip would be creating something false and quite other than the intention. He believed that most mistakes were derived from a lack of attention, and encouraged us to watch what we were doing and at the same time to have in mind that which was to be made.

In cutting my first inscription, I remember carefully carving serifs on the inside 'vee' of several M's. Just as I was about to cut yet another M, Laurie Cribb, Mr Gill's chief assistant, spotted my mistake and sent me to see Mr Gill. I was worried about the master's reaction, but I saw a way out of the difficulty. If I continued to put serifs in the same place on the rest of the M's in the inscription, my mistake would appear not as a mistake but as an intention. Mr Gill lost no time in telling me that this would not be fair or right, and that now that I knew the mistake it would, to say the least, be dishonest to continue. This all-pervading truth in the making of simple objects made a deep impression upon anyone that came into working contact with him.

Mr Gill's workshops at Pigotts amongst the beech woods of Buckinghamshire, were converted from fine eighteenth-century barns surrounding the farmyard where originally all natural things had been perpetrated. (I am reminded here that Mr Gill gave me the job of carving two inscriptions in shorthand. Unfortunately, we got the shorthand slightly wrong, and instead of it reading 'In the beginning was the word' it read 'In the beginning was the yard'.) Now, as if in honour of the pig, a sty was finely built of bricks in the centre of the yard, and his muck hummed and enriched the air – a little too much on a hot day. Mr Gill had his workshop and drawing office on the opposite side to us. At one end were the house and cottages. At the other, the Hague & Gill 'press' operated in a long, low outhouse.

Those that worked in the press were superior beings compared to us stonemasons. They did not, except at rare times, seem to be as busy – always a sign of superiority! Occasionally we were raided, and insults were hurled at us lower organisms. We, quite frankly, rather resented them and felt that we earned money which they in turn squandered. I'm sure there was little truth in this but it seemed that they always obtained what they wanted from Mr Gill whilst we had little to comfort us materially. For example, our fire for the winter was completely worn out, but it was fun collecting wood from the surrounding beech woods. Laurie Cribb would arrive trailing dead branches behind him – muttering always about the difficulties of an ever-increasing family and the Roman Church that made this inescapable. Laurie was certainly the finest letter-cutter of all time. He seemed to have learned all there was to know years before – his work had become instinctive. The exact opposite of his master, it seemed that he could only work in an unholy mess. He drew out his inscriptions apparently without any certainty of where the letters should be and rubbed them out with spit and thumb. Carving eventually through a black mass of pencil lead, he produced sublime letter forms and spacing.

Many inscriptions are by Lawrence Cribb though they may rightly be signed E G because, of course, we worked in a tradition and the tradition was Mr Gill's. Yet another contrast between Mr Gill and Laurie was that Mr Gill could not carve animals, but Laurie could. On the other hand, Laurie could not carve the human form so well. So it came about that Laurie carved and virtually designed the panel of *The Creation* on the League of Nations building at Geneva. The main panel was of man being touched by the hand of God, not an altogether unusual theme amongst painters. It is doubtful whether Mr Gill would have realised this at all, and he certainly designed this magnificent sculpture of man reawakening as he alone conceived it.

'Guess what', he said with a twinkle in his eye (he was holding a photograph of the same theme, painted by Michelangelo in the Sistine Chapel), 'some other bloke thought of this too!'

A large block of flats was being put up in London called Dorset House, and Mr Gill was asked to design some relief sculpture for the main entrance. The directors were not at all clear what they wanted and left it to the artist to suggest ideas. It was agreed that he would submit designs for the four basic activities that went on in such places, eating, drinking, washing, and sleeping. Sleeping and drinking were ruled out; I can't remember why – possibly his sketches frightened the directors! Even so, they found the cost of the remaining two more than they had budgeted for.

Mr Gill was invited to appear before the board of directors. One who had heard about Mr Gill's clothes thought he should warn his fellow directors. He explained that he wore a habit similar to, though shorter than, a monk's, and that being an artist of some distinction he should be treated with due respect. 'How could the cost be reduced,' they asked. At once Mr Gill said. 'Each leaf is £5, so if you do away with the whole branch that will save £25.'

The directors, already disappointed because Mr Gill had appeared in an overcoat, said bitterly, 'He is not an artist – he is a businessman! And moreover we have not seen his monk's habit!'

Mr Gill and I worked alone on these carvings late into the night by the light of the street lamps. He talked much to me and with little reserve. I was fascinated by all he said. It was clear that he felt misunderstood, and in his turn he had misunderstood the contemporary Roman Catholic Church. Though his faith remained firm, he was tending more and more to relate his faith to the early Church. It remained a burning shock to him that so much of his belief was unsupported by the Church, and what was worse, the Church, almost without exception, sanctioned that which he most strongly argued against.

His 'fellow travelling', as the phrase goes, with the communist view of life gained much from his understanding of early Christian communities, where material things were shared as between brothers. Undoubtedly, he was absolutely clear about the totally atheistic Communism in Russia, but he did not view the capitalist system of the West any more favourably. He thought both systems were out to achieve the same materialistic ends, and of the two evils he often appeared to favour Communism. This led him to frequent criticism and correction by the Roman Catholic hierarchy. However, Pope Pius XII has been quoted as saying, 'This man has understood our Encyclicals.' It was difficult to deny the point that the modern world, east or west, was predominantly atheistic and that those in power sought, by every means that modern technology produced, to seduce the masses of ordinary citizens to accept a form of slavery perhaps surpassing anything in the past. These view shocked and, my God, they stunned, my stockbroker father! Strangely enough, bricklayers, carpenters, and other craftsmen responded favourably in spite of the implication of slavery. All who worked with their hands instinctively and at once admired and felt at one with the champion of the underdogs of industrialism. By no means was it only that way round; on the contrary, he seemed drawn to them.

Back at Pigotts, I sat beside Mr Gill, drawing some of the fatter versions of Gill Sans for the Monotype Corporation. He could not bring himself to make the necessary changes. After all, his original designs were justified in his mind as being fool-proof as regards their mechanical manufacture and capability of being copied by men whose work was mechanical rather than free. But to have to introduce subtlety of a kind that was not easily measurable would defeat the whole purpose and make a nonsense of his reasoning. 'He who pays the piper calls the tune', he said, as he explained to me what was required. Would Mr Gill be proud of the fact, despite all the variations in monoline and sans serif that have been in and out of favour, that his Gill Sans is still found to be much the most legible? Yes, I think he would. In spite of everything, he really was a first-class industrial designer. He always wanted to know exactly how a thing worked and what it was for. For someone who so fiercely challenged the supremacy of machines, he took a remarkable interest in their design.

St John's College, Oxford, commissioned Mr Gill to carve St John the Baptist for a niche above their gateway. The honey-coloured Clipsham stone from Rutland slowly revealed the sturdy body of the beckoning John, clad in a skin and holding a strong staff. As I watched and, indeed, helped to find the hidden form, I knew that what was being created was as near to the image in his mind's eye as anything I'd seem him do. His attention was remarkable in degree and duration. No tool was used if a coarser one would do the work. No tool was every forced beyond its capacity. All stages were in process at once over various parts of the carving, the projections always being a stage ahead so that, for all the world, it appeared a simple question of removing a series of skins of differently textured stone. Strength and firmness of form were assured not only by the clarity of his vision but in no small degree through his technique. All form for Mr Gill was of a convex order. Concavities were the result of the meeting of two convexities. Bridging pieces of stone were as carefully carved as the rest and vanished as the carving matched its conception, leaving the stone ringing like a bell even if lightly touched, one thrill to reward the carver on the completion of work well done not usually shared by the sculptors of today! Mr Gill had no thought of self-expression or that the material should be emphasised, nor did he get involved in the relation of masses. He was not so much a sculptor as a carver making things in stone which he had conceived in stone from the start.

Pigotts was altogether an enchanting place: as I have said, a rectangular plan of buildings around the farmyard now grown over with grass. Orchards and a small space of surrounding green fields and then the dense beech woods of Buckinghamshire falling away, Pigotts surmounted the spur of a hill. A narrow lane, capable of only one vehicle at a time, led precipitously down through the woods to buses and a link with the outside world. It was a haven of peace and sensible occupations.

But there were contradictions between the theory and the practice. It could not of course be otherwise. Mr Gill was always very busy engraving, carving, or writing – preparing talks – and, of course there were letters to the press. Consequently he did not know the full extent to which the farm intruded on our work. He rebuked Mary, his wife, only occasionally and mildly. Sometimes, at Mary's desperate request, we fetched the cows back from distant lands. Then the calving became unplanned, and spells without milk called for treks down the hill to a neighbourly farmer. Other days, we would drive a cow several miles to a bull or hold a cow's tail whilst the vet would search her like a penny dip. All these occupations took up valuable time, valuable because the workshop earned money and the farm did not. Mr Gill knew this, and the odd pat of butter on the table, especially when an important visitor was coming, was somehow not sufficient compensation for all the trials and tribulations. It was a brave but unrealistic attempt to unite the workshop and the farm, and a drain on Mr Gill's income that he could ill afford. In this care of the farm the craftsman within Mr Gill seemed blind to the inefficient, amateur husbandry.

There were quite a few blind spots, in fact, and one I remember very well caused a lot of amusement. Mr Gill had a way of arguing himself into impossible positions. He had been invited to dine at the Royal Institute of British Architects. The dinner was in honour of Frank Dobson, another sculptor of the time. I was standing at the foot of the stairs as all these distinguished people came down into the hall to hear Dobson lecture. Mr Gill, escorting the president's wife, gave me a broad wink and missed a step! But this is not the point of my story.

Dobson, apart from speaking rather too long, put forward the theory that man had been interested in 'form' before anything else. Mr Gill could not take this at all! He jumped up and put forward his counter theory. 'Undoubtedly man had first scratched lines long before he was interested in form.' So the argument went on and on until someone pointed out, 'Was it not extraordinary that here were two grown men fiercely disputing something that could hardly be proved either way, and interesting in that the scratch theory so exactly fitted Eric Gill's predominantly linear approach to sculpture, whilst the mud-form theory so aptly fitted Frank Dobson's rounded clay forms.' It was still a matter of some importance as we drove back to Pigotts that night!

Mr Gill believed fervently in many things, and he used all the logic he could command combined with a very lucid style of prose. His overemphasis, perhaps through lack of maturity in early days and later through despair at the way the world was inevitably drifting into war, created many critics who otherwise might have been more tolerant of his religious and political views. In my opinion, he had the only tenable view of art which was in any way an alternative to the popular view in the contemporary west. The mainsprings of his belief were to be found at Chartres and Ajanta through his friend Ananda Coomaraswamy, that great exponent of Indian art.

Mr Gill's ideas were of a kind that turned the prevailing hypnotic acceptance of western art completely upside down. He thought and then he made his thought in stone. He put the intellect at least as high as the emotions. The artist was not a special kind of man, but man was a special kind of artist. Anonymity was an ideal and, insofar as a work expressed the personality of the maker rather than the subject, it had failed. Such things are an accident and a hindrance to a perfect rendering of an already complete visual concept within the mind.

Meister Eckart said of the carpenter that he, on building a house,

*Will first erect it in his mind and, were the house enough subject to his will, then, materials apart, the only difference between them would be that of begetter and suddenly begotten.*

Mr Gill's work was deliberate and intentional. He stood apart from it, being simply the executant. He was a balanced man bringing to his work an exceptional intellect, sensitivity, and skill. It was in stone that these three were best united. Personally, I regret that so much of his energy was encouraged into writing and that no one seems to have adequately suggested to him that we should all have been the more blessed through his stone work and engraving. Indeed, much of his writing, good and apt as it was, is too repetitive. As can be seen in his sculpture, he was a man not involved in the sense popularly understood today. He did not carve in a fury of passion, though he felt as deeply as any. He did not subscribe to any popular 'ism'. He was not interested in self-expression or in expressing the material in which he was working. And, above all, he was totally at variance with the teaching in art schools. It was not that he was negative to all these things; his system of thought had quite a different source and its fruits were wholly different. Today we are inclined to extol the virtue of total identification with what we are doing.

Once again Mr Gill fell foul of the majority of the Roman Church. He strongly opposed all that General Franco stood for in the Spanish War.

I had been approached by a Conservative member of Parliament about a memorial to commemorate those who were massacred in the Alcazar at Toledo. The finished memorial was to be exhibited in London to raise the funds for the Franco cause! As I remember, I wrote at some length to Mr Gill asking whether I should accept the commission, and how I felt and what my conscience would have to bear, until my dying day, if I undertook the job. Mr Gill's reply came by return on a postcard: 'Plenty biz no do! No biz. DO!' It was done!

Mr Gill never believed that war would come and he gave himself to the argument of pacifism. He maintained that one of the causes of war was the result of trade in things made for dividends rather than for human needs. But war came relentlessly, and it was bitter indeed for him to see the logic of his beliefs so totally denied. He died after an operation in 1940. One of his last letters contained the following prophetic words:

*It seems likely that if we win the war we shall have a dictator here to mop up the mess – we seem to be working in that direction. The Birmingham Post said, 'There can be no tolerable peace which does not mean a return to export trade.' I should like to know how they are going to work it!*

The war turned our thoughts away from all Mr Gill's ideas, for the time being, but I have little doubt that much of what he said and openly stood for will never die. For me, personally, I find it impossible to think of a man so vibrant with life as not existing. As one is confronted with the latest excesses of industrialism and war, I recall his calm, clear, and reasoning voice and see his quite unforgettable, steady, yet questioning eye.

One of Gill's
*Stations of
the Cross,*
Westminster
Cathedral

# David Pye

BORN 1914

Pye is a radical, non-conformist, amateur. A woodworker who makes boxes and bowls and dishes, and taught at the Royal College of Art in London for twenty-three years, part of the time as Professor of Furniture. He trained as an architect and spent most of his time as a student building wooden boats. His books are keen enquiries into the man-made world. *The Nature and Aesthetics of Design*, Barrie and Jenkins, London, 1978, swallows up *The Nature of Design*, Studio Vista, London, 1964. In their rational, reductive manner of enquiry lurks an impish spirit of contradiction: as when, in discussing the workmanship of risk, he suggests that 'it had doubtless been practised effectively by people of the utmost depravity'. He is properly critical of the lack of theory and imprecise standards associated with our ideas about craftsmanship and he pursues these failings back to their origins in the doctrines of the Arts and Crafts movement.

FROM

## THE NATURE AND ART
## OR WORKMANSHIP

# 1968

### DESIGN PROPOSES
### WORKMANSHIP DISPOSES

Extracts from *The Nature and Art of Workmanship*, Cambridge University Press 1968: Chapter 1: 'Design Proposes, Workmanship Disposes'; Chapter 2: 'The Workmanship of Risk and the Workmanship of Certainty'; Chapter 11: 'The Aesthetic Importance of Workmanship and Its Future'.

In the last twenty years there has been an enormous intensification of interest in Design. The word is everywhere. But there has been no corresponding interest in workmanship. Indeed there has been a decrease of interest in it. Just as the achievements of modern invention have popularly been attributed to scientists instead of to the engineers who have so often been responsible for them, so the qualities and attractions which our environment gets from its workmanship are almost invariably attributed to design.

This has not happened because the distinction between workmanship and design is a mere matter of terminology or pedantry. The distinction both in the mind of the designer and of the workman is clear. Design is what, for practical purposes, can be conveyed in words and by drawing: workmanship is what, for practical purposes, can not. In practice the designer hopes the workmanship will be good, but the workman decides whether it shall be good or not. On the workman's decision depends a great part on the quality of our environment.

Gross defects of workmanship the designer can, of course, point out and have corrected, much as a conductor can at least insist on his orchestra playing the right notes in the right order. But no conductor can make a bad orchestra play well; or, rather, it would take him years to do it; and no designer can make bad workmen produce good workmanship. The analogy between workmanship and musical performance is in fact rather close. The quality of the concert does not depend wholly on the score, and the quality of our environment does not depend on its design. The score and the design are merely the first of the essentials, and they can be nullified by the performers or the workmen.

Our environment in its visible aspect owes far more to workmanship than we realize. There is in the man-made world a whole domain of quality which is not the result of design and owes little to the designer. On the contrary, indeed, the designer is deep in its debt, for every card in his hand was put there originally by the workman. No architect could specify ashlar until a mason had perfected it and shown him that it could be done. Designers have only been able to exist by exploiting what workmen have evolved or invented.

This domain of quality is usually talked of and thought of in terms of material. We talk as though the material of itself conferred the quality. Only to name precious materials like marble, silver, ivory, ebony, is to evoke a picture of thrones and treasures. It does not evoke a picture of grey boulders on a dusty hill or logs of ebony as they really are – wet dirty lumps all shakes and splinters! Material in the raw is nothing much. Only worked material has quality, and pieces of worked material are made to show their quality by men, or put together so that together they show a quality which singly they had not. 'Good material' is a myth. English walnut is not good material. Most of the tree is leaf-mould and firewood. It is only because of workmanlike felling and converting and drying and selection and machining and setting out and cutting and fitting and assembly and finishing – particularly finishing – that a very small proportion of the tree comes to be thought of as good material; not because a designer has specified English walnut. Many people seeing a hundred pounds worth of it in a London timber yard would mistake it for rubbish, and in fact a good half of it would be: would have to be.

So it is with all other materials. In speaking of good material we are paying an unconscious tribute to the enormous strength of the traditions of workmanship still shaping the world even now (and still largely unwritten). We talk as though good material were found instead of being made. It is good only because workmanship has made it so. Good workmanship will make something better out of pinchbeck than bad will out of gold. *Corruptio optimi pessima!* Some materials promise far more than others but only the workman can bring out what they promise.

In this domain of quality our environment is deteriorating. What threatens it most is not bad workmanship. Much workmanship outside of mass-production is appallingly bad and getting worse, to be sure, and things are seen in new buildings which make one's hair rise. But at least it is easy to see what the remedies are, there, if difficult to apply them. Moreover, it is not the main danger, because it is outside the field of mass-production, and the greater part of all manufacture now is mass-production; in which, although there is some bad workmanship, much is excellent. Much of it has never been surpassed and some never equalled. The deterioration comes not because of bad workmanship in mass-production but because the range of qualities which mass-production is capable of just now is so dismally restricted; because each is so uniform and because nearly all lack depth, subtlety, overtones, variegation, diversity, or whatever you choose to call that which distinguishes the workmanship of a Stradivarius violin, or something much rougher like a modern ring-net boat. The workmanship of a motor-car is something to marvel at, but a street full of parked cars is jejune and depressing; as if the same short tune of clear unmodulated notes were being

1. Shape-determining systems are discussed in my book *The Nature of Design*, in which the chapters on Techniques and on 'Useless work' are relevant to the present subject.

endlessly repeated. A harbour full of fishing-boats is another matter.

Why do we accept this as inevitable? We made it so and we can unmake it. Unless workmanship comes to be understood and appreciated for the art it is, our environment will lose much of the quality it still retains.

David Pye
Drawing from workbook
1953

## THE WORKMANSHIP OF RISK AND THE WORKMANSHIP OF CERTAINTY

Workmanship of the better sort is called, in an honorific way, craftsmanship. Nobody, however is prepared to say where craftsmanship ends and ordinary manufacture begins. It is impossible to find a generally satisfactory definition for it in face of all the strange shibboleths and prejudices about it which are acrimoniously maintained. It is a word to start an argument with.

There are people who say they would like to see the last of craftsmanship because, as they conceive of it, it is essentially backward-looking and opposed to the new technology which the world must now depend on. For these people craftsmanship is at best an affair of hobbies in garden sheds; just as for them art is an affair of things in galleries. There are many people who see craftsmanship as the source of a valuable ingredient of civilization. There are also people who tend to believe that craftsmanship has a deep spiritual value of a somewhat mystical kind.

If I must ascribe a meaning to the word craftsmanship, I shall say as a first approximation that it means simply workmanship using any kind of technique or apparatus, in which the quality of the result is not predetermined, but depends on the judgement, dexterity and care which the maker exercises as he works. The essential idea is that the quality of the result is continually at risk during the process of making; and so I shall call this kind of workmanship 'The workmanship of risk': an uncouth phrase, but at least descriptive.

It may be mentioned in passing that in workmanship the care counts for more than the judgement and dexterity; though care may well become habitual and unconscious.

With the workmanship of risk we may contrast the workmanship of certainty, always to be found in quantity production, and found in its pure state in full automation. In workmanship of this sort the quality of the result is exactly predetermined before a single saleable thing is made. In less developed forms of it the result of each operation done during production is pre-determined.

The workmanship of certainty has been in occasional use in undeveloped and embryonic forms since the Middle Ages and I should suppose from much earlier times, but all the works of men which have been most admired since the beginning of history have been made by the workmanship of risk, the last three or four generations only excepted. The techniques to which the workmanship of certainty can be economically applied are not nearly so diverse as those used by the workmanship of risk. It is certain that when the workmanship of certainty remakes our whole environment, as it is bound now to do, it will also change the visible quality of it. In some of the following chapters I shall discuss what may be lost and gained.

The most typical and familiar example of the workmanship of risk is writing with a pen, and of the workmanship of certainty, modern printing. The first thing to be observed about printing or any other representative example of the workmanship of certainty, is that it originally involves more of

88

judgement, dexterity, and care than writing does, not less: for the type had to be carved out of metal by hand in the first instance before any could be cast; and the compositor of all people has to work carefully: and so on. But all this judgement, dexterity and care has been concentrated and stored up before the actual printing starts. Once it does start, the stored-up capital is drawn and the newspapers come pouring out in an absolutely pre-determined form with no possibility of variation between them, by virtue of the exacting work put in beforehand in making and preparing the plant which does the work: and making not only the plant but the tools, patterns, prototypes and jigs which enabled the plant to be built, and all of which had to be made by the workmanship of risk.

Typewriting represents an intermediate form of workmanship, that of limited risk. You can spoil the page in innumerable ways, but the N's will never look like U's, and, however ugly the typing, it will almost necessarily be legible. All workmen using the workmanship of risk are constantly devising ways to limit the risk by using such things as jigs and templates. If you want to draw a straight line with your pen, you do not go at it freehand, but use a ruler, that is to say, a jig. There is still a risk of blots and kinks, but less risk. You could even do your writing with a stencil, a more exacting jig, but it would be slow.

Speed in production is usually the purpose of the workmanship of certainty but it is not, always. Machine tools, which, once set up, perform one operation, such for instance as cutting a slot, in an absolutely predetermined form, are often used simply for the sake of accuracy, and not at all to save time or labour. Thus in the course of doing a job by the workmanship of risk a workman will be working freehand with a hand tool at one moment and will resort to a machine tool a few minutes later.

In fact the workmanship of risk in most trades is hardly ever seen, and has hardly ever been known, in a pure form, considering the ancient use of templates, jigs, machines and other shape-determining systems[1], which reduce risk. Yet in principle the distinction between the two different kinds of workmanship is clear and turns on the question: 'is the result predetermined and unalterable once production begins?'

Bolts can be made by an automatic machine which when fed with blanks repeatedly performs a set sequence of operations and turns out hundreds of finished bolts without anyone even having to look at it. In full automation much the same can be said of more complex products, substituting the words 'automated factory' for 'automatic machine'. But the workmanship[1] of certainty is still often applied in a less developed form where the product is made by a planned sequence of operations, each of which has to be started and stopped by the operative, but with the result of each one predetermined and outside his control. There are also hybrid forms of production where some of the operations have predetermined results and some are performed by the workmanship of risk. The craft-based industries, so called, work like this.

Yet it is not difficult to decide which category any given piece of work falls into. An operative, applying the workmanship of certainty, cannot spoil the job. A workman using the workmanship of risk assisted by no matter what machine-tools and jigs, can do so almost any minute. That is the essential difference. The risk is real.

But there is much more in workmanship than spoiling the job, just as there is more in music than playing the right notes.

There is something about the workmanship of risk, or its results; or something associated with it; which has been long and widely valued. What is it, and how can it be continued? That is one of the principal questions which I hope this book may answer: and answer factually rather than with a series of emotive noises such as protagonists of craftsmanship have too often made instead of answering it.

It is obvious that the workmanship of risk is not always or necessarily valuable. In many contexts it is an utter waste of time. It can produce things of the worst imaginable quality. It is often expensive. From time to time it had doubtless been practised effectively by people of the utmost depravity.

It is equally obvious that not all of it is in jeopardy: for the whole range of modern technics is based on it. Nothing can be made in quantity unless tools, jigs, and prototypes, both of the product and the plant to produce it, have been made first and made singly.

It is fairly certain that the workmanship of risk will seldom or never again be used for producing things in quantity as distinct from making the apparatus for doing so; the apparatus which predetermines the quality of the product. But it is just as certain that a few things will continue to be specially made simply because people will continue to demand individuality in their possessions and will not be content with standardization everywhere. The danger is not that the workmanship of risk will die out altogether but rather that, from want of theory, and thence lack of standards, its possibilities will be neglected and inferior forms of it will be taken for granted and accepted.

There was once a time when the workmanship of certainty, in the form colloquially called 'mass-production', generally made things of worse quality than the best that could be done by workmanship of risk – colloquially called, 'hand-made'. That is far from true now. The workmanship of a standard bolt or nut, or a glass or polythene bottle, tobacco-tin of electric-light bulb, is as good as it could possibly be. The workmanship of risk has no exclusive prerogative of quality. What it has exclusively is an immensely various range of qualities, without which at its command the art of design becomes arid and impoverished.

A fair measure of the aesthetic richness, delicacy and subtlety of the workmanship of risk, as against that of certainty, is given by comparing the contents of say, the British Museum with those of a good department store. Nearly everything in the Museum has been made by the workmanship of risk, most things in the store by the workmanship of certainty. Yet if the two were compared in respect of the ingenuity and variety of the devices represented in them the Museum would seem infantile. At the present moment we are more fond of the ingenuity than the qualities. But without losing the ingenuity we could, in places, still have the qualities if we really wanted them.


## THE AESTHETIC IMPORTANCE
## OF WORKMANSHIP,
## AND ITS FUTURE

In the foregoing chapters it has been suggested that the importance of good workmanship in its aesthetic aspect rests on there things:
1. Highly regulated workmanship shows us a thing done in style: an evident intention achieved with evident success. It is anti-sordid, anti-squalid and contributes to our morale.

To do a thing in style is to set oneself standards of behaviour in the belief that the manner of doing anything has a certain aesthetic importance of its own independent of the importance of what is done. This belief is the basis of ordinary decent behaviour according to the customs of any society. It is the principle on which one keeps one's house and one's person clean and neat, and so on. Regulation which, in general, the workmanship of risk can only achieve by taking a good deal of avoidable trouble, used undoubtedly to be a part of this idea of behaviour.

With the workmanship of certainty it is becoming easier to achieve high regulation and less determination is needed to do it; but still the quality of the result is clear evidence of competence and assurance, and it is an ingredient of civilization to be continually faced with that evidence, even if it is taken for granted and goes unremarked.

2. Free workmanship shows that, while design is a matter of imposing order on things, the intended results of design can often be achieved perfectly well without the workman being denied spontaneity and unstudied improvisation. This perhaps has special importance because our natural environment, and all naturally formed or grown things, show a similar spontaneity and individuality on a basis of order and uniformity. This characteristic aspect of nature, order permeated by individuality, was the aesthetic broth in which the human sensibility grew. Whereas in the early days of civilization highly regulated workmanship seemed admirable because it was rare, difficult, and exceptional, that situation is now completely reversed, and we might well try to make ourselves an environment which has more concord with our natural one.

3. Good workmanship, whether free or regulated, produces and exploits the quality I have called diversity, and by means of it makes an extension of aesthetic experience beyond the domain controlled by design, down to the smallest scale of formal elements which the eye can distinguish at the shortest range. Diversity on the small scale is particularly delightful in regulated workmanship because there it maintains a kind of pleasantly disrespectful opposition to the regulation and precision of the piece seen in the large: as when, for instance, the wild figure of the wood sets off the precision of the cabinet-work. Diversity imports into our man-made environment something which is akin to the natural environment we have abandoned; and something which begins to tell, moreover, at those short distances at which we most often see the things we use.

What changes can one foresee? Is there for instance any reason for the productive part of the workmanship of risk to continue doing highly regulated work? Why should it, when the workmanship of certainty is capable of higher regulation than ever was seen? Why, in particular, should it, considering that high regulation by the workmanship of risk is usually very expensive even where the best and the most ingenious use is made of machine tools? Imagination boggles at the thought of what it might cost to build any standard family car from scratch by the workmanship of risk. How many weeks would it take to make the carburettor, for instance, or one of the head-lamps?

It should continue simply because the workmanship of risk in its highly regulated forms can produce a range of specific aesthetic qualities which the workmanship of certainty, always ruled by price, will never achieve. The British Museum, or any other like it, gives convincing evidence of that. And one need not copy the past in order to perpetuate those qualities. People still use oil-paint, but they do not imitate Titian.

There is of course no danger that high regulation will die out in the preparatory branch of the workmanship of risk. Beyond that, the prevalence and immense capability of the workmanship of certainty will ensure that highly regulated workmanship continues and increases. Indeed there is already too much of it or, rather, there is too little diversity in it. The contemporary appetite for junk and antiques may partly be a sign of an unsatisfied hunger for diversity and spontaneity in things of everyday use. I do not think it can be quite explained either by the romantic associations of mere age or by an aversion from the ephemerality of contemporary designs. There is still comparatively so much diversity about that it is difficult to estimate how an environment quite devoid of it would strike us. The quality in design which is called 'clinical' is more or less the quality of no-diversity. A little of it, for a change, is pleasant, but a world all clinical might be fairly oppressive and such a world of design and workmanship without diversity is decidedly a possible one, now. Four things are going wrong:

1. The workmanship of certainty has not yet found out, except in certain restricted fields, how to produce diversity and exploit it.

2. Where highly regulated components are fitted and assembled by the workmanship of risk, in industries which are only part 'industrialized', such as joinery for buildings, some of the workmanship is extraordinarily bad.

3. Some kinds of workmanship, such as the best cabinet-making, which use the workmanship of risk to produce very high regulation and the most subtle manipulations of diversity, are dying out because of the cost of what they do. But what they do has unique aesthetic qualities.

4. Free workmanship also is dying out, for the same reasons, and it also has unique aesthetic qualities for which there can be no substitute.

It is, I submit, quite easy to see what might be done about the last three of these things but not about the first, which is undoubtedly the most important. The workmanship of certainty can do nearly everything well except produce diversity. Its only real success in that way at present is in weaving and in making things of glass or translucent or semi-translucent plastics such as nylon or polythene which show delightful diversification because of their modulation of the transmitted light and the interplay between it and the light reflected from their surfaces. Diversity in shapes and surfaces could also, no doubt, be achieved fairly crudely by numerically controlled machine tools, and perhaps something more can be hoped for there in course of time.

Much of the diversity in highly regulated work produced by the workmanship of risk used to be achieved through the manner in which it made use of the inherent qualities of natural materials. It is very probable that, if diversity were appreciated as much as economy, synthetic or processed materials would be made with an equally rich inherent diversification.

If industrial designers and architects understood the theory and aesthetics of workmanship better, and realized the importance of it, they would surely make better use of the opportunities offered by the techniques which are now available to them. One could almost believe that some industrial designers only know of two surface qualities, shiny and 'textured'; and that to them texture means something which has to be distinguishable in all its parts three feet away! They ought to reflect that so far as the appearance of their work goes its surface qualities are not less important than its shape, for the only part of it which will ever be visible is the surface.

The want of diversity is not so much to be blamed on the technologists as on the designers, who do not think enough about it, or do not think enough of it. Perhaps I think too much of it, but it is high time somebody spoke up for it. Art is not so easy that we can afford to ignore any and every formal quality which will not go on to a drawing board. Yet, the fact remains, I can offer no better suggestion than that, if people came to love diversity, they would find out ways of producing it.

The answer to the second problem, of bad workmanship in assembly and finishing off, is much easier to see. The first thing to be grasped is that the situation now is fundamentally different from what it was in the old days of good rough workmanship. The second thing is that the force of the long traditions of the workmanship of risk is now very weak in many trades. With some honourable but rather few exceptions, it no longer concerns a joiner's self-respect and standing in the eyes of his trade, that his work shall be done properly according to those traditions, and moreover he will be paid as well as before even if it is done badly.

This situation is regrettable, but it does not necessarily mean that the joiner is a bad man. It merely means that his education in his trade has been bad (for a trade learnt according to the traditions was an education, though a circumscribed one. It taught the principles on which one should act in certain circumstances and the difference between good and bad actions). The existing situation arises from the fact that the building trade is in transition in this country from the workmanship of risk to that of certainty, to the assembly of prefabricated components so made that neither care, knowledge or dexterity are required for their assembly; and such trades as the joiner's are in decline. There are now too few good joiners.

It is futile to hope that the process of decline can be reversed on a sufficient scale to match the size of the industry, and the action to be taken is unmistakable. We must stop designing joinery and other details of cheap buildings as though for such work we could command fully educated joiners whenever we wanted them. It is, for example, silly to design architraves which have to be mitred round door openings. Of all joints a mitre is sure to be badly done or to go wrong in cheap work. It is necessary for the architect to understand very clearly the limitations of the workmanship which the price of the building will allow, to understand that nothing can be left to the discretion of men without education in the trade, and to design within those limitations instead of asking for highly regulated traditional joinery like mitred architraves.

As for the third and fourth problems it is again not difficult to see a line of action, but it may not be easy to arouse interest and inform opinion so that the action gets taken. It will be a great loss to the world if at least a little highly regulated work does not continue to be done by the workmanship of risk in making furniture, textiles, pottery, hand-tools, clothes, glass, jewellery, musical instruments and several other things. It will equally be a loss if free workmanship does not continue. Most of such work will fall within the province of what are now called 'the Crafts'. What is now required is a more realistic conception of them.

The workmanship of risk can be applied to two quite different purposes, one preparatory, the other productive. Preparatory workmanship makes, not the products of manufacture, but the plant, tools, jigs and other apparatus which make the workmanship of certainty possible. Productive workmanship actually turns out products for sale.

The preparatory branch of the workmanship of risk is, of course, already far the more important of the two, economically. Without it we should starve pretty quickly because without it the workmanship of certainty would cease, and only by way of that is mass-production possible. The productive branch on the other hand is declining, and in the course of the next two or four generations it may well have become economically negligible as a source of useful products. But, though, after that, the workmanship of risk may never again provide our bread, it may yet provide our salt. It will no doubt provide our space-craft too, and our more enormous scientific instruments.

The term 'crafts', that sadly tarnished name, may perhaps be applied to the part of the productive workmanship of risk whose justification is aesthetic, not economic (and not space-exploratory or particle-pursuing). The crafts on that definition will still have a slight indirect economic importance, in that they will enable designers to make relatively expensive experiments which the workmanship of certainty will deny them, and also to try out materials it denies them. But economics alone will never justify their continuation.

The crafts ought to provide the salt — and the pepper — to make the visible environment more platatable when nearly all of it will be have been made by the workmanship of certainty. Let us have nothing to do with the idea that the crafts, regardless of what they make, are in some way superior to the workmanship of certainty, or a means of protest against it. That is a paranoia. The crafts ought to be a complement to industry.

For the crafts, in the modern world, there can be no half measures. There can be no reason for them to continue unless they produce only the best possible workmanship, free or regulated, allied to the best possible design: in other words, unless they produce only the very best quality. That quality is never got so quickly as more ordinary qualities are. The best possible design is seldom the one which is quickest to make, or anything like it; and, even where it is, the best quality of workmanship can usually be achieved only by the workman spending an apparently inordinate amount of time on the job. There are exceptions. Pottery, some hand-loom weaving and some jewellery, for instance, can be produced relatively cheaply. Moreover, in pottery at least, industry offers no serious competition, since the aesthetic qualities of 'studio pottery' are as yet rarely attempted in industrial production. Consequently these crafts flourish — though too seldom they produce the very best quality, or the best design — and people are making a reasonable living at them. But they are exceptions. The rule is, and always was, that the very best quality is extremely expensive by comparison with things of ordinary quality.

It is very probable that most people are beginning now to associate the word 'crafts' simply with hairy cloth and gritty pots. It is not quite realized perhaps that modern equivalents of the multitude of other kinds of workmanship we see in museums could and should be made: nor how astronomically expensive many of them would be.

Now the crafts, even when they do produce the very best quality, are in direct competition with producers of ordinary quality. The crafts are in no way comparable to the fine arts, a separate domain: far from it! The crafts are a border-ground of manufacturing industry, and nearly every object they make has its counterpart and competitor in something manufactured for the same purpose. In all but a very few trades exceedingly high quality is the last remaining ground on which the crafts can now compete.

Two of the fundamental considerations which will shape the future of the crafts are the time they must take over their work and the competition they must face. The differential in price between a product of craft, of the best quality, and a product of manufacture varies, naturally, according to the trade; but it is always large and sometimes huge. It ought to be and must be. Unless it is, the craftsman has no hope of anything approaching a modest professional standard of living, and he will never be able to command a better living than that.

The crafts will therefore survive as a means of livelihood only where there is a sufficient demand for the *very best quality at any price.*

eg. where
expensive crafts
are accepted
vs. mass produced

struggling
crafts

That sort of demand still exists in some trades. *Haute couture* flourishes. Certain musical instruments, yachts, guns, jewellery, tailoring, and things of silver, are still in that kind of demand. But the demand is not large, by comparison, for instance, with the demand for contemporary paintings, or for antiques, at comparable prices. The situation of the craftsmen who make these things of the best quality is evidently precarious. The West End tailors and bootmakers are not finding it easy to exist any more.

In other fields that kind of demand has very nearly ceased in Britain. Cabinet- and chair-making, blacksmith's work, carving, hand-tool making are examples. These are all cases where the differential is very large. Here the potential buyers have turned to antiques or else spend their money on things of other kinds.

It is not always clear why the demand has persisted in some fields but not in others. We may suspect that where it does persist the reasons are not always very creditable ones. But we need not concern ourselves with that, for it is absolutely certain that no demand for the best quality at any price can be re-created, or stimulated where it still persists, until it becomes a fact that a fair amount of work of that quality is being done and can be had.

Now, considering the time that is needed to do it, how can such work be made? It is obvious that it must be done, at first and for a long while afterwards, for love and not for money. It will have to be done by people who are earning their living in some other way.

It is sometimes hoped that a man can set up as, say, a cabinet-maker and aim at making a few pieces of the very best quality each year, so long as he keeps himself solvent by making other furniture to order, or for sale in competition with the manufacturers. This can be done and is being done. Some good furniture is being made in this way, but very, very little of the best. The man who does it is likely to find that to make a moderate living he has to become a manager more than a maker – sales manager, works manager, despatch manager, buyer and accountant, as well as secretary, all rolled into one. Whatever he does of the very best quality will have to be done as a side line, very likely at week-ends. It will not increase proportionately to the other. If it were not for being his own master he might about as well make his living working in some other office or at some other trade, and make his two or three pieces of the very best quality in his spare time.

That is the logical conclusion. With certain exceptions, some of them precarious, the crafts, like the fine arts, are not fully viable. Only a very small proportion of painters can make enough money, by painting alone, to bring up a family, and that in a time when there is a climate of educated opinion very favourable to painting and a whole apparatus of distribution specifically for them: and when, above all, high prices for them are paid. None of these advantages is yet available to the crafts. Moreover, they are under a disadvantage which the painters are free from: the pressure of competition just mentioned.

Nearly all craftsmen, as nearly all painters and poets already do, will have to work part-time, certainly in the opening years of their career. One of the best professional cabinet-makers in Britain, Ernest Joyce, started as an amateur and learnt his job at first from books. 'Amateur', after all, means by derivation a man who does a job for the love of it rather than for money, and that happens also to be the definition, or at least the prerequisite, of a good workman. There is only one respect in which a part-time professional need differ from a man who can spend his whole working life at the job. He who works at it part-time must be content to work more slowly in his early years. Constant practice gives a certainty quite early in life which takes much longer to attain if one is working intermittently. Until he does attain it he must make up for the want of it by taking extra care and therefore extra time. In consequence his output will necessarily be very small; but that is unimportant. The only reason for doing this work is quality not quantity.

No one will find the patience to become a proficient workman of this sort unless he has a lively and continual longing to do it, and, given that, ways of learning the job will be found. There are books, there are examples of the work, and there are workmen. With the help of all these and with practice he will learn to do work of the highest standard. I doubt whether there is anything which a determined part-time professional could not attain to, except speed, and even that comes in time.

It is still commonly believed that a man cannot really learn a job thoroughly unless he depends on it for his living from the first and gets long experience at it. It is untrue. Two minutes experience teach an eager man more than two weeks teach an indifferent one. A man's earning hours and his creative hours can be kept separate and it may be that they are better separated. Painters and poets separate them. Are painting and poetry really so much easier than craftsmanship? Part-time seamen are making ocean voyages in small craft which any professional seaman of the days of sail would have highly respected. Is not that a parallel case? Astronomy, to take but one other example, has owed an immense debt to amateur observers and telescope makers from Newton and Sir William Herschel onwards. No one in that science would subscribe much to the idea that amateurs are apt to be amateurish. It is high time we separated the idea of the true amateur – that is to say the part-time professional – from the idea of 'do-it-yourself' (at its worse end) and all that is amateurish. The continuance of our culture is going to depend more and more on the true amateur, for he alone will be proof against amateurishness. What matters in workmanship is not long experience, but to have one's heart in the job and to insist on the extreme of professionalism.

That this kind of workmanship will be in the hands of true amateurs will be a healthy and promising state of affairs, not a *faute de mieux*, for if any artist is to do his best it is essential that his work shall not be influenced in the smallest degree by considerations of what is likely to sell profitably. What concerns us is the very best. It is that which must somehow be continued because the aesthetic quality of it is unique, and the tradition of it must be kept alive against a time when it will put out some new growth. The part-time professional will be in a position to do the very best even though he can turn out very little of it, and even though at first he will have to sell it at a price which pays him very little for his time. Why not? Whom will he be undercutting? Will there be placards saying 'Craftsmen Unfair to Automation'? That can't be helped.

Along this road there will still be pitfalls. The crafts and craftsmen have been bedevilled, ever since Ruskin wrote, by a propensity for striking attitudes. The attitude of protest I have mentioned already. Another one is the attitude of sturdy independence and solemn purpose (no truck with part-time workers: they are all amateurs; social value; produce things of real use to the community); another is the attitude of holier-than-thou (no truck with machinery; no truck with industry; horny-handed sons of toil; simple life, etc). Another is the snob attitude, learnt from the 'fine' artists (we who practise the fine crafts are not as other craftsmen are). These are ridiculous nonsense by now, but who has not felt sympathy with them, all but the last at one time or another? For nostalgia is always in wait for us. The workmanship of risk *was* in many ways better in the old days than it is now, there is no sense in pretending otherwise. Moreover, many of the trades we ought to set ourselves to continue are already taking the complexion of survivals from an older world. That should not prevent us from looking ahead. We must think of the future more than the past. Some trades which are dead economically are all alive in human terms, and still have much to show the world.

It remains to notice the most disastrous illusion which was encouraged by Ruskin's chapter, whether he meant it to be or not; and which has done the most harm: the illusion that every craftsman is a born designer. There are no born designers. People are born with or without the makings of a designer in them, but the use of those talents is only to be learnt very slowly by much practice. Any untrained but gifted man can knock up something which looks more or less passable as a design but the best design for industry is done by people who have really learnt their job; and it looks like it. The crafts are always liable to comparision with industry and they cannot afford to come off second best in design as well as in price.

Design is so difficult to learn now simply because the arts are in a state of violent flux and because there are great interests vested in constant innovation. There is no settled tradition. If there were, the profession would be far more quickly learnt. If the crafts develop as I envisage, perhaps few craftsmen will be able to go through a designer's training, but surely there will be designers who will work for them, and be glad of the chance even if they make no money by it at all. There will have to be an alliance between the craftsmen and the designers.

Some things, of course, can only be designed, or at any rate designed in detail, by the workman himself. Writing and carving are obvious examples. Other things, such as musical instruments, ought to go on being made to traditional designs (not 'reproduction' designs, which are quite a different thing. Tourte's pattern of violin bows has been in use ever since he evolved it: it is not a mere revival of something which had died out).

The whole future of the crafts turns on the question of design. If designers will only come to recognize it, the crafts can restore to them what the workmanship of certainty in quantity-production denies them: the chance to work without being tied hand and foot by a selling price: the chance to design in freedom. There is nothing more difficult or more necessary for the modern designer to attempt.

If the crafts survive, their work will be done for love more than for money, by men with more leisure to cultivate the arts than we have. Some of them will become designers, some not: that is not important: a designer is one sort of artist, a workman another. Instrumentalists do not feel any sense of inferiority because they are not composers. But the scale of what craftsmen could achieve by concerting their efforts, and the opportunity it would give designers, would be something not dreamt of. Cathedrals were built, if not with joy in the labour (*pace* Morris), quite certainly by concerted effort unaided by any plant to speak of but what the workmen made themselves. People are beginning to believe you cannot make even toothpicks without ten thousand pounds of capital. We forget the prodigies one man and a kit of tools can do if he likes the work enough. And, as for those trades by the workmanship of risk which do need plant, it is not impossible to imagine that associations of workmen will set up workshops by subscription.

The great danger is that spurious craftsmen, realizing that the workmanship of certainty can beat anyone at high regulation, will take to a sort of travesty of rough workmanship: rough for the sake of roughness instead of rough for the sake of speed, which is rough workmanship in reality. This can be seen already in some contemporary pottery.

One rather feels that painting, whatever else it does nowadays, has to take care to look as different as possible from coloured photographs. Have the crafts got to take care to look as different as possible from the workmanship of certainty? If that is the best aim they can set themselves, let them perish, and the quicker the better! If they have any sense of their purpose they will look different, right enough, without having to stop and think about it. It is infinitely to be hoped that free and rough work will continue, but not in travesty. One works roughly in order to get a job done quickly, but all the time one is trying to regulate the work in every way that care and dexterity will allow consistent with speed.

Free workmanship is one of the main sources of diversity. To achieve diversity in all its possible manifestations is the chief reason for continuing the workmanship of risk as a productive undertaking: in other words for perpetuating craftsmanship. All other reasons are subsidiary to that one, for there is increasingly a vacuum which neither the fine arts nor industry and its designers are any longer capable of filling. The contemporary passion for anything old, for junk and antiques, is no doubt symptomatic. The crafts in their future role may yet fill the vacuum but only if craftsmen achieve some consciousness of what they are for, only if they will set themselves the very highest standards in workmanship, and only then if they attract the voluntary service of the best designers. Workmanship and design are extensions of each other.

———————————————

The patron does not turn to the craftsman until he wants a mace, or a presentation object of some kind; the craftsman will not regain some of his lost position until he is approached for day-to-day spoons and pots. The craftsman will be nearer success when he gets back to where the thatcher was, or the garage mechanic is. If he confuses himself with Michelangelo, then he is under an obligation to be, at least, a competent artist.

Ken Baynes: review in *Crafts Review* 5, 1960

———————————————

The glory of the rhythm of the hand with its infinite capacity for adaptation and change is something which is fading. Instead we are getting a universal tidying-up, a reduction to a common denominator of texture and finish which is forced onto materials as a sort of mechanistic skin: even the rough textures of pots go on as a sort of gimmick, rather than as an organic part of the whole.

Sam Smith, letter in *Crafts Review* 6, 1961

# Hans Coper

1920-1981

This was Coper's only publicly acknowledged utterance. Underwritten by the authority of his work it has come to be a touchstone for many in considering his work and their own. However, in his biography *Hans Coper* (1983) Tony Birks recalls that Coper had 'serious misgivings' about the statement, and that he burned all his writings shortly before he died. In *Modern Potters* (1967, revised 1976, 1982) Birks reports the evolution of Coper's feelings about pottery (his first interest had been painting and sculpture):

*His first contact with pottery came in 1946 when he went to assist Lucie Rie in her London studio. Gradually, and unexpectedly, he began to find that pottery encompassed the particular problems which he had found most challenging in sculpture. He did not turn to pottery as a substitute for sculpture, and feels, like many other potters, that there is very little in connection between the two. For him pottery is the opposite extreme as an art form – an accumulation of sensations and not an expression of emotion.*

## 1969

Coper's catalogue statement from the Collingwood/Coper exhibition at the Victoria and Albert Museum, London in 1969.

A pre-dynastic Egyptian pot, roughly egg-shaped, the size of my hand: made thousands of years ago, possibly by a slave, it has survived in more than one sense. A humble, passive, somehow absurd object – yet potent, mysterious, sensuous. It conveys no comment, no self-expression, but seems to contain and reflect its maker and the human world it inhabits, to contribute its minute quantum of energy – and homage. An object of complete economy made by MAN; Giacometti man; Buckminster Fuller man. A constant. This is the only pot which has really fascinated me. It was not the cause of my making pots, but it gave me a glimpse of what man is.

My concern is with extracting essence rather than with experiment and exploration.

The wheel imposes its economy, dictates limits, provides momentum and continuity. Concentrating on continuous variations of simple themes I become part of the process; I am learning to operate a sensitive instrument which may be resonant to my experience of existence now — in this fantastic century. Practising a craft with ambiguous reference to purpose and function one has occasion to face absurdity. More than anything, somewhat like a demented piano-tuner, one is trying to approximate a phantom pitch. One is apt to take refuge in pseudo-principles which crumble. Still, the routine of work remains. One deals with facts.

---

Some embroiderers feel that the word 'embroidery' is evocative of a 'tatty hobby' and that it should be changed; indeed this is slowly happening . . . By changing the word, although threads might still be incorporated in the work, the art and skill of embroidery might be lost. I would prefer to retain 'embroidery' and to raise standards to give the word its proper stature.

Constance Howard, in *Artifex: Journal of the Crafts*, volume 2, 1969

# Soetsu Yanagi

1889-1961

Yanagi and Leach met in the spring of 1910 at a Tokyo exhibition arranged by the Shirakaba (Silver Birch) Society. Yanagi edited the Society's magazine. He and Leach exchanged enthusiasms and insights: Blake and Whitman; Lao Tze and Chuang Tse – as Leach wrote 'We dealt authors and artists like playing cards'.

Yanagi's aesthetics grew out of Buddhism; indeed, objects were considered as aspects of human life and work at levels where the mystical and the ordinary faded into one another. This led Leach to compare Yanagi's position in Japan to that of Ruskin and Morris in England. Certainly this extract is an essential ingredient of his philosophy, as *The Nature of Gothic* represents the centre of Ruskin's beliefs.

FROM
## THE UNKNOWN CRAFTSMAN
# 1972

### THE KIZAEMON TEABOWL

The central section of the essay 'The Kizaemon tea-bowl' (1931) as it appears in *The Unknown Craftsman*, Kodansha International, 1972, the selection from Yanagi's writings made by Bernard Leach who also adapted the translations.

In 1931 I was shown this bowl in company with my friend, the potter Kanjirō Kawai. For a long time I had wished to see this Kizaemon bowl. I had expected to see that 'essence of Tea', the seeing eye of Tea masters, and to test my own perception; for it is the embodiment in miniature of beauty, of the love of beauty, of the philosophy of beauty, and of the relationship of beauty and life. It was within box after box, five deep, buried in wool and wrapped in purple silk.

When I saw it, my heart fell. A good Tea-bowl, yes, but how ordinary! So simple, no more ordinary thing could be imagined. There is not a trace of ornament, not a trace of calculation. It is just a Korean food bowl, a bowl, moreover, that a poor man would use every day – commonest crockery.

A typical thing for his use; costing next to nothing; made by a poor man; an article without the flavour of personality; used carelessly by its owner; bought without pride; something anyone could have bought anywhere and everywhere. That is the nature of this bowl. The clay had been dug from the hill at the back of the house; the glaze was made with the ash from the hearth; the potter's wheel had been irregular. The shape revealed no particular thought: it was one of many. The work had been fast; the turning was rough, done with dirty hands; the throwing slipshod; the glaze had run over the foot. The throwing room had been dark. The thrower could not read. The kiln was a wretched affair; the firing careless. Sand had stuck to the pot, but nobody minded; no one invested the thing with any dreams. It is enough to make one give up working as a potter.

In Korea such work was left to the lowest. What they made was broken in kitchens, almost an expendable item. The people who did this were clumsy yokels, the rice they ate was not white, their dishes were not washed. If you travel you can find these conditions anywhere in the Korean countryside. This, and no more, was the truth about this, the most celebrated Tea-bowl in the land.

But that was as it should be. The plain and unagitated, the uncalculated, the harmless, the straightforward, the natural, the innocent, the humble, the modest: where does beauty lie if not in these qualities? The meek, the austere, the unornate – they are the natural characteristics that gain man's affection and respect.

More than anything else, this pot is healthy. Made for a purpose, made to do work. Sold to be used in everyday life. If it were fragile, it would not serve its purpose. By its very nature, it must be robust. Its healthiness is implicit in its function. Only a commonplace practicality can guarantee health in something made.

One should correctly say, perhaps, that there is no chance for it to fall sick; for it is a perfectly ordinary rice bowl used every day by the poor. It is not made with thought to display effects of detail, so there is no time for the disease of technical elaboration to creep in. It is not inspired by theories of beauty, so there is no occasion for it to be poisoned by over-awareness. There is nothing in it to justify inscribing it with the maker's name. No optimistic ideals gave it birth, so it cannot become the plaything of sentimentality. It is not the product of nervous excitement, so it does not harbour the seeds of perversion. It was created with a very simple purpose, so it shuns the world of brilliance and colour. Why should such a perfectly ordinary bowl be so beautiful? The beauty is an inevitable outcome of that ordinariness.

Those who like the unusual are immune to the ordinary, and if they are aware of it at all, they regard it as a negative virtue. They conceive active beauty as our duty. Yet the truth is odd. No Tea-bowl exceeds the Ido bowl in beauty.

All beautiful Tea-bowls are those obedient to nature. Natural things are healthy things. There are many kinds of art, but none better than this. Nature produces still more startling results than artifice. The most detailed human knowledge is puerile before the wisdom of nature. Why should beauty emerge from the world of the ordinary? The answer is, ultimately, because the world is natural. In Zen there is a saying that at the far end of the road lies effortless peace. What more can be desired? So, too, peaceful beauty. The beauty of the Kizaemon Ido bowl is that of strifeless peace, and it is fitting that it should rest in that chapel, the Kōho-an for in that quiet place it offers its silent answer to the seeker.

From my heart I am thankful for those discriminating eyes of the men of Tea who chose their Tea-bowls. It was by an extraordinary honesty and depth of perception that they formed their standards. In the whole world I know of no parallel. In their appreciation lay an astonishing creativity. Emerging from a squalid kitchen, the Ido bowl took its seat on the highest throne of beauty. The Koreans laughed. That was to be expected, but both laughter and praise are right, for had they not laughed they would not have been the people who could have made such bowls, and if they had not continued to laugh they could not have gone on making them: and on the other hand if they had not been made as commonplace crocks the Tea masters would not have selected them. The Koreans made rice bowls; the Japanese masters made them into Tea-bowls.

The Tea masters liked the fine netting of crackle on Ido bowls for the warm, fresh friendliness it gives. They found a charm when the glaze skipped in firing, and when a 'landscape' formed in the pattern of mended cracks. They enjoyed free, rough turning and felt that many pots are incomplete without it. They gave great attention to the cutting of a footring, and delighted in natural runs and drips of congealed glaze. Then again they developed a high appreciation for the internal volume and curves of bowls; they looked to see how green tea settles into them. They were particular how the rims of bowls feel to the lips and how the endless ring is varied. They embraced the shape and kissed the thickness. And they knew what heart's ease there was in a gentle deformity. Finally, they worked out the conditons that made a bowl beautiful; for all beauty is inseparable from laws.

If Ido bowls had not be recognized in Japan, their beauty might not have been perceived in Korea or elsewhere. Japan became the native land of the Ido Tea-bowl. In the Gospel of Matthew, it says Jesus was born rather in Bethlehem than in Nazareth. In this statement there is truth.

So far I have looked at the character of the Ido Tea-bowls from the point of view of the users, the Tea masters. Now I would like to consider them from the potter's angle. By whose hands was that remarkable beauty produced, to be later discovered by the sharp eyes of men of Tea? Whence came that power?

It is impossible to believe that those Korean workmen possessed intellectual consciousness. It was precisely because they were not intellectuals that they were able to produce this natural beauty. The beauty in them springs from grace. Ido bowls were born, not made. Their beauty is a gift, an act of grace. The seven rules evolved by the masters of Tea were born by nature rather than made by man. They did not own the laws of beauty. Laws exist in a realm that transcends the self and ownership. Laws are the work of nature, not the product of human ingenuity.

It is nature that makes laws work. To observe them is appreciation. Neither is a matter of the maker's intellectual ingenuity. The artistic qualities inherent in a Tea-bowl belong to nature in their origins and to intuition in their perception. There is no objection to seeing seven 'things to see' (i.e., points that constitute the aesthetic appeal) in the Ido bowls. But this should not lead one to believe that they were made for the sake of these seven points. Nor should one assume that so long as these seven points are all present the result will be a beautiful bowl; for the points are a gift of nature, and not the product of conscious artifice. Yet how often in Japanese Tea-bowls have people laboured under the obvious delusion that you could create beauty by artificially lining up these seven qualities.

The Tea masters assert that Korean bowls are the best. It is an honest admittance. Why, one asks, do they surpass Japanese bowls? And the answer is that Japanese potters strove to make good pots according to accepted canons, or rules. To confuse the two approaches to pots, that of the maker and that of the user, is quite wrong. Production was poisoned by appreciation. Japanese bowls bear the scars of awareness. Raku Chōjirō, Honami Kōetsu, and other individual potters all to a greater or lesser degree suffer from the same sickness. It is all very well to find irregularities of form in Ido bowls charming, but to make pots with deliberate distortions is to immediately lose that charm. If glazes skip during the firing of a pot, it is natural, it may be a blessing in disguise, but deliberately to cause it to do so with the misguided idea of following some Tea master's rules is quite another matter.

The foot-ring of an Ido bowl is exceptionally beautiful, but to set out to copy its spontaneous irregularities is fatal; the beauty vanishes. All these wilful sorts of deformation are to be found in Japanese pots above all others. It is our specialized kind of ugliness, all in the pursuit of misconceived beauty. There are few parallels anywhere in the world. It is ironical that the Japanese Tea masters, whose appreciation of beauty was more profound that anybody else's should have perpetuated, and still be perpetuating, this evil. There is hardly one bowl stamped with the Raku seal that escapes ugliness. By contrast, every single Ido Tea-bowl escapes. The Kizaemon Ō Ido bowl is the antithesis of and challenge to Raku.

# Bernard Leach

1887-1979

These two extracts, probably owing their origin to the tape-recorder, have the confident, genial flow of Leach's conversation. Written down, there is a characteristic tone of assertion, enquiry and recollection. Blithely didactic, it suits his roles as teacher or master of a workshop or just as a craftsman proudly conscious of the worth and resonance of his work.

FROM

## THE POTTER'S CHALLENGE

# 1976

Two extracts from The Potter's Challenge, writings and tape-recordings by Leach, edited by David Outerbridge, Souvenir Press, London 1976.

In making pots one of the great pleasures I have had is in using a good clay to pull a handle. Pulling is done by taking a slightly hardish lump of clay with a wet hand constantly dipped in water to keep it lubricated. Take that lump of clay and from it by the thumb pressing it inside the hollow of your hand on the outside until it looks like you are milking the teat of a cow. You put pressure down the edge on one side, then you do it on the other side until it has the desired thickness and ribbing, so that the handle will be nice to use, nice to pour with. You get pleasure in the making, there is pleasure to you in using, pleasure to your friends, pleasure in the work. That is the kind of pleasure I have had, and I think perhaps the greatest. I am fairly good at making a handle and I have taught many potteries of Japan how to make a handle of the pulled kind, which they never had in their past. The pleasure comes in keeping the same width to hold comfortably when pouring. How the jug balances best, not only empty but full of liquid, is determined by the handle and its line, which should swing through to the spout or lip. The handle should be strong in attachment so that it carries the weight. Its base should come off the side like the branch of a beech tree. I like to see where the angle is, not just the slick S-curve. Every curve has a bone in it, just as every arm has a bone in it, and to make it a sweet line of single or double curve is not giving enough appreciation of construction and materials. Usually it is well to have an inch or more coming straight off an extra ridge along the top of the jug. That is the natural jumping off place. It should be half the width of the average hand for a full-size jug, and it should stay far enough away from the pitcher so that your knuckles won't be burned. Yet the handle must not stick out like an airplane wing. It must be comfortable to hold. It can convey beauty, and provide use and pleasure in combination.

Presuming that the form is complete, we are left with the problem of whether the pot needs further decoration. Take a look at it and consider whether it is better left plain or whether it would be improved by any of the dozens of methods available. Perhaps it could be engraved. What with? A piece of split bamboo or other wood sharpened into the shape of a wooden chisel. After the bowl has half hardened dampen the head of the wheel, centre the pot, give it a tap to fix it onto the wheel, and with plain bamboo or metal chisel head, or fine comb, you may band or engrave the surface of the clay almost as if it was ice and you a skater. Such treatment, if brushed broadly with a slip or glaze, will give darker colors in the scored recesses of the surface. Of course the surface is sufficiently soft to take the imprint of any mould made of biscuited clay or carved wood. There is also the whole field of brushwork. One of your first techniques will be banding, whether by engraver or brush. Done with a single turn of the wheel and one touch at one spot, this forms a new defined area asking perhaps for a pattern. What is a pattern? Where do we seek such a motif? What is the difference between it and the drawing of, let us say, a bird or fish or flower?

This is a point which I feel needs to be stressed, for that which I consider to be pattern is in its piquancy different from the object depicted. Museums are full of magnificent examples which stir the imagination as no reproductive drawing does; an element of pure make-believe is employed whether consciously or not. It is like good miming, melody or dance. The word 'pattern' does not merely mean repetition but may yet well be the repetition of the simplification and sharpness of which I write. Hardly ever during the last sixty years have I been able to persuade a student to pursue this strange bird, fish or flower, of man's imagining. It is no mere simplification of a drawing of dead flowers in a vase. Has it died upon us like that flower in the vase in the art room? Is it merely out of fashion? Whatever the reasons, I dare to say that the loss is considerable. We have had generations of bad patterns since the industrial revolution. They are contrived. We need a return to simplicity and our own given hands and hearts.

---

Having lost the single-mindedness of the primitives, we tend to blame our whole civilisation because we cannot produce anything of comparable beauty. But this is unjust to our civilisation, and unjust to ourselves. Civilisation is essentially an enlarging of consciousness; we should try to enlarge it a little more. The very fact that we are capable of feeling this nostalgia for primitive pottery, proves that we also have the capacity, if we set ourselves to work in the right way, to carry the process of civilising ourselves a few steps further, until at last we shall wake up and find that we too can make good pots.

Michael Cardew: Pioneer Pottery, 1969

# Breon O'Casey

BORN 1928

This amicable exchange of views about the basic stuff of craft is rather like two people wringing a piece of washing: by standing at opposite ends and twisting the cloth in opposite directions their adversarial stances become complementary. The debate about spirit versus substance is one of the motivating forces of the modern crafts: it is such questioning and comparing – through work as well as words – that makes these crafts develop as new, hybrid arts. The original Crafts Revival was essentially a hybridisation: the beginnings of our experimental mingling of pre-industrial traditions and post-industrial sensibilities. These new arts are aesthetic mongrels – the result of the awkward union between modern theory and older hierarchies of skill.

O'Casey provides a good bibliography. I would like to add Collingwood's own *Textile and Weaving Structures* (1987) as a marvellously condensed source book that can be used to support both sides of this argument.

## WEAVING IS EASY

# 1978

*Crafts*, January/February 1978, plus Peter Collingwood's letter in reply from the March/April of *Crafts*.

Weaving is easy. It really is. (Ramses Wissa Wassef has proved that.) Of all the crafts, it must be the easiest. It is easier to weave a rug than throw a pot, or make a chair, or build a wall, or bind a book, or bake a cake: it is certainly far easier than knitting. Because of this simplicity, it is cursed with people anxious to make it as difficult as they possibly can. Also, in our time and place, it is burdened with that monster, the horizontal frame loom, which, with its complicated shedding devices, batten, and temple, makes weaving of any value virtually impossible.

In his wonderful book, *Small is Beautiful*, discussing Buddhist economics, E.F.Schumacher quotes from *Art and Swadesh*, by Ananda K. Coomaraswamy, and I repeat the quotation here; 'The craftsman himself,' says Ananda,

> can always, if allowed to, draw the delicate distinction between the machine and the tool. The carpet loom is a tool, a contrivance for holding warp threads at a stretch for the pile to be woven round them by the craftsmen's fingers; but the power loom is a machine, and its significance as a destroyer of culture lies in the fact that it does the essential human part of the work.

There are two reasons why work done with tools is to be preferred to work done with a machine: firstly, it ennobles the work; and secondly, it ennobles the worker.

Is a modern horizontal frame loom with its mechanically operated sheds, its batten and temple (taking all the flavour – and control – out of the beating) a tool or machine? I have no doubts at all, delicate or otherwise, having used one of the damned things, that it is a machine.

In Collingwood's book, *The Techniques of Rug Weaving*, he says:

> In some rugs woven on primitive equipment (for instance kilims woven on a horizontal ground loom) the selvages curve and waver. A rug may lose a foot in width between its starting and final end. This may have a certain charm to sophisticated eyes but it is only the result of weaving without the physical help of a batten and temple, and without the mental

105

*concept of symmetrical edges. It should not be cited as an excuse for irregular selvages on a rug woven on a better equipped loom.*

No. But perhaps it should be cited as a reason for abandoning the better equipped loom for the old horizontal ground loom! Let me twist Peter Collingwood's words a bit, if he will forgive me, to try and show what I think is the fallacy in his argument. Suppose he were talking not about weaving, but about pottery. The same paragraph would then read:

'In some pots thrown on primitive equipment (for instance, a Hamada thrown on a Japanese hand-powered wheel, or pots by Leach thrown on a primitive kick wheel) the sides of the pots curve and wave. This may have a certain charm to sophisticated eyes but it is only the result of throwing without the physical help of an electrically operated wheel, and without the mental concept of symmetrical edges. It should not be cited as an excuse for irregular shaped pots made on a better equipped wheel.' That is to say: what is the point of making things by hand, with all the labour involved, if they don't look handmade? And if the only way to make them look handmade is to use primitive equipment, then one must use primitive equipment.

For I say unto you: if you are sitting at an horizontal frame loom, with a limited number of mechanical controlled sheds, even if these sheds are tied up irregularly in an attempt to disguise the monotony of the look of the weaving (but just as two minuses multiplied together make a plus many similar irregularities make a regularity), and you have designed your rug, and are following your design, and each row of weft you weave is pounded into place by your batten, and your selvages are kept straight, not by your eye, but by your temple; then, however much the birds sing in the trees outside your white-washed cottage and your free-range hens cluck away, and your organically grown vegetables flourish in your garden; however beautiful your wool, however dyed with natural dyes, you are a drudge and you might as well be working with a Japanese high speed water-jet loom and be done with it; because what you are using to weave with is a machine, and what you are weaving is therefore dead. If you study any fine rug, it is not only the selvages that curve and waver: the whole rug curves and wavers, just as does a fine pot. It is the wobbles that make it a work of art. A mathematically perfectly shaped pot or rug has nowhere for the spirit to enter.

So it follows that if you want to ennoble yourself and your work, you must simplify your loom. As Luther Hooper says in his book *Hand Loom Weaving*:

*Each step towards the mechanical perfecting of the loom, in common with all machinery in its degree, lessens the freedom of the weaver, and his control of the design in working.*

It is paradoxically true that the simpler the loom, the more sophisticated its capabilities. You can play on a simple loom like a harp: a complex one like a barrel organ.

But, alas, this is only the beginning. If the yarn you weave with has been machine made – and is therefore lifeless – it is very diffcult to give the weaving any flavour. Bland flour makes bland bread. To quote Bernard Leach from his *Potter's Book*:

*A potter's prime need is good clay... upon the quality of clay depends the strength and still more the character of the finished pot. Eastern potters, whether by design or accident, have generally used clays which when fired respond pleasantly to the touch, whereas Western potters from the early days of industry and epecially in making porcelain, have travelled further and further away from a natural conception of clay towards an ideal or over-refined mixtures which are aptly called pastes.*

106

Which means, we must handspin our own yarn, we must dye our own yarn, and God help us, we must keep our own sheep! All of which would be only child's play and only common sense to a Navaho or a Peruvian or an Ethiopian weaver; but it's a prospect that I find frightening. But I see no escape. St Theresa said: 'The first step to on the road to Heaven is humility: the second step on the road to Heaven is humility: The third step on the road to Heaven is humility. . .' I say: the first step on the road to making a good rug is to buy a flock of sheep; the second step is to tend and shear them; the third step is to sort and spin the wool; the fourth step is to dye it; and only the fifth step is to weave it into a shape. And each of these steps is of equal importance to the excellence of the finished rug. So you do all of that, and then you'll see I'm right: the actual weaving is easy.

Anni Albers, in her lovely book *On Weaving*, says:

*Our materials come to us already ground and chipped and crushed and powdered and mixed and sliced, so that only the finale in the long sequence of operations from matter to product is left to us: we merely toast the bread. No need to get our hands on the dough. No need – alas, also little chance – to handle materials, to test their consistency, their density, their lightness, their smoothness. No need for us, either, to make our implements, to shape our pots or fashion our knives. Unless we are specialised producers, our contact with materials is rarely more than a contact with the finished produce. We remove the cellophane wrapping and there it is – the bacon, or the razor blade, or the pair of nylons. Modern industry saves us endless labour and drudgery but, Janus-faced, it also bars us from taking part in the forming of materials and leaves idle our sense of touch and with it those formative faculties that are stimulated by it.*

Now because we merely toast the bread, or in our case merely weave the yarn, this limited part of the process takes on an exaggerated importance, which in turn tends to lead to over-complication. What is in fact only a part, and a very small part of the process of making a rug, we see as the whole, and over-balance. A beautiful rug could be made simply of one plain colour in one plain weave; but it would be difficult to convince yourself of this unless you were celebrating your own handspun yarn. It is simply this over-emphasis on making the toast that leads to the desperate and tortured creations (dread word!) that are woven by craft weavers these days. (Question: When is a tapestry not a tapestry? Answer: When it is woven by Archie Brennan).

The great strength of crafts is that they are useful; and to throw this away, to make a rug that cannot be used on the floor and call it creative weaving; or a pot that holds no water, and call it ceramic sculpture, is conceited folly. As I was walking up Fish Street, whom should I meet but Bernard Leach; and in the course of our conversation he was bemoaning the fact that his pots were now so expensive that people dare not use them. 'I would far rather see a housewife make her stew in one of my pots than have it gather dust in a museum,' he said. How many weavers today would far rather see their rugs trodden over by careless feet than hung up on a museum wall to be gazed at? How many weavers today make constructions that can't be trodden on, however softly?

The trouble is that although weaving is the easiest of the crafts to do, it is the hardest to sell. Every addition to the looms of old has been made for one reason – to push the business on. Time is money. and it may well be impossible for a weaver living today in Britain to tend and shear his flock, spin his wool, weave it on a primitive, and therefore time-consuming loom, and earn a living. But if he doesn't, it may also be impossible for him to make a decent rug.

# Peter Collingwood

BORN 1922

Dear Editor

Breon O'Casey's article *Weaving is Easy* deserves some response. But your publication deadline allows me too short a time to make a reasoned reply. So here are a few points.

1. Yes, compared to the potter's wheel, the modern hand-loom is an extremely advanced bit of equipment. It certainly does not require the manual skill of the potter to work it. (The textile equivalent of throwing a pot is, I think, spinning with a spindle; in both operations the fingers directly shape the raw material.) But I would suggest it is only Mr O'Casey's brief encounter with weaving which makes him find a loom a dominating machine, rather than a useful tool. Being more mechanical, it needs little skill to work it, but a great deal of time to *understand* it. And it is only with understanding that the 'damned thing' reveals that it can confer freedom as well as speed.

2. Luther Hooper was wrong. Mechanical additions can be made to the loom which indubitably do increase the weaver's freedom. He was probably thinking only of those devices which *speed* up the operations, not those which increase the weaver's *control* (such as the shaft switching method).

3. As to the 'wobbles making it art' and trying to make textiles 'look hand made', I feel I am back fighting the battles of twenty years ago, when such attitudes were prevalent among handweavers – thank goodness, no longer. (Though I was recently told by an American potter that he bashed his perfectly thrown pots to give them 'sculptural significance') If Mr O'Casey only appreciates wobble-weaving, that is sad for him, because he is thereby missing so much in textile history. What about the Sassanian silks, the Venetian two-level velvets, woven by professionals on looms far more complex than any used by handweavers today? Do their perfect selvages and incredible craftsmanship put them beyond the pale?

I do not think anyone has the right to say at a certain point in the development of weaving, 'Right, folks, that's it. You can use all the tools we've got, but nothing new that gets invented.' At what moment in time does one say it? One could argue that surely it is more 'ennobling' to darn your weft across the warp than use the leashes on a primitive loom. Or why not grow the trees specially to make the loom that will carry your handspun warp from your own sheep? What if you want to use cotton, do you have to move to Egypt to grow your own? Where does it end?

4. Machine-spun yarns can be beautiful, and a weaver who has handled fibres and learnt to spin can pick these out. They are not 'lifeless' unless by that is meant they show even spinning, which is after all the aim of hand spinners, though not often achieved.

5. I agree entirely that rugs are for use and I do not think anyone weaves them *in order* that they be hung as wall art. That decision lies with the exhibition and museum arranger and sometimes with a customer.

6. Is weaving the hardest craft to sell? Only, I think, if your insistence on ancient wobble-inducing methods makes your production so slow that you have to charge excessively high prices. This is the nub of the matter. To me, weaving is dead, if it is producing 'perfect' rugs in such a way that they are too expensive for their meagre sale ever to support their maker. That is the wrong turning to take. It ignores the modern handloom's gift of speed; but

that is nothing unless coupled with a hard-won understanding of its other capabilities. I cannot help wondering if Mr O'Casey allowed himself enough time to discover the latter, as I see in the same issue of *Crafts* that he is selling his loom 'as new'!

Yours, etc

Peter Collingwood

# David Pye

## 1978

### [ THE CRAFTS ]

The 1978 preface to the paperback edition of *The Nature and Art of Workmanship*, Cambridge University Press, 1978.

In the last ten years there has taken place quite suddenly a great increase in the practice and appreciation of the Crafts. When this book was written, twelve years ago and more, this could not be foreseen or even hoped for. Consequently some passages about the future of the Crafts in Chapter 11 can now be seen to have been far too pessimistic. 'If the Crafts survive. . .' I wrote, and more in the same strain. *Survive* indeed! How oddly that reads now! But other things that were written there about the Crafts still seem pertinent: about design: about the high importance of the amateurs: about the best work being done for love not for money: about the necessity of aiming high: about 'gritty pots and hairy cloth' and the travesties of rough workmanship. For the sake of these I hope my failure in the matter of prophecy may be excused. At least they are a convincing demonstration that things can change for the better, and change fast – for now there is indeed quite a strong demand for the best quality and not a discreditable one either. Some few people do make a living by supplying it, and the Crafts, by and large, are becoming decidedly viable. All that is to the contrary of what I could expect and what I wrote those few years ago. It has not been practicable to rewrite the text for this paperback edition, beyond making minor corrections, and so Chapter 11[1] has been allowed to stand as it was originally written.

1. 'The Aesthetic Importance of Workmanship, and its Future', reprinted in this anthology.

---

Why don't our commercial craftsmen have the courage to wear their colours and call themselves what they are? They would not lose by it. The world being what it is, there will be a demand for their wares for a long time yet; and it would leave the way clear for craftsmen simply to do their proper job, which is to create a folk art relevant to the second part of the twentieth century.

Sam Smith, letter in *Crafts Review* 6, 1961

# Christopher Frayling

# and Helen Snowdon

BORN 1942

There *is* a Crafts Movement; there *is* a crafts world with its own qualities detected by its own evolved sensibilities; this book, like most craft publications except the unmentionable 'How-to-do-its', has been written by insiders *for* insiders. Frayling and Snowdon have opened up the arguments to outsiders: it is a brave attempt to end the closed shop of craft discussion.

PERSPECTIVES ON CRAFT

# 1982

1

## THE MYTH OF
## THE HAPPY ARTISAN

A series of five articles with the general title 'Perspectives on Craft'. Published in *Crafts* throughout 1982, as follows:
1. The Myth of the Happy Artisan. January/February
2. Crafts: With or Without Arts. March/April
3. Skill: A Word to Start an Argument. May/June
4. Crafts in the Market-Place. July/August
5. Nostalgia Isn't What It Used to Be. November/December.

In a recent survey of *The State of the Language*,[1] the word 'crafted' is described as one of those words which 'beguile as well as inform.' When advertising people use 'crafted' as a substitute for 'manufactured,' the survey goes on, they are attempting to 'delude the public into believing that something has been made by hand, in a carefully old-fashioned way.' The hoardings do not actually *say* this – they simply 'smuggle it in.' Hence the slogans 'handbuilt by robots' and 'more space, more craft' – in which the reassuring connotations of 'handbuilt' and 'craft' seem calculated to offset the less reassuring connotations of 'robots' and space-age technology. Craft is trustworthy, microchips are not – at least not yet. It is as if the advertisers are deliberately creating a confusion between William Morris, artist craftsman, and William Morris, automobile magnate, and in the process selling our own nostalgia back to us at a profit.

Perhaps the campaign which has made the fullest use of this marketing strategy is the series of 45-second films promoting Hovis on television: by means of this campaign, some mass-produced goods are associated in consumers' minds with the brass-bands in rural Yorkshire during the early part of this century, bakeries run by elderly craftsmen and their even more elderly apprentices, technicolour 'villages of the mind'[2] to beguile the supermarket shopper into believing that 'it's as good today as it's always been.' If the strategy works – and it seems to, even if it does create problems when a new product is being launched – it says a lot about the continuing potency of craft as an idea. Assembly-lines may be manned by robot, the corner grocery-shop may have long since been demolished, convenience foods may seem too processed for comfort – but the advertisers can rely on the simple word 'crafted' to relieve for a moment the complex anxieties which social and economic processes have created.

Of course, the word 'crafted' is not confined to the billboards, and the ad-men did not conjure this imagery from out of thin air. As a result of the

1. *The State of the Language* ed. Leonard Michaels and Christopher Ricks, University of California Press, 1980, pp.383-5
2. The phrase comes from Howard Newby's two books on the sociology of rural life, *Green and Pleasant Land* and *The Deferential Worker*.

110

recent 'craft revival,' the word can be seen wherever there is a corn-dolly or a bean-bag, wherever teenagers still hope to become Janey Morris lookalikes in their new Laura Ashley frocks, wherever pine is stripped, and wherever post-Glastonbury hippies congregate to sing about what they imagine it was like before the war memorial took over from the maypole in the village square. Confronted by these disconnected bits of the olde worlde, with only the *AA Book of the Village* and BBC social history to locate us, we may well be tempted to echo the drunken sentiments of Lucky Jim:

*The point about Merrie England is that it was about the most un-Merrie period in our history. It's only the homemade pottery crowd, the organic husbandry crowd, the recorder playing crowd who. . .*[3]

In other words, there's not much use in being a 'homecomer' (like Schumacher, Illich and to some extent Pirsig) unless we know exactly what or where 'home' is.

Lucky Jim's famous lecture – dealing as it did with the 'integration of social consciousness' and 'the identification of work with craft' – was intended, in part, as a satire on the style of literary history (just as fashionable in the early nineteen fifties as it is today) which was really a sustained lament for 'the world we have lost,' a history (or rather a nostalgia) in which today's synthetic, entrepreneurial culture is always compared unfavourably with the culture of yesterday's 'organic community.'[4] In pointing out that the 'organic community' of old England never existed, that it is always 'over the last hill,' Raymond Williams has recently drawn attention to an unbroken chain of 'retrospective regret' for an age which had just passed – and which was usually thought to have been on its last legs during the childhood of the writer or historian. *The Country and the City* shows how this unbroken chain leads from John Betjeman (in our time), via F.R.Leavis, George Sturt and Thomas Hardy, all the way back to Oliver Goldsmith's *Deserted Village* in 1769 – and probably beyond that to the Garden of Eden.[5] Where the world of the craftsman is concerned, we can perhaps construct our own parallel chain of 'retrospective regret,' which leads from, say, Edward Barnsley, via Ernest Gimson and C.R.Ashbee, to William Morris, thence to a Sussex furniture-maker named Ephraim Coleman and, by a huge imaginative leap, to Merrie England in the reign of Edward I. William's purpose is not to condemn such nostalgia out of hand, but to look closely at 'each kind of retrospect as it comes' in order to understand when *la mode rétro* is a strategy for criticising the present, and when it is simply an escape from the present.

The recent 'craft revival' is clearly based on a certain reading of English history, using evidence of the aesthetic (as well as moral and ritual) value of certain English artefacts from the past as evidence of how these artefacts must have been both produced and consumed. It is implicitly based on a series of contrasting images – between 'the craftsman' and 'the industrial worker,' 'doing is designing' and 'thinking is designing,' 'happy artisans' and 'unhappy machine-minders.' Robert Blauner has commented on some of these contrasts, which lie hidden at the centre of many a history of craftsmanship:

*It is remarkable what an enormous impact this contrast of the craftsman with the factory hand has had on intellectual discussions of work and workers in modern society, notwithstanding its lack of correspondence to present and historical realities. For, indeed, craftsmen, far from being typical workers of the past era, accounted for less than ten per cent of the medieval labour force, and the peasant, who was actually the representative labourer was. . . practically nothing more than a working beast. . . . In modern society there is far greater scope for skill and craftsmanship than in any previous society.*[6]

3. Kingsley Amis, *Lucky Jim*, Penguin, 1981, pp.17,195,223,227.
4. The satire seems to have been directed mainly against the literary criticism of F.R.Leavis: see, in particular, F.R.Leavis and Denys Thomspon, *Culture and Environment* London, 1933, esp. pp.71-80.
5. Raymond Williams, *The Country and the City* (Paladin,1973), pp.9-22.
6. Robert Blauner, 'Work Satisfaction and Industrial Trends in Modern Society' in *Labour and Trade Unionism*, ed. W.Galenson and S.M.Lipset, London, 1960, pp.352-5. When Blauner writes about the scope for skill and craftsmanship today, we take him to be referring to activities outside the industrial sector: the controversial question of what a skill is, will be discussed in a later article.

Perhaps the most obvious example of how historically misleading these contrasts can be is provided by the contemporary image and status of the craft potter who sees himself as the inheritor of traditional skills. For, although craft pottery is today the most popular of handicrafts, it played a negligible part in the urban economy of Merrie England. The Guilds do not seem to have given any protection to clay potters (since there was very little demand for their products in the towns) and when clay was worked by medieval craftsmen, it was mainly to produce tiles and bricks (for those who could not afford stone). Only in the countryside, where neither the work nor the products were subject to Guild inspection, did potters spend a significant proportion of their time serving the domestic needs of the local community by making vessels for the kitchen or the peasant's hut.[7] From the sixteenth century onwards, this kind of production was mainly based in small workshops and rural households. As the family economy (which continued what there was of the medieval 'craft' tradition) became linked through merchant investment with the capitalist organisation of trade, putting-out, and the marketing of products, 'proto-industrial families' developed more and more extreme methods of unregulated self-exploitation in the production of craft goods. Eventually, according to the most recent researches, they managed in times of scarcity to sustain a work output 'even beyond the amount which is customary in an economic system depending on developed capitalist wage labour,' a primitive kind of mass production of handicrafts.[8] The myth of the happy artisan – like the 'artist craftsman,' craft guilds to which select potters could belong, and the confusion of rural workers with guild craftsmen – did not exist until the nineteenth century, when it became part of a romantic reaction against the spread of industrial capitalism. And the history which underpins much of the 'craft revival' is, in fact, nostalgia masquerading as history.

Most of the 'artist craftsmen' or 'designer craftsmen' we interviewed have disassociated themselves completely from the popular image of the craftsman, from Merrie Englandism in all its various incarnations. Typical comments have been:

'It's essential that we are not seen as folksy alternative people who can't get it together, who have opted out as a reaction against rather than a complement to industry;' 'I avoid the word 'craftsmanship.' Craft shops are full of very good examples of very bad craftsmanship. A lot of makers prefer not to use it – David Pye's 'workmanship' is better;' 'It's the people making for love that ruin the market.'

But many of these 'artist craftsmen' and 'designer craftsmen' – whether they like it or not – belong to a tradition which invented Merrie Englandism as a way of giving craftsmanship some respectable origins, and they depend on clients who may be 'reacting against' mass-produced goods by investing in well-made, well-designed, scarce domestic objects; these clients may also be reacting against the wilder excesses of Modernism when they decide to own a piece of art which they understand and which is tangible. In short, the self-image of the 'artist craftsman' may be at odds with the recent tradition of which he is a part, and the expectations of the people who buy his work. We will be attempting to resolve this, and other apparent contradictions, in a constructive way, as we continue to explore 'each kind of retrospect as it comes' in the next four articles.

7. On craft pottery and the Guilds, see, among many others, S.Kramer, The English Craft Guilds Colombia University Press, 1927, G.Unwin, The Guilds and Companies of London London 1963, J. Harvey, Medieval Craftsmen London 1975. On medieval rural pottery, see P.Brears, The English Country Pottery Newton Abbot, 1971. For a useful discussion of the issue, see Brian Ranson, Craft, Occupational Ideology and Self Identity: a study of English potters, typescript conference paper, Lanchester Polytechnic, 1980.
8. See Hans Medick, 'The Proto-Industrial Family', Social History, 3 October 1976, esp. pp.296-313.
9. As part of Helen Snowdon's MA thesis Craftmanship in the Machine Environment, Royal College of Art, May 1979, and since. Most of the artist craftsmen interviewed are engaged in the design and making of furniture.

# 2

# CRAFTS:
## WITH OR WITHOUT ARTS

Towards the end of the nineteenth century, the craftsman was given a new image and status, both of which were the product of a particular kind of 'retrospective regret:' in order to draw attention to contradictions in an industrialising society where 'shoddy is king,' and to provide an example for manufacturers to follow, a small group of Fine Art workmen (as they called themselves) adopted the strategy of giving craftsmanship some respectable origins, by associating the activity with a particular version of English history and a philosophy of design which was as much social as aesthetic.

The legacy of this 'Arts and Crafts Movement' has been thoroughly documented by design historians – with reference to the artefacts produced by twentieth-century artist-craftspeople whose occupational ideology has its roots in this attack on 'shoddy is king,' rather than in traditions which go further back. But, as we tried to show in our first article, it is an ambiguous legacy which has (under various pressures) led to widespread confusion about the meaning of craftsmanship today – at a time when 'the craft revival' has provided advertising people with a powerful set of images to associate with anything from automobiles to sliced bread and when, as Bernard Leach pointed out in the 1940s, those who are most attracted by handcrafts are no longer simple peasants in the vernacular tradition, but self-conscious art students who want to make a name for themselves. Just as some of the 'artist-craftsmen,' 'studio-craftsmen' and 'designer-craftsmen' we interviewed tried to disassociate themselves from the ad-people's image of ye country craftsman, or from the professional craftsman's image of dear Emily, they also expressed a variety of opinions about the value of attaching the label 'art' to what they do. For, as the quotations below illustrate, the association between art and craft has as many meanings as the different traditions which have come to be lumped together under the catch-all label of the artist-craftsman. These include

the *Arts and Crafts tradition* (Cotswold version),

the *Council of Industrial Design* tradition (Haymarket version),

the tradition of the *Oriental Mystic* (Cornish version), and

the *Craftsman's Art* tradition (South Kensington version) which rejects – and sometimes makes fun of – both the social philosophy of a Morris and mysticism of a Leach.

The Arts and Crafts people, following Ruskin, appear to have believed that 'he who works with his hands only is a mechanic; he who works with hands and head is an artisan; and he who works with hands, head and heart is an artist.' These commonsense classifications were decisively challenged by the philosopher R.G.Collingwood, when he launched an all-out attack on the theories of Ruskin and Morris which encouraged.

*People who write about art today to think that it is some kind of craft; this is the main error against which modern aesthetic theory must fight.*[2]

For Collingwood, 'the technical theory of art' – which implied that the art activity had something to do with 'the power to produce a preconceived result by means of consciously controlled action' – only succeeded in confusing 'what I shall call craft' with 'art proper:' 'a technician is made, but an artist is born.' If the 'theory of art' continues to lay so much stress on mere craft technique, he concluded , 'it is no more to be

1. The interviews in this series of articles were taped and transcribed as part of Helen Snowdon's MA thesis *Craftsmanship in the Machine Environment*, Royal College of Art, May 1979, and since. Although most of the 'artist-craftsmen' interviewed are makers in wood, their comments are perhaps characteristic of makers in other materials as well. They include (among others) Gordon Russell, Edward Barnsley, David Pye, John Makepeace, David Field, Rupert Williamson, Desmond Ryan, Fred Baier and Richard La Trobe-Bateman.
2. See R.G.Collingwood, *The Principles of Art*, London, 1938, pp.9-41.

called art criticism, or aesthetic theory, than the annual strictures in *The Tailor and Cutter* on the ways in which Academy portrait-painters represent coats and trousers:' the words 'artist' and 'artisan' may have the same linguistic origin, but that is where the similarity ends.

Some of today's artist-craftsmen, working in the *Craftsman's Art* tradition, would agree with much of what Collingwood has to say. Others, working in the *Arts and Crafts* tradition, would presumably try to bridge precisely those gaps between art and craft which the philosopher was seeking to widen. Yet they are all known as artist-craftsmen, whether they happen to believe that motorcycle maintenance is an art or a craft, and whether they identify most closely with traditional craftsmen, industrial designers, or sculptors. Not surprisingly, they argue amongst themselves about the meaning of what they do.

"*If we compare a chair made forty years ago to a modern one, the modern one is technically more accurate and is better made, but there is something missing: that missing something is man's personal labour. This 'something' that is lost is difficult to express: we can only call it 'art'. . . I would like to think that craftsmanship is skill, used in the best sense; after all, the original meaning of 'art' is skill. I prefer the term 'maker of things.' Makers have a particular awareness that is very rare these days.*"

"*I recently read somthing that said, 'the need to improve the design of manufactured articles has almost nothing to do with art and little to do with craft.' How Mr Gradgrind would have approved ! It has certainly been true in the past and still holds true in many places today. But I agree with Eric Gill who said, 'the artist is not simply a person with ideas, he is a person who has the skill to make his ideas manifest.' The designer has often a great choice of efficient shapes, but in selecting one that is also beautiful he must, to some extent, be an artist.*"

"*It is very difficult to find a term which does not lead to misunder-standing – I suppose 'designer-craftsman' is the only term which indicates to people what one does.*"

"*I find making art a challenge, not making furniture. It is just the joy of doing it.*"

"*Something happens to the object that is being made, but what that something is – the art I suppose – is very difficult to explain.*"

"*Most of us start out as artists and find ourselves having to find techniques to express our ideas, and becoming craftsmen.*"

"*I make what other people call furniture; utilitarian furniture in the sense that it is something they are going to need and use. What I think I'm making is sculpture or art. . . . The first perception of the object is 'chair, 'table' and so on; the artist proceeds from that perception. For example, one artist is particularly good at knowing how far an object is not like a table whilst we still have a basic perception of it as 'table.' It is rather like a poet pushing language to the extremes of language where it becomes meaning-less. Some tables now have four legs on the wall, three on the floor. This is playing the game. . . .*"

114

*"I'm trying to produce a sculptural object; it has got nothing to do with playing games. I'm trying to invent new forms and new decorations."*

*"If you make a table, it has got to be used as a table – if you don't use it as a table, it is a failure – you might as well do your sculpture another way. For example, a table which has legs that project out beyond the corners of the table – it is very unsatisfactory as a table because you would be forever walking into the legs. People buying this sort of work are buying the illogic rather than the logic. I find this unacceptable."*

*"Furniture can't be a joke or amusing because you would have to live with the same joke every day."*

*"There is a perversion about now, where much of the craft furniture seems to be highly engineered pieces of jewellery rather than furniture."*

*"The relationship that I and others have with objects is a very subtle, long-term, unselfconscious thing that one doesn't get with art. Art doesn't relate to one in such a specific way. That is what makes me a better artist. I've discovered that people who are bagged as 'artist' by society are on to a loser because they are not making the most potent form of artefact. Most artists are doing it for reasons of social currency – that is the way they see themselves."*

These comments, made by artist-craftsmen engaged in the design and making of furniture, give an idea of the confusion which is caused when the word art becomes part of the craftsman's everyday vocabulary (or, conversely, when the word craft becomes part of the artist's everyday vocabulary) – as it has, ever since the late nighteenth century. The craftsman, we are told, is an artist when he is fighting the tendency of automated industry to de-skill man's personal labour; when he can select (and execute) the most beautiful design solution, from among the many which are available to industry; when his training took place at an art college and when he is expressing himself through making. Conversely, the artist is a craftsman when he makes a table rather than an abstract sculpture; when his work is exhibited and sold as art; when he transforms a material object into something different. Those artist-craftsmen who react most strongly against the implied association of their work with developments in the fine-art world, prefer the word to mean 'well-made and well-designed' – 'art' as a standing example to mass-production industry: and they sometimes end up rejecting the world out of hand, because it leads to so many misunderstandings. Let's face it, any word which can be said to apply in different ways to the process, the product, the state of mind of the maker, and the place where he sells his work, is not much use as a description of anything. Unless, that is, you agree with Humpty Dumpty in *Through the Looking Glass*:

> When I use a word, it means just what I choose it to mean – neither more nor less. . . . The question is, who is to be master – that's all. . . . Impenetrability! That's what I say![3]

3. Lewis Carroll, *Through the Looking-Glass*, 1896 edition, chapter VI.
4. Howard S. Becker, 'Arts and Crafts', *American Journal of Sociology*, Chicago, January 1978, pp.862-888.

Howard Becker, a social scientist researching the equivalent 'ambiguities and contradictions' in the American arts and crafts scene has found a way of making the concepts mean something again.[4] In his analysis, the terms art and craft are no longer intended to be descriptions of aesthetic or personal experiences. Rather, they refer to 'two contrasting kinds of work organisation and work ideology, differing in their emphasis on the standards of utility, virtuoso skill, and beauty.' Normally, he suggests, we can rely on common-sense folk classifications of what the arts and crafts actually involve. According to these classifications, members of the craft world possess a body of knowledge and skill which can be used to produce useful objects and they have the ability to perform in a way which meets someone else's practical needs; members of the art world, by contrast, have no interest in the conventional standards of practical utility, they downgrade 'the old craft standards of skill,' and their work is done 'in response to problems intrinsic to the development of the art and freely chosen by the artist.'

These folk definitions are only seriously called into question when the two activities, craft and art, are undergoing social change, for example when concerns 'characteristic of the folk definition of art' (standards of beauty) begin to merge with concerns 'characteristic of the folk definition of craft' (standards of utility and skill). Such a 'typical historical sequence' may eventually lead to a situation where craftsmen turn to 'the art world itself as a source of value,' and begin to lay emphasis on 'the relative freedom of the artist from outside interference with his work.' Once this has happened, 'the organisational form of the craft world becomes more complicated than it might otherwise be,' involving two distinct groups of people, opening up 'new organisational settings in which to work and gain support for one's work,' and encouraging kinship between craftspeople and fine-art institutions. All this is reflected in publications and institutions, exhibitions and shows, which are exclusively associated with one group or the other.

Becker writes:

The American Craft Council identifies itself as the organised voice of the artist-craftman. Its influential magazine, Craft Horizons [now American Craft] emphasises questions of beauty and artistic merit in contrast to a more purely craft-oriented magazine like Ceramics Weekly.

As part of the 'historical sequence,' a craft world – defined according to the folk classification – develops a new segment; the new segment's members add to the basic aesthetic an emphasis on beauty, and develop some 'additional organisational elements;' eventually these artist-craftsmen develop 'a kind of art world around their activities;' as members of this world they can earn more money from their products and can attract grants and subsidies as well. It is not, of course, possible for all craft worlds to go through this process (the concept of the artist-plumber seems a little far-fetched, for example): but the important thing is, that the same activity, using the same materials and skills in what appear to be similar ways, may be called by either title, as may the people who engage in it; the activity may look the same from the outside, but the organisational setting has changed, as has the emphasis on concerns 'characteristic of the folk definition of art,' and this has led to a new image and status.

Matching this social movement of some craftsmen into the art world, there is a parallel movement the other way round as 'some artists look for new media in which to explore a current expressive problem.' This new breed of artists produces standards that are 'aggressively non-utalitarian,' and the organisation of their work remains within the art world proper.

It becomes a virtue not to display conventional craft virtuosity, and the artist may deliberately create crudities either for their shock value, or to show that he is free of that particular set of conventional restraints.

At this stage, the artist may well be in a position to pose as 'a heroic individualist' – for

artists working in conventional craft media are relatively freer than artist-craftmen who work in the same media; for example, in the diversity of *objects they can make.*

And the previous generation of craftsmen is likely to become enraged at this invasion of their world.

These twin processes – craftsman enters the art world, while artist hi-jacks craft – are not simply a matter of one social group replacing another. 'Instead, a new and more complicated world comes into being, in which craft segments, artist-craftsmen segments and art segments coexist.' At this point, the current folk definitions cease to have any meaning in the real world.

*Such shifts are successful only in so far as they involve enough people to take over an established art or craft world or create a new one. For most of the people involved, the experience is much more one of choice among alternative institutional arrangements and working companions than of creative expressive leaps.*

Throughout the historical sequence, the emphasis on 'utility, virtuoso skill, and beauty' (or combinations of the three) will 'express an organisational reality.' So, Becker's conclusion is that the terms 'art' and 'craft' refer at the same time to

*contrasting ways of bringing to bear in particular work situations the standards of utility, virtuosity and beauty and to contrasting situations of work. These appear in all kinds of combinations, depending on historical circumstances.*

Howard Becker's work on American arts and crafts refers specifically to the example of ceramics in the 1960s and 1970s, when a small group of artists launched a successful invasion on an unsuspecting craft world. It is intended as a prelude to further research into the conditions under which 'typical historical sequences' like these usually occur. As such, it provides a useful starting point for reevaluating the terms art and craft, in the light of the significant changes of direction which have occurred over the last ten years in America and Britain. The point is that the distinction between an artist and a craftsman – which seems so obvious until we examine it closely – may, at base, be a sociological distinction rather than an aesthetic or a technical one.

We may wish to question some of Becker's assumptions, and to emphasise the differences between the American experience and our own (both in the late nineteenth century, and today). But at least he has found a useful way of reopening the discussion about art and craft with those who continue to sit on the wall.

3

# SKILL: A WORD
# TO START AN ARGUMENT

The word 'skill,' wrote David Pye in 1968 in his book on workmanship,[1]

*does not assist useful thought because it means something different in each different kind of work. To a smith, dexterity is important but rarely in the extreme; but his judgement of certain matters, particularly heat, has to be brought to a pitch and decisiveness rarely needed or matched in woodworking trades, in which, however, more dexterity is often needed. Moreover, much of what is ordinarily called skill is simply knowledge, part of 'what can be conveyed by words or drawings' . . . You can make it mean what you please. It is a thought-preventer.*

1. David Pye, *The Nature and Art of Workmanship* Cambridge, 1968, pp.23-4.

By the time he reissued his book on design in 1978,[2] David Pye had made a firm decision about whether the concept of skill could most usefully be applied to 'know-how', 'simply knowledge,' 'manual dexterity,' or a shifting combination of the three: the word, he wrote,

*excludes any reference to 'know-how' and indicates simply a particular application of dexterity. The old usage of the term did refer to know-how, and certainly the modern usage does. I think however that it is necessary to differentiate between 'skill' as the exercising of constraint on movement and 'skill' as know-how, for know-how, in making, is design. Anybody has 'skill' enough to build a good dry-stone wall, but few know how to design one . . .*

In this way, Pye felt impelled to divorce manual skill from *mental* skill (know-how), going directly against the grain of established Arts and Crafts movement opinion. Most theorists who analyse skill today (from whatever perspective), take a different point of view. A psychologist (school of David Legge) is likely to define skill in terms of the *coordination* of perceptual and motor activity – thinking and making. A philosopher (school of Michael Oakeshott or Michael Polanyi) might think of skill in terms of the distinction between knowledge and know-how – the kind of information which can be found in books and the kind which can't – and to stress the importance of craft skill as an example of know-how, or tacit knowledge. A sociologist (school of Harry Braverman) is likely to think of skill in terms of the tendency of monopoly capitalism to drive a wedge between mental and manual labour – deskilling and degrading the work-force – and build a critique of monopoly capitalism on these grounds. An educationalist (especially one interested in craft – school of Robert Witkin) is likely to think of skill in terms of the expressive training of both mind and body – the intelligence of feeling – and to warn curriculum planners that they ignore skill at their peril.

Some of the artist craftspeople we interviewed,[3] aligning themselves with David Pye, dismiss such views, suggesting that these theorists of skill are all projecting onto 'skilled labour' the satisfying experience of an hour or two's labour in the garden on a Sunday afternoon: the theorists had, we were told, treated skill with too much respect because they lacked experience in the real world of work (rather like Oscar Wilde, who went to work in an Oxford road gang in order to test Ruskin's idea about the dignity of manual labour). One or two of these artist craftsmen even thought that our questions about skill were *really* about marketing strategy – whether or not to show the customer he was getting something hand made for his money by laying on the human thumb-prints: skill as packaging. Clearly skill, like 'craftsmanship' is, as David Pye says 'a word to start an argument with.'[4]

If there is one development which radically separates some of the 1970s artist craftspeople from the roots of the Arts and Crafts movement, it is this progressive downgrading of the concept of skill in the last ten years. While the generation of artist craftspeople working in the Arts and Crafts tradition (Cotswold version) and the Council of Industrial Design tradition (Haymarket version) still find it difficult to think about the design process in isolation from the making process, many artist craftspeople do not find it difficult at all: they are busy reinforcing precisely those distinctions – between brain and hand, design and making, design management and skilled labour – which the Arts and Crafts movement was originally trying to break down, or at least challenge. (Collingwood's *Principles of Art*[5] appear to have become a new orthodoxy, *in the craft world* of all places, just at the time when Robert Pirsig's best-selling *Zen and the Art of Motorcycle Maintenance* was stressing the importance of craft – or a personal relationship with

2. David Pye, *The Nature and Aesthetics of Design* London, 1978, p.52.
3. As part of Helen Snowdon's MA thesis *Craftmanship in the Machine Environment*, Royal College of Art, May 1979 and since. Direct questions about the value attached to 'skill' (or the meaning of 'craftsmanship') were sometimes rejected outright by these interviewees ('impossible to answer,' 'the words do not mean anything,' 'I really don't know what to think,' 'I don't accept the question,' 'these are the sort of questions designed to bring out the most airy-fairy pretentious long-winded rubbish') – an admission, perhaps, that in the art-and-craft world of today, these really are words 'to start an argument with . . .'
4. David Pye, *The Nature and Art of Workmanship* pp.4-6.
5. See R.G. Collingwood, *The Principles of Art* London, 1938, pp.9-41, and our brief comments in *Crafts*, March/April 1982.

technology – as a means of adjusting to life in an automated economy.)

These craftsmen, designer craftsmen and artist craftsmen are, of course, talking about differing things when they explain their attitude towards skill: we give a range of their views below. Analysing skill becomes a way of bringing into focus their ideas about life in general, their philosophy of design, or their self-image as artists. The makers with the most direct line to the Arts and Crafts movement tend to think of craft skills as a challenge (social and aesthetic) to automated industry, and to the social structure which sustains it: in a society where a worker is likely to use more skills driving to work than he uses while minding the machine which turns out parts for his car, the defence of skill can be seen as one way of 'teaching the machine manners' (in Gordon Russell's words).

The designer craftsmen who are concerned about the relationship of their work to more industrialised forms of design tend to think of craft skills as an essential component in the design process or, less commonly, as 'the therapeutic bit in between the struggle of designing': they seem to be less interested in 'the inner man' than the Arts and Crafts people, but still find unacceptable (for other reasons) any clear separation between thinking and making.

Some of the artist craftsmen, by contrast, see their work as 'pure creative potential,' based upon the principle that 'making is no problem': if they are going to call themselves craftsmen at all (and one or two of them deeply resent the connotations of the term), it is important for them to add that 'the quality of thought is really the craftsmanship today.' The other 'craft part . . . is merely a mechanical skill' – an altogether different and lower order of skill.

Each of these attitudes matches both the tradition to which the craftsmen may be said to belong – reinforced by the recent subdivision of the craft world into artists, artist craftsmen, designer craftsmen and designers – and developments within the art colleges from which many of the craftspeople originally came. The following quotations exemplify the different attitudes, characterised by training and age, of these three distinct types of craftspeople.

"I recall my first vivid impression of skill just about eighty years ago. I was a small boy who had stopped in a London street to watch something happening. Three burly navvies – the genuine article, not the tidied-up, suburban, pre-Raphaelite variety – were standing in a group holding heavy sledge hammers. One bent down, placed a large steel chisel upright and tapped it gently with his hammer held close to the head. When it stood of its own volition, he rose, and gave it a mighty blow followed by others, one-two-three, one-two-three. It was a faultless rhythmic exercise, exquisitely timed and with a ringing thud at each blow. When the chisel had sunk sufficiently, the exercise stopped. The leader tapped it on the side and a large section of the road came loose. Should I ever achieve such skill? It looked easy . . ."

"A skilled person using simple tools will make it look easy, and, furthermore, it is easy when you know how. It's like riding a bike. It's very difficult to ride a bicycle when you can't and it's very difficult to fall off when you can. To get to that point – getting the knack to a degree that comes genuinely easy – what David Pye calls the 'habit of attention' which makes it easy – one can't not attend to the right bits if one is attending. I'm continually thrilled when I succeed – I was always the boy whose model aeroplane never flew."

"The Arts and Crafts leaders tried to bring designer and maker together, in itself a worthy objective, but by insisting that the craftsman should design everything that he made they went a bit too far. I knew that many first-rate craftsmen were not highly imaginative. In any case it became clear that the designer must have a thorough knowledge of methods of production, whether by hand or machine."

"I sometimes find myself a reluctant maker; going through the process to develop the idea – it's the idea that is all important. The excitement for me is seeing it in three dimensions. It's not the process itself that satisfies. A high percentage of the work is donkey work and working down a surface absolutely square and straight is the hardest thing . . . Design and craft are totally intermeshed, an extension of one another. However beautifully made, if the object is not well designed, it is a waste of time, and vice versa. There must be a synthesis of each, meshing at a high level of design thinking and craft."

"The machine has absolutely dulled our sensitivity: people in the work situation are not allowed to decide or take personal responsibility. Most people's lives today are extremely monotonous and pre-determined – just like machines. But we are still trying to maintain the ideologies of William Morris carried on by my father and Gimson, giving the man a direct personal interest in his job. It's just the manner of doing it that's changed. How do you describe and convince anybody of what has happened to the work we do? What is it exactly? I don't know. Jobs made today are extremely accurate, made with accurate power tools that cut down so much time . . . but there is something missing: that missing something is man's personal labour . . . Craftsmanship will survive – if it doesn't we really are in trouble."

"Pride and excellence in workmanship is very much part of it. Why should Coventry Cathedral be so much less extraordinarily touching in feeling than Salisbury or Winchester? There are some very clever chaps around, but somehow the work is not right."

"The problem today is that designers produce the designs and others solve the problem of making, and you get a totally artificial separation. For me, I have to solve problems and the end product is a logical conclusion of shape and materials."

"The most potent form of plastic art is plastic art. It is not an idea. I'm concerned with actual objects. The idea is never there in the first place – that's the whole point of creative activity; you are finding ideas. The concept of ideas happens after the event. The ideas come from the making situation – that's where you get the kick-back."

"I admire the achievement of something well-made, but one that is a good solution to a problem, which is design not craftsmanship. The diversity we achieve in our work is nothing to do with craftsmanship – it's art and design. Craftsmanship is just the way of doing it. I do like the doing – I suppose it's the therapeutic bit in between the struggle of designing: it is a great struggle. The working out is a design job, but the cutting in a straight line is the craft."

"I think craft is the actual physical making – being able to do it – and design is imagining the object. The craft is just the mechanical part. Design goes all the way through ... the craft part is just doing it. It's merely a mechanical skill. What is important is that you achieve what you set out to do – the actual process by which you achieve this isn't important."

"The designer is in a sense the craftsman today ... but most of the good designers do tend to be able to make."

"Skill in the sense it is usually used doesn't interest me really. The sheer making bit doesn't interest me all that much. It's seeing the creative potential in what you're doing and the new things that can be sparked off from that ..."

"I never really think of myself as a craftsman because it tends to split the operation as I know it. To me making is only part of the process. It starts in the head, then it goes down on paper and it's not finished until the object is made. I've never been able to visualise totally what's in my head, what's been on paper, and what the thing is actually going to look like – this is one of the reasons for making it."

"The making is no problem. It's technical, controllable and measurable so we make it as well as we are capable of doing. Craftsmanship as technique can be learned."

"I think the only way you can realistically judge the workmanship of a piece is not by some absolute standard that exists for all time but by a standard implicit in the piece itself and obviously the standards are different in each piece. Because the standard in my work is so much lower therefore the standard I have achieved may still in fact be a far better piece of workmanship."

"The quality of thought in the design is really the craftsmanship today."

It may be necessary to re-examine the analysis by Ruskin, Morris and others of the degradation of work in general during the late nineteenth century (de-skilling) in order to find a generally applicable definition of skill in today's complex art-and-craft world. The invention of the artist craftsman was indirectly based on their analysis of the labour process, so, if there is any comon ground, it is likely to emerge from the same sources.

On the face of it, the Arts and Crafts line on de-skilling remains persuasive. If we place a plate from Diderot and d'Alembert's mid-eighteenth century *Encyclopedia* of a textile manufactory next to a late nineteenth-century print of a textile machinofactory, the main difference is obvious. In the *Encyclopedia* plate, the weaver's relationship to the loom is that of a musician to a musical instrument; in the Victorian print, the weaver's relationship to the power loom is that of a cog or lever to the machine being operated.[6]

Equally, if we read accounts of the traditional crafts at the time of the Industrial Revolution and compare them with accounts of similar activities written a hundred years later, the contrast seems to tell us much about the degradation of work which had happened in the interim. The eighteenth-century craftsmen were

*not on the whole the unlettered tinkerers of historical mythology. Even*

6. The difference is striking, even if we take into account changes in the conventions of illustration during the intervening period.

*the ordinary millwright was usually a fair arithmetician, knew something of geometry, levelling and mensuration, and in some cases possessed a very competent knowledge of practical mathematics . . .[7]*

By the end of the nineteenth century, however, the separation of the craftsman's 'craft knowledge' from his 'craft skill' was complete, in many areas which contributed significantly to the economy; and some articulate critics of this separation at the time thought they were clear as to the reasons why.

*We think of craftsmanship ordinarily as the ability to manipulate skilfully the tools and materials of a craft or trade. But true craftsmanship is much more than this. The really essential element in it is not manual skill and dexterity but something stored up in the minds of the worker. This something is partly the intimate knowledge of the character and uses of the tools, materials and processes of the craft which tradition has given the worker. But beyond this and above this, it is the knowledge which enables him to understand and overcome the constantly arising difficulties that grow out of variations not only in the tools and materials, but in the conditions under which the work must be done.'[8]*

Instead of this combination of knowledge and dexterity, the craftsman in industry was faced with the tendency to gather up

*all this scattered craft knowledge, systematising it and concentrating it in the hands of the employer and then doling it out again only in the form of minute instructions, giving to each worker only the knowledge needed for the performance of a particular relatively minute task. This process, it is evident, separates skill and knowledge even in their narrow relationship. When it is completed, the worker is no longer a craftsman in any sense, but is an animated tool . . .[8]*

This description, and indeed the whole deskilling thesis, is open to question on several counts. It assumes skills are always lost rather than redistributed; it depends on the belief that all pre-industrial activities were once highly skilled;[9] it baldly contrasts something called 'craft' with something called 'industry,' and, above all, it does not sufficiently emphasise what may have been the most important consideration for pre-industrial craftsmen fighting for the status of a way of life – *control at the point of production.* Whether or not the pre-industrial craftsmen were protecting their skills when they became machine-breakers, they were certainly defending the measure of control they exercised over their work.[10]

The most useful concept of skill, then, might encompass not only "a combination of knowledge and dexterity' (the process itself) but also 'a high discretion content' (the circumstances which make possible any skilled activity). Today's various types of craftspeople may argue forever about the process itself – does skill involve mental or manual dexterity or both? – but they all seem to have in common a strong belief in the importance of exercising control over every aspect of the work they do.

If the analysis of skill shifts to the circumstances which make possible any skilled activity, the word may prove to be less of a 'thought-preventer' than many post Arts and Crafts people believe. But if this aspect is taken up, the phenomenon of the artist craftsman will have to be related, at long last, to the dynamics of the labour process in general.

7. Quoted in David Landes, *The Unbound Prometheus* Cambridge, 1969, pp.63,104.
8. Quoted in Harry Braverman, *Labour and Monopoly Capital* London and New York, 1974, pp.136-7. Of course, Braverman goes much further than either Ruskin or Morriss would have done – and argues from a theoretical perspective which was not available to them (with historical data which is not entirely appropriate to the English experience): but a 'de-skilling' thesis of this kind seems to us to lie behind much of what Rusin and Morris wrote concerning the degradation of work at the point of production.
9. The most famous example is plain handloom weaving; that this activity required very little skill in the early nineteenth century is established by Duncan Bythell, *The Handloom Weavers*, Cambridge, 1969, pp.42-5.
10. See E.P.Thompson, *Time, Work Discipline and Industrial Capitalism* in Past and Present, No.38, December 1967, and the introduction to Charles More, *Skill and the English Working Class*, Croom Helm, 1980.

# 4

# CRAFTS IN THE MARKET-PLACE

At the Centre for Alternative Technology, near Machynlleth in Wales, visitors to the blacksmith's shop are told of the great attractions of small-scale production units which serve local needs:

*Small workshops like this can have, in a small way, far-reaching effects. They keep money and work in the area. They help spread skills more evenly over the country thus reducing the pressures of urban living. They enable us to prolong the life of 'obsolete' equipment and produce 'special' components. Job satisfaction is increased; being involved with the complete process has advantages for the individual and the community. Scrap metal can be re-used in many ways.*[1]

This reassuring image of the craft workshop in relation to the community at large, with its emphasis on decentralisation, appropriate techology and job satisfaction, comes directly from 'homecomers' like Schumacher. In the early 1970s these 'homecomers' challenged the more established view of the post-industrial technology and a regime of profession-als. Since then, they have tended to assume that the decentralisation of craft production will have a magical effect on the market-place ('workshops like this can have . . . far-reaching effects'): If goods are produced by craftsmen and women in small-scale production units which 'serve local needs,' 'the advantages of customisation will, it is claimed, automatically become apparent to re-educated consumers, and the values implicit in the work of the craftsmen and women will help spread the gospel of conviviality – a new social ethic – to the world outside. In other words, the creator, owner, and user will all have the same, intimate relationship with the products of the workshop.

This non-fiction version of the happy ending may seem to resolve the problems of our post-industrial future, but in fact it merely restates an age-old contradiction – between craft production and the consumer patterns of an industrialised society. This is the contradiction of which William Morris became acutely aware mid-way through his adult life. The disjunction between Morris's aims for his own craft workshop and the market which consumed its products prompted him to become involved in the 1880s debate about socialist ethics and public aesthetics. Morris's realisation that the value of objects produced by 'Fine Art Workmen' actually *depended* on the capitalist organisation of the economy (in the sense that Morris's Firm conferred a social status on its products which industry could never confer, since everyone, in principle, had access to the products of industry) forced him to play down his achievements in the design field[2]. And it encouraged him to ask, over and over again, "whether the tremendous organisation of civilised commercial society is not playing the cat and mouse game with us socialists".[3]

The remarks made by Morris about catering to 'the swinish luxury of the rich' by producing nothing but 'ingenious toys' have often been quoted by biographers. It was a view shared by C.R.Ashbee, who later wrote:

*We have made of a great social movement a narrow and tiresome little aristocracy working with great skill for the very rich.*[4]

He had only to leaf through a copy of *Country Life*, to wander past expensive 'vernacular' dwellings in the stockbroker belt, or to visit the latest examples of Public-School Baronial, to see that it was true. What had seemed

1. National Centre for Alternative Technology, Visitors' Guide, Machynlleth 1979, pp.8-9, and caption at the Centre itself.
2. See Helen Snowdon, William Morris and the Firm in *William Morris and Kelmscott*, Design Council 1981, pp.73-81, and the relevant sections of E.P. Thompson's *Wiliam Morris* revised edition, London, 1977.
3. A.L. Morton (ed.) *Political Writings of William Morris* London, 1973, p.230. We are grateful to David Brett for drawing our attention to this key lecture by Morris, which was delivered in March 1893.
4. See Nikolaus Pevsner, *Pioneers of Modern Design* Middlesex 1978, pp.24-6; also Edward Lucie-Smith, *The World of the Makers* London 1975, p.24.

123

at the outset to be "a great social movement", the vanguard of a new social ethic, had rapidly turned into a branch of *haute culture*, in the process providing a style which suited well the aspirations (and the sense of history) of consumers who wanted to show the world that their social status was not achieved but ascribed. An attempt to challenge the concept of anonymous marketing – 'you could have the things such as the Firm chose they should be, or you could do without them'[5] – ended up by avoiding the mass market altogether.

The Arts and Crafts people felt guilty about this contradiction: Morris devoted the rest of his life to lecturing about it, while Ashbee implied that members of the art and design élite *could* have done something about it if they really wanted to ('We have made . . .'). Today, 'homecomers' may dreamily wish away the contradiction (to a chorus of 'stop the world, I want to get off'), but in the real world of artist craftspeople it is considered poor taste even to mention the misplaced evangelical zeal which made an issue out of it.

By their attitude to their work and its presentation in the market-place, these artist craftsmen and women have inherited the 'Morris dilemma', whether they care to acknowledge the fact or not. For, the work of most contemporary artist craftspeople (and especially those who belong to what we have called the Craftsman's Art tradition) now belongs firmly in that sector of the economy – known in the trade as the 'positional economy' – where the individual enjoyment of goods is directly affected by the extent of their use or availability. This is a sector which is dependent on scarcity of supply and the containing of demand by the auction process, and is in contrast to the material economy where the individual enjoyment of goods is divorced from the number of persons consuming them, and where supply is dynamic and capable of great expansion.[6] If everyone can, in principle, have a mass-produced chair, the buyer of a unique or limited production chair, made by an artist craftsman or woman with a reputation (preferably one who signs his or her work) is buying status as well as the object, and thereby demonstrating a particular set of values which the buyer reckons is embodied in the work. As one economist has neatly put it, 'If everyone stands on tiptoe, no one sees better.'[7] In this respect, the work of these artist craftsmen and women belongs in the same sector of the economy as the work of the successful fine artist. But in other respects, the parallels between the artist craftsperson's market and the fine artist's market can be pushed too far – after all, only a tiny percentage of the art-and-craft population, about ten artist-craftsmen and women *in toto*, making furniture, pots and books, is deemed by investors to be in the gilt-edged superstar bracket. The rest may *aspire* to have their work inspected in the best auction houses and museums, but they are usually content to sell their work in interior-design shops where it represents a viable (and better-quality) alternative to the mass-manufactured product – often at prices which do not even cover the time put into it. Our discussions with retailers suggest that the pressure of the market to conform to the fine-art model may not really serve the best interests of these artist craftspeople: better to be a first-eleven artist craftsperson, whose work is respected for what it is, than an unsellable second-eleven artist.

While the 'Morris dilemma' is inescapable for artist craftsmen and women, other types of craftspeople manage to avoid it because both the nature of their work and the way they market it are different. Some individual rural craftspeople – notably basketmakers, thatchers and cabinet-makers – continue to 'serve local needs' by producing customised goods or performing skilled services in traditional ways; some others, notably potters, try to reach the

5. See William Rossetti's comments on the Firm in *The Furnisher*, iii, 1900-1, pp.61-2.
6. The contrast between 'the positional economy' and 'the material economy' is taken from Fred Hirsch, *The Social Limits to Growth* London, 1977. Although the basis for Hirsch's distinction can be found in nineteenth century writings on economics (for example Ricardo's theory of rent), in Alfred Marshall's (1920) concept of 'quasi-rent' and in Roy Harrod's famous essay on The Possibility of Economic Satiety (1958), Hirsch extends the distinction in order to question the work of 'homecomers' like Schumacher, and also develops the useful concept of 'the auction process.'
7. Fred Hirsch, *op cit*, p.5.

mass market through craft shops for tourists or through direct selling from local workshops, which operate like small-scale assembly lines. A few individual craftspeople, especially those who belong to what we have termed the *Council of Industrial Design* tradition, are still attempting to improve the quality of design in industry through the high standard (and reproducibility) of their products.

In addition to all these, there is the large group of craft merchants who are not necessarily themselves craftsmen or women, but who know a good marketing ploy when they see one. Down the road from the Centre for Alternative Technology, tourists may buy both local *and* mass-produced wares in a 'craft shop'. Up until the craft revival of the late 1960s such shops were always known as 'souvenir shops', but the mythology of 'craft', Merrie England-style, provided entrepreneurs with a powerful new marketing concept, and the 'world we have lost' was used to create and fill a space in that particular market-place. 'Craft shops' of this kind may be stocked with moulded plaster pixies, local pottery, mass-produced pottery which *looks* local (or at least rural), do-it-yourself embroidery kits of the Royal Family, wholefoods and Third World products which have been made by the cheapest kind of labour and bought by wholesalers at knock-down prices – the range of 'natural' goods on offer may vary from place to place, but the same allusion to – and illusion of – 'craftsmanship' encourages consumers to invest in *crafts* (of whatever origin) as souvenirs of their holiday in Wales.

The comments that follow[8], made by a range of practising artist craftspeople, will help to illustrate the ways in which they see their own relationship with the market-place. In our previous articles, we have suggested that these artist craftsmen and women belong to three main traditions – 'Arts and Crafts', 'Council of Industrial Design' and 'Craftsman's Art'.

*"Craft shops are full of very good examples of very bad craftmanship."*

*"I prefer people to have thoroughly bad furniture which they like rather than something they think is fashionable. Good design is not a luxury. I believe that well-designed objects should be reasonably priced. Good design is a social as well as an aesthetic matter."*

*"My desire was to set up a workshop to make decent furniture for ordinary people. I would have liked a small country workshop . . . but it's difficult today – some governments are determined to stamp out all small concerns. They have the fatuous idea that size and speed are all, and that it is socially irresponsible to buy something that everyone can't have."*

*"The point was, to make an impact on my generation, and to alter, in however small a degree, the thinking of the furniture trade. This meant going out to sell things – ideas first, goods second – instead of waiting for an exclusive clientele to insist on buying."*

*"Our emphasis is still on individual pieces of the first quality: nearly all are direct order sold from the workshop . . . But in the last ten years, due to economies, we've had to adopt a different approach, which is to try to make small batches because the price is considerably less this way than doing one at a time. My clients know my work, they see what we are after and they discuss what they want. We don't advertise or use publicity. We don't need it."*

8. From interviews taped and transcribed as part of Helen Snowdon's MA thesis *Craftmanship in the Machine Environment*, Royal College of Art, May 1979 and since. An interesting example of the special definitions attached to words describing the 'market-place' – by makers from all the three main traditions – arose in the varying response to our questions about 'speculation': those who had been involved in the manufacturing and selling of batch-production furniture thought the word meant 'introducing an adventurous new line' or 'venturing into the open market'; most of the artist-craftsmen thought it meant making pieces 'for the galleries,' working 'for an exhibition,' or embarking on a new project without pre-selling the idea to a client. In other words, changes in the normal pattern of work ('speculations') were defined with particular reference to what the normal pattern of work entailed.

125

"I'm trying to work speculatively to do small batches – or limited editions as the artists call them. That means I will have to sell them through galleries and retail outlets. I'm certainly not concerned with making good art cheap, so that everybody can have it: that's irrelevant to me . . . If the machine produced millions of one beautiful thing, it ceases to be beautiful. For example, a beautiful piece of music played over and over again can become ghastly. The music/design/score versus execution/playing/practice is the best analogy because it is removed from all that function and utility crap."

"If I designed one beautiful table I would not like five thousand others to have it, apart from the kudos . . . You might get a one-off that is beautiful but if you see it one thousand times it's something else . . . Some people might say it was nice because it was seen by many, but I can't waste my time on that sort of low visual thinking."

"What we ought to be doing, or trying to do, is making the furniture we like making but also that other people like it. I'm making for me but also for others."

"Really? I couldn't give a hoot for others . . ."

"I would take a great deal of care to please my client if I didn't have a clear idea of what I wanted to do myself. If the commission fitted in with what I wanted to do at the moment, then I would take a great deal of trouble to convince the client that my idea was his idea."

"I have a feeling that when it's right for me it's right for the client. If it's not right for the client then he's an idiot."

"One of the reasons why many people are commissioning individual craftsman's work is that they know the result – apart from any intrinsic merit it may have – is extremely noticeable: That it draws attention to itself, and, indirectly, to the person who has commissioned it. I would like very much to get rid of this ignoble motive: it's a bad piece of art and it's bad human behaviour."

"They are paying for the quality of thought in the design, plus the workmanship. I think part of the interest of the client is being part of creating something new. They then have a personal identification with the piece because they know it does not exist elsewhere. Everyone likes to feel they have something unique; it's a desire to own something not available to everyone."

"I decided to specialise in the things I make because there was no one else doing them . . . My work can show off the client: the client is buying the status that the one-off object implies."

"It does not matter to me whether the human mark shows, but it does to the client. He always wants the piece signed and dated and wants to be sure it is hand made and hand polished."

"Most customers are prepared to pay for useless work but may not value or understand the qualities they are paying for. The maker will be able *to sell nothing if he reduces his prices by omitting as much of the useless work as it is possible to omit. Few people realise how nastily things can be made and yet work well enough. Good workmanship is taken for granted."*

*"Speculative work is important – not having to worry about the market. Other concerns can displace the activity out of proportion, and blunt creativity."*

*"Today there seems to be a breed of craft superstars who have the opportunity to be preoccupied with perfection and are, as a result, achieving the highest levels of craftsmanship in history . . . Because you are not working to the limitations of industry or the market you can take it to the highest degree of perfection possible."*

*"The only reason why we all try to get publicity and acclaim is so that we can command a price that our self-indulgence costs. It's not for the glory of being famous – it's just to be able to be paid for our standards."*

*"I would find it difficult to buy from fellow-craftsmen because if I accepted the fact that there was something worth buying, it would diminish me in some way – so it is competitive. Production furniture is anonymous – it's not a competitor."*

*"It's an ego trip, I enjoy being in magazines and I'm absolutely staggered at the thought of one of my pieces going directly in the V and A."*

It is clear from these comments that most of the Craftsman's Art people we interviewed see themselves as operating within the positional economy – whether through direct-selling from workshop or studio ('if it's not right for the the the client then he's an idiot') or through retail outlets ('I'm trying to do . . . limited editions as the artists call them'). They have little time for the evangelism of the Arts and Crafts people ('all that function and utility crap') or for improving the quality of design in industry ('I can't waste my time on that sort of low visual thinking') and no time at all for the commercialised folksiness of the tourist Craft Shop. One or two of these artist craftspeople had some experience as industrial designers before they set up on their own – but tend to look back on that period of their lives as a time when they were 'boring, sensible, and rational people, who design the sort of products that make the world such a dreary place.'

In contrast, makers who uphold the Arts and Crafts tradition, still talk of 'good design' as a social and aesthetic matter. They resent being cast in the rôle of 'fashionable' designers working for an 'exclusive clientele' (which offends their nonconformist conscience), but are also aware that William Morris's disillusionment with the market pressures of civilised commercial society may have been based on 'the fatuous idea . . . that it is socially irresponsible to buy something that everyone can't have.' In short, they would like to be 'homecomers', but are too realistic (and concerned about the good design of individual pieces) to swallow the philosophy whole. They share with the Council of Industrial Design tradition an aim to 'alter . . . the thinking of the furniture trade' by selling the idea of 'well-designed objects.' Where the traditions differ is over the question of producing prototype pieces which are intended to be batch- or mass-produced elsewhere by other people.

9. See, in particular, Raphael Samuel's The Workshop of the World History Workshop Journal, iii, 1977).

Most of the answers given by *all* these craftspeople to our questions about crafts in the market-place are based on a series of basic oppositions: mass production *versus* craft production; industrial design *versus* art; the material *versus* the status-giving economy; anonymous marketing *versus* direct selling; ethics *versus* aesthetics. This tendency to think about the market in either/or terms seems partly to come from a traditional reading of the history of craftsmanship in the last 150 years. According to this reading, the process of industrialisation involved a sudden, dramatic shift from workshop to factory (or from craft to machinofacture), which had the immediate effect of forcing the crafts into a marginal position in the economy. However, as most of the recent research has shown,[9] the process of industrialisation was much more likely to have affected different activities in different ways at different times – with craft-based sectors of the economy existing side by side with those few sectors which were thoroughly automated. The recent debate about the 'two paths' which society is likely to face in the future (the 'homecoming' model *versus* the 'post-industrial' model) has to some extent inherited these terms of reference from the traditional literature – which misleadingly was always searching for something it could call an industrial *revolution*.

It also seems that the either / or account of the options which are open to practising craftspeople today is very much in the interests of those makers who see themselves as artists – the market for their work *is sustained by* a rejection of the part of both producers and consumers of mass production, industrial design, the material economy and anonymous marketing; as Morris realised a century ago, this market is as much about social status as it is about beautiful objects. (Note how the Morris designs which *have* at last reached the mass market via Morris and Company, Liberty's and Sanderson's, and fabric shops in the high street – have also lost their aura of exclusiveness, the very quality of course which lost them any association with a new social ethic in the first place.)

If the tourist Craft Shops have created a space in the market by exploiting their consumers' sentimental attachment to the folk culture of Merrie England, some artist-craftspeople have created a space further up the market by setting themselves apart from the material economy in their role as artists creating one-offs or 'limited editions' (often in reassuringly traditional materials). By choosing this particular marketing strategy, they have set themselves apart from other artist- and designer-craftspeople who aim to produce well made, well designed objects *to compete with* the industrially-produced equivalents. In order to widen their marketing opportunities, all these artist-craftsmen and women might do well to consider an option which is now becoming available to them: with the development of increasingly sophisticated 'robots' (or numerically controlled technologies), they will be able to design and make individual pieces which can be produced in large batches of which *each one* is different – a 'batch-produced' one-off. If they do take up this option, they will no longer have to call themselves artists, or produce goods for the exclusive luxury market in order to engage effectively in the *personal* production of well-designed pieces for a market which expects special attention.

# 5

## NOSTALGIA ISN'T WHAT IT USED TO BE

A browse along the crafts shelf of a high street bookshop shows at a glance both the range of activities covered by the magic word 'crafts' – from matchstick houses to the latest avant-garde jewellery – and the usual ways in which writings about craftsmanship have been presented to readers in recent years. Most of the shelfspace is devoted to recipe books ('painted eggs and how to paint them') or coffee-table surveys of the state of one particular craft. The rest of the shelf is crammed with collections of faded photographs ('the country diary of an Edwardian thatcher') or reminiscences by famous studio craftspeople about the things they think were going on in their heads when they made the objects which made them famous.

All these publications are really about the circumstances *surrounding* the crafts: recipes, catalogues, albums and autobiographies; reassuring souvenir brochures about what goes on before or after the event. There seems to be no books on the shelf about craft *as an activity*.

There are good reasons for this. Commentators writing about design have for a long time made the distinction between design as an activity which involves a kind of knowledge which *can* be formalised (or generalised) in a systematic way, and craft as an activity which involves a kind which cannot – because it is informal, tacit, individual and demonstrable only through the actual process of making. Whether or not we accept such a hard-and-fast distinction, it's clear that the concept of craft *as a special kind of knowledge* has proved extremely difficult to write about. Which in some cases makes it vulnerable.

'In the craft tradition,' writes one design theorist,

*Since there are no radical departures from the repeated type, it is possible for artefacts to be made which are technically very sophisticated, which exploit physical principles, chemical processes or the properties of materials in very subtle ways – but without any of their makers having a theoretical understanding of how these effects are achieved. The principles have been discovered empirically and are embodied in the inherited design. We might speak, in a sense, of information being conveyed within the forms of the artefacts themselves. The craftsman knows how to make the object, he follows the traditional procedure (the recipe): but in many respects he literally does not know what he is doing.*[1]

This account of what's involved when we perform a 'craft' – a characteristic passage from academic literature on design – assumes that because craft knowledge is not easily expressible in a formal and systematic way, it is not to be counted as knowledge at all. It's just something you do with your hands.

The philosopher Michael Oakeshott, who has written a great deal about the distinction between 'knowing that' (or formal knowledge) and 'knowing how' (or tacit knowledge) – a distinction between design and craft in the passage quoted above – has used similar arguments to come to a very different conclusion. When giving a lecture on knowledge and know-how, he is reputed to have read out the recipe for an omelette, then demonstrated how little the recipe told us about the making of an omelette by cooking one on the stage of the lecture theatre. The point of this bizarre exercise was to show that the really important information about the omelette was only demonstrable in the process of making, and that while it might be possible to say – after the event – 'I learned about the ingredients of an omelette when I read the recipe book,' it was not possible to say 'I learned about how to turn on the gas, how to

1. See Philip Steadman, *The Evolution of Designs*, Cambridge, 1979, pp.231-236; and, for an earlier example of a similar argument, J. Christopher Jones, *Design Methods*, Wiley, London, 1970, pp.15-24.

hold the frying pan by its handle, how to judge whether the butter had melted, how to change the consistency of the omelette, how to know when it was just "right" to serve' and countless other things which simply aren't absorbed in the form of bits of information all at the same time. Oakeshott's conclusion was that this kind of knowing was in no sense inferior to the formal kind (indeed, he thought that it was if anything *more valuable* in educational terms), but it was different. And it could only be transmitted by repeating the experience in full, and by becoming aware of all the tacit 'rules' which governed it.[2] The same could be said of any craft activity, where the proof of the craft lies in the good performance of it.

The special problem of writing or talking about craftsmanship itself, as opposed to its recipes, its procedures and its results (the most exciting of which may not have been anticipated by the maker), struck us very forcibly when we interviewed practising artist craftspeople and asked them what sort of knowledge they thought they needed.

*"I don't see much place for theory or knowledge, knowledge can interfere. Sometimes it's better not to know too much in order to be able to feel. The Bible says 'By thy work shalt thou be known, by the word shalt thou be confused.' I think this happens to be true. My foreman teaches the young by examples and experience. There is no theory. In my workshop the lads can only learn to follow excellence."*

*"Love is the most necessary ingredient, and that cannot really be learned. As D.H. Lawrence said, 'things men have made with wakened hands and put soft light into, are awake through years of transferred touch and go on glowing for long years, and for this reason old things are lovely, warm still with the light of men who made them . . .' "*

*"Training and learning are not enough. One day you feel it, and that's what it's all about. You get a feeling for the job, your fingers become sensitive so that you feel the bumps you cannot see. You can go on for years using a plane and all of a sudden you've got it – you know what it's about."*

*"Our theory has been founded on abstractions taken from the fruits of inventions made without theory . . . We can only go on if we are capable of reasonable preliminary assumptions based on experience."*

*"In the past, we tried to establish a valuable precedent by mixing theory and practice, establishing close links between architectural students and cabinet-makers. Looking back at the men who have done interesting furniture, under the inspiration of William Morris, all were architects – Lethaby, Voysey, Mackintosh, Gimson and the Barnsleys. They had all made a special study of the subject and they had all worked at the bench."*

*"I wanted to learn more about what goes into designing and making, but I was forced to learn how to run a business."*

2. The distinction between 'knowledge' and 'know-how' is best presented in Michael Oakeshott's collection of essays *Rationalism in Politics*, London, 1967, esp. pp.2-36. See also *Knowing and Being: Essays by Michael Polanyi* (ed. Marjorie Grene, London), 1969, especially the essay *Tacit Knowing*, pp.159-180, and Michael Polyani, *Personal Knowledge*, London, 1962, pp.49-65.

*"When you see a drawing translated into three-dimensions, there are inevitable changes which you want to make. This is very common: the ability to draw something comes with experience of course. The three-dimensional reality comes as an awful surprise sometimes to an inexperienced designer – the more experienced designers get it right first time. It also depends on whether the designer has had physical experience of manufacture and has actually made things."*

*"You are really asking why we go into making in the first place. I suppose it is because most craftspeople have been told, at some stage in their lives, that they are 'good with their hands', so they've already had some sort*

*of failure in one sense, which tends to make them limit their expectations from that point on. They get a lot out of making because it is something that is directly measurable and forseeable – something they can control and is relatively simple to comprehend. They can make a direct value judgement about this ability and this is what gives the ability meaning."*

*"In making things, people are involved in something which they can readily understand and identify with. Something that does not seem remote. Doing is one of the best ways of learning for this reason – provided it is for the purpose, like improving what exists both in terms of the object and improving the quality of life."*

*"Theory? It just happens in the course of work. I suppose I think about it. It's a philosophy in a way. To me it's part of the process – it's just a logical happening when you're waiting for inspiration. 'Doodling' is just the linking-up of the brain passages in a way. I suppose I do just fiddle around but really that's a kind of drawing in three-dimensions. I couldn't do any kind of designing unless I knew how I was going to make something . . . I've always wanted to do, there is something in me wanting to fiddle, mend things, work things out, take things apart and put them together again – that sort of mental attitude."*

*"There is so much to learn. I would like to know a lot more about the actual stuff – trees, wood yards, tools, machines. The requirements are always changing. I'd like to know more about how things were made in the past. I feel the need to draw. But it's all a question of time. All these things are competing for one's time – one staggers from one incomplete investigation to another, of necessity."*

*"The idea is never there in the first place – that's the whole point. You are finding ideas. The concept of idea happens after the event. One becomes wiser by doing and one therefore becomes launched into investigating the potential of the qualities one has discovered. That is what I mean by creativity."*

*"Theory? Read* The Painted Word *by Tom Wolfe to see what I think about theory!"*

These different groups of craftspeople which in our series we have named after the three traditions: Arts and Crafts, Council of Industrial Design and Craftsman's Art – may differ in the actual words they use ('reason versus feelings', 'theory which grows out of good practice', 'theory versus practice'), and in the reasons why they use them, but all are agreed that craft activity represents a type of knowledge the effectiveness of which can be demonstrated rather than articulated in a verbal way.

This unusual measure of agreement brings out into the open two questions which are becoming more and more urgent at a time when craft practitioners, educators and administrators are being pressed from many sides to argue convincingly about what they do.

The first question concerns the nature of craft knowledge, and the ways in which this knowledge can effectively be described. Whatever our artist craftspeople may claim, the distinction between craft and other types of knowledge is not one between theory (or reason) and practice (or feeling) – and it may well be disastrous to suggest that it is. The distinction is between two ways of knowing. But if one of these ways is locked up in a black box labelled 'experience', then it is in constant danger of not being counted as knowledge at all – as some design theorists and most of the people

131

responsible for the information explosion have shown. Some attempts have been made to penetrate the black box: through research into how children can best develop the intelligence of feeling; through the sociology of 'doing craft' (as opposed to the sociology of craftspeople); through the history of how craft traditions are passed on; the psychology of visual perception; the science of why materials behave as they do; and through an understanding of what the Victorians called 'the grammar of ornament'. These attempts may seem to reduce craft knowledge in one way or another (and in consequence may be greeted with hostility by craftspeople), but they are essential if the relationship between rules and applications – the root of all craft activity – is to become clearer.

The second question concerns the widespread temptation to find substitutes for the analysis of craft knowledge in a series of attitudes or postures which are based on the mythology of craft – to put the black box on a pedestal and call it magic. Could it be that these attitudes, in the 1980s, sustain the makers, their market and indeed the whole crafts revival?

Our articles in Crafts this year have tried to look at most of these attitudes (with a lot of help from artist and designer craftspeople who hold strong views about them) and to say something about their significance. In The Myth of the Happy Artisan, we described the artificial history which has been constructed around the crafts – by some ad-men and makers alike – and speculated on the imporance of this history for today's investors in well-made objects. In Crafts – with or without Art, we described a Cinderella-like transformation scene which has occurred in recent years (originally in competition with the Ugly Sisters of modernism, but increasingly looking more and more like them) and explored some of the problems of definition which this transformation has caused, such as: What does count as craft today? Who decides? Has craftsmanship become simply a matter of skill? In Skill – A word to start an argument we looked at the many different versions of that elusive concept (and the many different attitudes towards it since Cinderella's transformation), and noted that the crafts in education seem to be going in the opposite direction to the crafts which have joined the art world. Our conclusion was that the most constructive way forward is to discuss craft skills in the broad context of the labour process as a whole, and the related issue of 'control'. In Crafts in the Market-Place we analysed the market pressures which have helped to sustain 'the crafts revival' and concluded that, with the development of robots, there are now unprecedented opportunities for artist craftspeople to start batch-production without loss of quality – opportunities which might be lost if too much emphasis is given to fine-art values and the aura of original artworks. Perhaps the best example of how this might work is 'the middle Italy' – an economic area which is distinct on the one hand from the heavy-metal North and on the other from the rural South of Italy – where a group of small workshops, each equipped with numerically-controlled machine tools, have linked up to produce high-quality craft goods: these workshops have the great advantages of flexible production, smallness of scale, and imaginative individuals who control all the stages in the production of prototypes.

The argument throughout all our articles has been that, while most accounts of craftsmanship depend for their support on sentimentality and conservatism and while most discussions of craft knowledge remain at the level of hippie folk-wisdom, proper assessment of craft and its contemporary value and significance will forever remain obscured.

Sixty-three years ago, in reply to the Bauhaus message to 'return to the crafts', the designer/critic Adolf Behne made some remarks about the crafts which seem peculiarly apt for the 1980s:

*Craftsmanship has become a catchword. Today, we have ascribed everything positive to the word craftsmanship, everything negative to technology. But as telling as these sympathies and antipathies are of the mood of the times, they still have nothing to do with the matter at hand. Craftsmanship is not the good angel, nor is technology the evil demon of art and culture. Of course, to listen to the champions of the former, craftsmanship is in itself the guarantee of artistic quality, while technology has the monopoly on artistic rubbish. Craftsmanship is equated simply with loving, inspired, conscientious, engaged work; technology with the hasty, mechanical and soulless. But why? Can one really dispute the fact that there are innumerable handcrafted products which are loveless, indifferent, banal, and superficial? Is there not also mechanical work in handiwork, and can one maintain that work aided by technology cannot be exceptionally inspired and conscientious? If the difference between craft and technology is not a simple, qualitative one . . . what is the actual difference?*[3]

A crude version of the craft-versus-technology (or art-versus-industry) argument is still number one on the agenda, and it is depressing to be reminded that the debate has progressed so very little in the last sixty years.

3. Adolf Behne, Art, Handicraft, Technology, Kunst, Handwerk, Technik, first published 1922, translated by Diane Blaurock for *Oppositions*, 22, Fall 1980, pp.96-104. A welcome translation of a neglected text.

## ACKNOWLEDGEMENTS

The Crafts Council is very grateful to the following for their kind permission for the reproduction of work in this book:

Cambridge University Press
Breon O'Casey
Peter Collingwood
Crafts Magazine
Dartington Hall Trustees
Faber & Faber
Christopher Frayling and Helen Snowden
Jane Gate
David Kindersley
Angela Lane
Janet Leach
John Leach
Kate Russell
Studio International